In Search of Utopia

Du frembes Land, im Traum der Nacht geschaut,
In dem mein Volk sich seine Hütten baut,
Wie ein Geheimnis blickst du ernst mich an;
Ein Bild in schwarz und weiß: dein Schnee — dein dunkler Tann.

                                        Jakob H. Janzen*

(Thou foreign land in dreams of night revealed,
In which my people build and till the field,
Some secret in your somber mien lies hid.
So white in snow, so black in firs that pyramid)*

*The motto is taken from the poem "Canada" included in
Janzen's book *Durch Wind und Wellen* (Waterloo, Ontario,
1928). The translation is by Jacob Suderman and was
published in *Mennonite Quarterly Review*, January, 1945,
p. 72.

In Search of Utopia

The Mennonites In Manitoba

BY

E. K. FRANCIS

Professor of Sociology
University of Notre Dame

1955

THE FREE PRESS
GLENCOE, ILLINOIS

TO MY FRIENDS

Foreword

THE Historical and Scientific Society of Manitoba welcomes the appearance in print of a portion of the extensive and scholarly study of the Mennonite community of Manitoba by Dr. E. K. Francis. The study was the first undertaken under the Society's grants, made possible by the Government of Manitoba, for research in the history of the ethnic groups of Manitoba. The difficulties which have delayed its appearance are now overcome, and the fruit of the author's patient work is to be available both in the present volume and in an edition in microfilm of the complete study. The latter, it is hoped, will be published under the imprint of the University of Toronto Press, for the use of scholars who may wish to avail themselves of the whole body of Dr. Francis' researches.

The Society is grateful to Dr. Francis for the service he has rendered to the documentation and interpretation of a distinctive and important element of the Manitoba community. A newcomer to Canada, he threw himself into this work, begun in 1945, with great eagerness, and by his published research in the field soon made a name for himself among North American historians and sociologists. It is to be regretted that Canada can find no further use for his talents; Dr. Francis is now Professor of Sociology at the University of Notre Dame.

The Society is no less grateful to D. W. Friesen and Sons Ltd. who with other friends of Mennonite history, when other means of publication had seemed impossible, came forward and made this book possible. It is to be hoped that their contribution to its appearance will be rewarded in every way.

While the Society can assume no responsibility for the book or anything in it, and claim no credit except for having made the study possible, it is happy to be associated with its appearance, in the assurance that it is a book which will be a source of pride to members of the Mennonite faith in Manitoba and elsewhere, and a valuable aid to the study of Manitoban and Canadian history.

W. L. MORTON

President, Historical and Scientific Society of Manitoba

Winnipeg, August, 1954

Preface

THIS book is based upon research carried out from September 1945 to March 1947. I am indebted to the Manitoba Historical and Scientific Society for the grant of a fellowship, one of several offered for the study of ethnic groups in Manitoba, and for the permission to use materials included in my final report for the preparation of the present volume. The full, and much more exhaustive, report, which has been submitted several years ago, is deposited in the Provincial Archives at Winnipeg.

The original version has been shortened drastically to make a book publication at all feasible in face of high printing cost. Most details, including much of the evidence for summarizing statements, references to unpublished sources, particularly field notes, and other important elements of the scholarly apparatus had to be omitted. A small list of selected publications has been appended for the guidance of the general reader; those more interested are referred to the bibliographical essay in the July, 1953, issue of the *Mennonite Quarterly Review*. While the general outline of the report has been retained, the second part which deals with contemporary conditions observed in the course of the author's field research had to be condensed to less than half its size. The sociological scope of the revised presentation has thus been reduced in favor of a stronger historical emphasis. But by making ample use of oral traditions, the recollections of eye-witnesses and the participant-observer method of the cultural anthropologist, the conventional sources of historical research have been greatly expanded. What is still more important, care has been taken to preserve the basic design of this project and its underlying intention of describing and analyzing a social system in process.

In community studies of this kind great care is frequently taken to conceal the identity of individuals and groups who have a right to be protected in their privacy. The nature of this project has made this impossible. The best I could do under the circumstances was to combine impartial objectivity with due regard for understandable sensibilities. I hope that I have not unwittingly misused the trust of my many informants.

This book is dedicated to my friends, the living as well as the dead. It is also intended as a token of gratitude to the Canadian people among whom I have found generous benefactors and friends during trying years. It is not possible to name them all; for I have been very fortunate in having experienced real friendship and loyalty among men and women of many nations and races, in good days as well as in danger and need. Their friendship has become part of what I am and whatever little I may have accomplished.

I feel deeply obliged to the publishers, to Dean Harold S. Bender, of Goshen College, Professor W. L. Morton, of the University of Manitoba, Professor S. D. Clark, of the University of Toronto, and to the Canadian Social Science Research Council for having made this publication possible. I also wish to thank the University of Notre Dame, in particular the Reverend Philip S. Moore, C.S.C., Vice-President, Academic Affairs, for having provided facilities for the preparation of the manuscript, and Mrs. Bertha Halley Ross for invaluable assistance in editing the present revision and preparing it for the printer.

During earlier phases of this project the following have given generously of their time and experience to advise and assist me in many ways: Professor Aaron I. Abell, Professor Russel Barta, Miss Laura Beaulieu, Professor Herbert Blumer, Mr. Louis P. Carney, Professor Hugh McD. Clokie, Miss Clementine Combaz, the Reverend Antoine d'Eschambault, Professor J. E. L. Graham, Professor K. F. Helleiner, the Reverend and Mrs. Foster Hilliard, Professor E. C. Hughes, Mr. Michael Hunt, Mr. J. A. Jackson, Mr. Victor Kroeger, Professor A. R. M. Lower, Mr. H. P. O'Brien, Dr. R. O. MacFarlane, Professor Frank O'Malley, the Reverend G. B. Phelan, Professor Robert Redfield, Professor Ruth Riemer, Mrs. E. E. Sandeen, Professor Solomon

Sinclair, the Honorable I. Schultz, Dr. David S. Solomon, Mr. Paul Stoner, Dean W. J. Waines, Mr. Ted Whitley, and in particular Miss Rhoda Stirling without whose encouragement and devotion the project could not have been completed.

It is difficult to express in a few words my obligation to the staffs of several libraries, archives, and statistical bureaus. Mr. O. A. Lemieux, of the Canadian Bureau of Statistics at Ottawa, not only has made available much unpublished information but has made several checks of my tabulations and computations. Mr. J. L. Johnston, Miss Lillian Buggey, Miss Clementine Combaz, and Miss Marjorie Morley, of the Provincial Library at Winnipeg, Miss Elizabeth Dafoe and Miss Mary Hughes, of the University Library at Winnipeg, and Dr. Melvin Gingerich and Mr. N. P. Springer, of the Archives of the Mennonite Church and the Historical Library, at Goshen College, have shown a deep personal interest—going far beyond professional concern—in facilitating my work. Above all, the late J. L. Johnston has contributed much rare information out of the wealth of his great knowledge of local and Canadian history. Some additional material has been made available by Dr. Cornelius Krahn and the Bethel College Library, North Newton, Kansas.

Valuable documentary material was also made available by the officers of the Rural Municipalities of Hanover, Rhineland and Stanley; the towns of Altona, Winkler and Steinbach; the Canada Colonization Association, Winnipeg; the Chortitz Waisenamt, Blumengart; the Concordia Hospital, Winnipeg; the Clerk of the House of Commons, Ottawa; the Federation of Southern Manitoba Coöperatives, Altona; the Mennonite Collegiate Institute, Gretna; the Land Titles Office, Morden; the Provincial Legislature of Manitoba: Department of Agriculture and Colonization, Department of Education, Department of Health and Public Welfare including its Vital Statistics division, Survey Branch of the Department of Natural Resources; the Rhineland Agricultural Association, Altona; the archives of the Winnipeg Free Press; also by the bishops of the Old Colony and Chortitz churches; and by the publishers of the Steinbach Post and the Christian Press, Winnipeg.

Several private individuals have generously permitted the use of their treasured collections of rare documents and publications, including the late D. W. Friesen, Mr. Arnold Dyck, the Reverend Benjamin

Ewert, the Reverend Jacob J. Froese, Mr. H. H. Hamm, Mr. G. G. Kornelsen, Mr. K. J. B. Reimer, and Mr. B. J. Schellenberg. The Reverend I. I. Friesen has permitted me to make extensive use of his unpublished thesis. Many of these same persons together with their families, and scores of other volunteers, in addition to spending many hours and days in conversation with the author, have extended to him their hospitality, served as guides and provided transportation in their private cars. The great number of my informants and aides makes it unfeasible to mention each; but none has been forgotten. There remains to add a few names of those to whom I am especially indebted: Mr. and Mrs. G. S. Derksen, Mr. and Mrs. D. K. Friesen, Mr. and Mrs. Ted Friesen, Mr. and Mrs. Victor Peters, Mr. and Mrs. Vern Rempel, Mr. and Mrs. J. J. Siemens, Mr. and the late Mrs. John Siemens, Miss Helen Siemens, Dr. J. K. Friesen, Dr. Nicholas Neufeld, Dr. S. S. Toni, the Reverend J. F. Barkman, and Messrs. K. A. Dack, Lou Erk, Dave Friesen, T. O. Hertzer, J. J. Hildebrand, the late C. F. Klassen, J. A. Penner, G. H. Peters, J. E. Regehr, J. C. Reimer, Paul Schäfer, Armin Sawatzky, David Schellenberg, and John Toews.

Finally, I apologize to those whose assistance goes unacknowledged through my oversight.

E.K.F.

Innsbruck, Summer, 1954

CONTENTS

LIST OF TABLES

CHARTS

Introduction

THE Mennonites in Manitoba are a small but distinctive group within the ethnic mosaic of the oldest of Canada's Prairie Provinces. Unlike the Amish, the Hutterites or the Pennsylvania Dutch, to whom they are related, most of them are not conspicuous for their particular dress, long hair or beards. Nor do they attract attention by unusual conduct in public, or by appearing in horse-drawn buggies on the main streets of neighbouring cities. The great majority dress like other Canadians, are able to converse fluently in English without accent, and drive cars and tractors like anybody else. Even their farms and villages have, as a rule, quite a conventional appearance. It requires a trained eye to single out a Mennonite in a crowd, or to recognize one of their settlements along the road. Only when he penetrates into the old core of the Mennonite Reserves will the casual visitor recognize the remnants of their neatly arranged farm villages, the tall growth of exquisite shelter belts, or the old-world architecture of some of the buildings. But even here the traces of by-gone days and other unusual sights are rare.

In 1941, there were about 40,000 Mennonites in Manitoba,[1] or 5.4 per cent of the total population (8.7 per cent of the rural population). The Mennonites were the sixth largest of the ethnic components of Manitoba's population, and ranked next to the English, Scottish, Ukrainians, Irish, and French. The group was highly concentrated in an economically important region between Winnipeg and the American border. The Mennonites came to Manitoba only four years after its incorporation as a separate province, and were the first large group of immigrants from the European continent who added to its then small

---

[1] The Canadian census lists the Mennonites under the heading "religion" but not under "racial origin." In 1881 the Mennonite population of Manitoba was 7,776, in 1886: 9,112 in 1901: 15,246, in 1911: 15,600. in 1916: 16,541, in 1921: 21,295, in 1931: 30,352, in 1941: 39,336, and in 1951: 44,667.

number of white residents. In 1881 they represented almost 13 per cent of Manitoba's total population, and ranked fourth among its ethnic components. The Manitoba Mennonites, out of proportion with their actual numbers, have played a significant role in the development of the province.

Neither the Mennonites themselves nor their neighbours in Manitoba will ever have the slightest difficulty in determining precisely who is one of them and who is not. The distinguishing characteristics which provide the cues for their social classification are generally known and accepted: their Low German vernacular, their religious affiliations, a characteristic pattern of attitudes and values, some typical folk customs. More often than not, a tell-tale family name and residence, or at least birth, in one of the Mennonite settlements will suffice to identify a Mennonite.

While there is little controversy about the question of who is a Mennonite, few would be prepared to say what the Mennonites really are; for somehow they do not fit any of the conventional concepts commonly used to classify people. That the word "Mennonite" indicates primarily a certain religious affiliation is, of course, generally known. A few individuals are recognized as Mennonites, however, who may be Adventists or Pentecostals, or even belong to the United Church of Canada, or perhaps to no religious community at all. Moreover, there are at least nine branches of the Mennonite church in Manitoba which are completely independent of each other. On the other hand, one might occasionally find a member of some Mennonite congregation who, when asked whether he is a Mennonite, would affirm the fact, though with the qualification that he really is of German or Scottish descent. Just as there are Irish and German Catholics and Protestants, it is quite conceivable, theoretically at least, that one can be a Mennonite Scotsman, or a Presbyterian Mennonite. The word "Mennonite" evidently suggests the notion of a distinct religious affiliation in one case, but something quite different in another.

While firmly interwoven in the web of the larger society, the Mennonite group in Manitoba is not only well defined socially as to its personnel, but has preserved a high degree of inner coherence. It is a social and cultural subsystem functioning to some extent independently of Manitoba's society at large. Its social and cultural homogeneity should, however, not be overrated. The Manitoba Mennonites are divided not only into several religious bodies with somewhat different

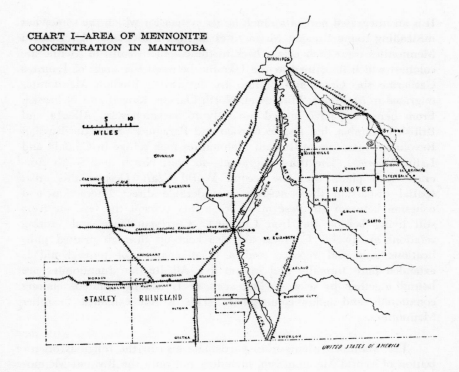

CHART I—AREA OF MENNONITE
CONCENTRATION IN MANITOBA

cultures, but also into two major sections, referred to as *Russländer* and
Kanädier. The expressions are German and quite descriptive. Although
nearly all Manitoba Mennonites are descended from the same cluster
of colonies in the Russian Ukraine, they came to Canada in different
stages. The first group arrived between 1874 and 1879, and these as
well as their descendants are now called "*Kanädier*." Those who left
Russia after the Revolution, that is, between 1923 and 1930, and their
Canadian-born children are the "*Russländer*." The time lapse between
these two migrations was sufficient to create real distinctions in the
whole outlook on life between the two groups. But the deep gulf which
existed in the years following the *Russländer* immigration has been
largely closed. Thus the Manitoba Mennonites appear as a social
microcosm with a well differentiated structure.

The Manitoba group of Mennonites is not really defined by the
boundary lines of the province, which follow the geometric designs of
the surveyor rather than the natural topography and culture areas.

It is an integrated part of a much larger system for which the somewhat misleading name Russian Mennonites has been adopted.[2] All Russian Mennonites trace their origin back to the commonwealth of Mennonite colonies which flourished in the Ukraine between the times of Empress Catherine the Great and Stalin. In the 1870's Russian Mennonites migrated to Manitoba, Minnesota, North Dakota, Kansas and Nebraska. From here they have moved not only to Saskatchewan, Alberta and British Columbia, but also to Mexico and Paraguay. After the Russian Revolution many more Russian Mennonites took refuge in Canada and Latin America. The third migration—to both North and South America—took place after the second World War. Despite this great spatial dispersion there exists a considerable direct interaction and cohesion between all these many fragments (except the few survivors still living behind the Iron Curtain). Correspondence and visiting relations are lively. Contacts are also kept up through printed publications and oral reports, and a great amount of mutual aid is extended both formally and informally. All Russian Mennonites are bound together by a we-feeling such as is usually common among conationals and fellow-countrymen. This is not extended to other Mennonites.

The Manitoba Mennonites participate also in the religious organization of World Mennonitism, including not only the Russian Mennonites but many other Mennonite congregations in Germany, Holland, France, Switzerland, Ontario, Pennsylvania, Ohio, Indiana, and elsewhere. The difference between them and the Russian group is in part ecclesiastical, in part ethnic. While the Russian group are descended from originally Saxon, Flemish and Frisian folk elements, the Mennonite communities in the eastern parts of Canada and the United States are mostly of Swiss German and South German origin. They are organized into separate religious bodies despite the fact that their creed and religious practices have the same Anabaptist-Mennonite root. At one time, both groups used literary or High German as their cult language; now most Mennonites in the east have adopted English. Pennsylvania Dutch, spoken by the eastern Mennonites as their vernacular, is sufficiently different from the West Prussian Platt of the Russian Mennonites to make communication difficult. Their folkways and mores also differ. The culture of the Amish in Lancaster County,

---

[2] The German equivalent *Russländische Mennoniten* or *Russland-Mennoniten* (not *Russische Mennoniten*) is more adequate.

Pennsylvania, for instance, is just as much an object of curiosity to a Manitoba Mennonite as to any other Canadian or American. Still, the various Mennonite religious bodies consider each other as brethren, and occasionally coöperate in church affairs and charities. As a rule, however, this coöperation takes place on an institutional level through agents and representatives of the different branches of the Mennonite church, and not between individual members of the different groups. The social system of World Mennonitism, in which the Manitoba Mennonites participate, is of the same order as the Lutheran World Federation or the Baptist World Alliance. It refers to a specific religious organization which lacks the more intimate, direct and informal relationship characteristic of the Russian Mennonite group.

As a whole it may be said that the Mennonites of Manitoba participate in no less than three or four separate social systems: the religious organization of World Mennonitism, the social system of the Russian Mennonites, and the large society of Manitoba and Canada. At the same time, the Manitoba Mennonites participate in the ethnic system of the Germans in Western Canada. The relationship between the social system of the Russian Mennonites and the German people is difficult to describe abstractly. At this point only this much can be said: in the compact Mennonite settlements in Manitoba there exist enclaves of German Lutherans which are almost completely segregated from their Mennonite neighbours. This multidimensionality and complexity of the social pattern must be kept in mind in studying the Mennonite group in Manitoba.

The title of this book was suggested by the chance remark of a student who served the author as a guide on some of his visits to Mennonite settlements. This young man, a veteran of World War II, had been brought up as a Mennonite but had left the group. To him his life in a Mennonite community was Paradise Lost, a Utopia never to be recaptured. The title "In Search of Utopia," rather than "The Mennonite Utopia," was chosen because Mennonite history is determined not so much by a preconceived ideal of a perfect society, but by the indefatigable search for a form of social life which would allow man to realize the ideal of a Christian life according to the Bible. Their story is one of search and hope, not of rigid insistence upon one definite form of perfection, and thus permits a more general application because it is so deeply human. Moreover, at no time during their wanderings do the Mennonites strike us as mere escapists from reality. With the sober common sense of Low German merchants and farmers they went about the business of organizing their social life. Perhaps it was a lack of imagination, often ascribed to their race, which prevented them from devising any unusual or extravagant methods such as communism or polygamy. As long as they were allowed to follow their rather simple religious ideals, they were disinclined to deviate too much from the accepted pattern of the society within which they happened to live. This caution is probably another reason for their survival.

While the author was engaged in his research, he was often asked by non-Mennonites: "When will they become good Canadians?" Modern nations lack the stability and the cultural homogeneity of folk societies. Precisely what makes a "good Canadian," is difficult to say. The ideal is also subject to change even if all foreign intrusions were carefully excluded. It is very true that a certain minimum of cultural homogeneity and social stability must be preserved in every society. It is equally true that large-scale immigration may throw the social order off balance, and this regardless of whether such immigrants are classified as desirable or undesirable. Social policy must strive, not to prevent social change at any cost, but to eliminate real dangers to national integrity.

The aim of a rational immigration policy should be the integration of all ethnic components into the social body of the nation at the least cost in human suffering, rather than their assimilation at any price and with maximum speed. The study of the Mennonite group in Manitoba proves (what social scientists have known for a long time) that ethnic communities perform a valuable function in adjusting immigrants to the ways of their adoptive country, and in maintaining social controls during the crucial period of transition following immigration. If the Mennonites today are relatively well-adjusted to Canadian social and economic life, and constitute hardly any problem, this is largely due to the fact that they were allowed to settle in solid communities, and that these communities have been preserved. This may retard complete assimilation. But the advocates of rapid absorption forget that assimilation means more than the adoption of the official language of the country, of uniform habits of eating, dressing, fighting wars, celebrating Dominion Day, intermarrying or playing baseball. It also may mean, and often does mean, loss of family ties, disruption of local community organization, weakening of religious convictions, moral and mental insecurity, personal maladjustment, social disorganization, perhaps pauperism, perhaps insanity, perhaps crime . . .

It seems bad policy, therefore, to break down ethnic communities deliberately or to prevent their formation by distributing immigrants with the same ethnic backgrounds over wide areas. As this study will clearly show, the preservation of strong ethnic ties does not necessarily prevent adjustment to the pattern of the dominant component of a total society. It is only that adjustment, when achieved by the group as a whole instead of individually, does not lead to the sudden breakdown of social organization but to gradual, imperceptible (and thus often all the more effective) change, until a certain equilibrium is reached which is acceptable to both, the large society and the minority.

What makes mutual understanding between different ethnic elements so difficult is ethnocentrism and provincialism. The impetuous query: When will you become good Canadians? means, of course, nothing else than: When will you conform to my own culture and norms of conduct? This attitude of the dominant component of a society has often only increased resistance to adjustment by the minorities. No society, it is true, can possibly survive without the conviction that its own mores are right, a conviction which involves some opposition to the mores of others. Yet, as L. G. Brown says, there is an alternative to this fundamental source of conflict, wherever different peoples meet: a scientific, rational understanding of human nature. "If we understand human nature," he writes, "and the process by which it develops, and acquire this knowledge before we are too old, then there is some possibility of a certain amount of tolerance."[3] Even if it should be impossible to eliminate all tensions between the ethnic components of a New World nation, this profoundly Christian and democratic attitude will at least avoid patent injustices and unnecessary hardships, and more often than not ultimately lead to mutual adjustment.

---

[3] *Immigration* (New York, 1933), p. *372*

CHAPTER I

From Religious Movement To Ethnic Group

Anabaptist Origins

MENNONITISM is an offshoot of the social and religious movement which, in the sixteenth century, revolutionized the social fabric of Western Civilization. While the more moderate majority of the reformers under the leadership of Luther, Zwingli and Calvin soon entered into alliances with secular power, the radical wing continued protesting against "incompleted" Protestantism and against all institutionalized religion. To them the establishment of the new Protestant state churches of Wittenberg, Zürich and Geneva seemed almost as evil as the old church of Rome, and a betrayal of the true ideals of the Reformation. As R. J. Smithson remarks, their principles "were in reality the principles of the Reformation carried to its logical conclusion."[1]

The religious communities of the Protestant left wing became known as Anabaptists. The movement spread like wildfire through the Holy Roman Empire. There were two camps which differed from each other mainly by the manner in which they expressed their rejection of the existing social order. On the one hand, there were "the various mystical, spiritualistic, revolutionary, or even antinomian . . . groups which came and went like flowers of the field in those days of the great renovation."[2] Others, however, disclaimed any attempt to change the "world" either by means of violence or of

---

[1] *The Anabaptists: Their Contribution to Our Protestant Heritage* (London, 1935), p. 217.
[2] Harold S. Bender, "The Anabaptist Vision," *Mennonite Quarterly Review 18* (1944): 67-88.

power politics, but preached the peaceful withdrawal from it. German writers on the subject usually refer to the latter sects as *Täufer, altevangelische Brüder* or *Taufgesinnte* to distinguish them both from the Anglo-Saxon *Baptisten* (Baptists) and from the *Wiedertäufer* like the Münsterites. The phrase "Evangelical Anabaptists" has been suggested as an appropriate translation of the traditional term *Täufer*.

It is difficult to state precisely the characteristic religious beliefs and practices which distinguished the Evangelical Anabaptists from other Protestant groups. For there never was an Anabaptist church or confession in the same sense that one may speak, for instance, of the Lutheran Evangelical church or the *Confessio Augustana*. On the contrary, the Evangelical Anabaptists were unable and unwilling to mobilize political forces in support of any large-scale socio-religious institution or of any doctrinal uniformity. Nevertheless, doctrines and religious practices of the various branches of Evangelical Anabaptism were remarkably similar. They were opposed to the excessive emphasis on grace and the inner experience of justification, together with election, as expounded by Luther and Calvin, but stressed freedom of the will, individual responsibility for moral conduct and, above all, the imitation of Christ. In this respect they seem to be more closely related than most other Protestant groups to mediaeval asceticism and the Catholic reformers in the Netherlands, like Thomas a Kempis. Furthermore, the Evangelical Anabaptists always were strict fundamentalists in the exegesis of the Holy Scripture. While the interpretation of the Bible was left to the individual, illumination by the Holy Spirit was required and presupposed. But the question regarding which of two or more contradictory interpretations is to be upheld as divinely inspired has remained the crux of Anabaptist fundamentalism, and is largely responsible for the many divisions throughout their history.

The Anabaptists rejected tradition and a thousand years of church history, and insisted upon a revival of the Apostolic church as described in the New Testament. To them, the only true church was the community of those who had been regenerated by the Holy Spirit, a brotherhood of the saved and saints bound together by the precepts of the Sermon on the Mount. This concept of the church of Christ is also responsible for their practice of adult baptism upon personal profession of faith and proof of consecration. Since they denied both the doctrine of original sin and the sacramental character of Baptism and the Lord's Supper, the ceremony of baptizing new members was considered as but a symbol of spiritual rebirth and commitment to discipleship, and as a rite of admission to God's visible church. Similarly, they believed that anyone who committed a grave sin after his admission to the church was, *ipso facto*, excluded from it until he made full repentance and restitution. This explains the rather lavish use of the church ban by most Anabaptist groups; through it church membership was publicly revoked for all those who, because of their evil conduct, had already ceased to belong to the church.

The state they considered an institution of God which must be obeyed but it was, to their mind, an order outside the Christian church. Thus government, police and military force were thought to be necessary only for sinners, while brotherly advice and, at the most, excommunication were sufficient social controls within the community of saints. Evangelical Anabaptists refused to participate in public affairs or to hold any civil office. By taking literally Christ's words in the Sermon on the Mount, "Swear not at all," they refused to take any oath, even a civil oath. Their principle of non-resistance is based on the Fifth Commandment and Christ's words: "Love your enemies," and "Resist not evil."

The organization of the Anabaptist communities was strictly congregational and democratic. While other Protestant churches accepted appointment of their ministers by the secular authorities, Anabaptist ministers were always either elected by the congregation or, in some instances, chosen by lot from the rank and file. Many of the early leaders of the movement, such as Menno Simons, the founder of Mennonitism, had been Roman Catholic priests, although laymen were not uncommon among them, as the example of Jakob Hutter, founder of the Hutterites, proves. But continued persecutions by both Protestants and Catholics soon robbed the Evangelical Anabaptists of their trained leadership. Thus unpaid lay ministers became the rule, although some form of ordination and ministerial hierarchy has been preserved in most of their churches. The puritanical simplicity of their religious services is due in part to this lack of an educated clergy, in part to the necessity of attracting the least possible attention to their meetings in times of persecution.

In or about the year 1525, many Protestants in widely dispersed regions of Central and Northern Europe leaned toward Anabaptism, although most of them soon joined the more successful Lutheran and

Zwinglian parties. Anabaptist ideas were spread quickly to distant parts by refugees fleeing from persecutions in their home country. Southern Germany and the German cantons of Switzerland were the first centers of the movement. Swiss refugees transplanted it to the neighbouring provinces of Austria, mainly Tyrol and Salzburg. From here it was carried as far as Moravia, where it found the ground well prepared by the earlier Hussite movement of the preceding century, and by the indigenous Moravian Brethren. Simlarly, the reform movement in the Netherlands was at first fed by Swiss and South German sources. In fact, Anabaptism was the leading factor of the Reformation in the Netherlands until 1566, when it was gradually replaced by Calvinism.

One of the outstanding leaders of the Evangelical Anabaptist movement in the Netherlands was Menno Simons. Born in 1496 in a Frisian village, he became a Roman Catholic priest in 1536 but renounced his faith to join an Anabaptist congregation in Leevwarden and Groningen. He was called to the office of elder (bishop) and eventually succeeded Obbe Philips, who recanted as the leader of all Evangelical Anabaptists in the Netherlands. When the counter-Reformation under the Duke of Alba (1544-1572) forced him and many of his followers to flee the country, they found a haven and new fields for their missionary zeal in several of the more tolerant principalities of Northwest Germany. It is to the merit of Menno Simons that he provided a rallying point and a solid institutional basis for the Evangelical Anabaptists in the Netherlands both among his fellow countrymen and among the leaderless mass of refugees. His brotherhood spread to many parts of Northern Germany, making converts among other Protestants, some of whom were exiles or earlier emigrants from the Netherlands. Eventually, even Anabaptist congregations having no direct connection with Menno's movement became known as Mennonites, a generic term used today as synonymous with Evangelical Anabaptists.

At the end of the Middle Ages, the feudal and semi-feudal territories into which the Holy Roman Empire was divided, were not nation-states in the modern sense, but within their boundaries they permitted the coexistence of many different folk societies. While political boundaries were subject to frequent changes, the local cultures and languages remained quite stable or changed only gradually and imperceptibly. In the area covered by the Spanish Netherlands, several distinct folk dialects were spoken (and are still spoken) which are known to philologists as Frisian, Low Franconian, and Low Saxon. The same vernaculars were used in the adjoining parts of Germany, properly speaking, such as the Rhineland and Westfalia. Frisian is considered a separate Germanic language, while both Low Franconian and Low Saxon dialects belong to the Low German family of dialects which differs so greatly from the so-called High German dialect family as to constitute almost a separate language.[3]

The emergence of the modern German and Dutch national languages, which contributed to the rise of national feelings and ultimately to the formation of separate nation-states, is mainly a result of the Reformation. The increasing importance of the written word since the invention of the printing press had fostered the development of literary languages which could be understood in ever wider areas. This trend was intensified by the desire of the Protestant reformers to spread the knowledge of the Bible among the masses. In fact, Luther's Bible translation has set the standard for the language of modern German literature which also became the language spoken by the educated classes. As ever wider strata of the population were made literate, literary German was adopted as the means of communication among all Germans regardless of the particular folk dialects which have remained their real mother tongue. In quite a similar manner modern literary Dutch was introduced as the official language for all the peoples of the Netherlands after that country had become completely independent of Germany, and was standardized in the Dutch version of the Holy Scripture. Thus the question of whether the Russian Mennonites are of Dutch or of German ethnic origin, is misleading. Neither the Swiss and South German Anabaptist refugees reaching Moravia, nor the Dutch Mennonites migrating to Northern Germany and even Poland were thought of as nationals of a foreign country in the same way as they would be in our time. Moreover, the natives of the Netherlands, who formed the bulk of the membership of the early Mennonite congregations were themselves ethnically and culturally less

---

[3] While speakers of High (that is, both Middle and Upper) German folk dialects find it easy to acquire a knowledge of literary German in school, those who speak a Low German vernacular, such as the Mennonites, have to learn literary German almost like a second language. The more common designation of literary German is High German, a term which has been avoided here in order to distinguish it from the High German folk dialects on which it is actually based.

homogeneous than the common use of Dutch in their writings might suggest.

From Prussia to Russia

During the Reformation period, Mennonite communities made their appearance in the northern part of the Kingdom of Poland and in the Duchy of Prussia. Mennonite colonies existed before 1600 in the Vistula-Nogat Delta, the territories of the cities of Danzig and Elbing, the low lands of Graudenz, Schwetz and Kulm, and in the region of Thorn. More colonies branched off in the following two centuries. They continued to flourish until the wholesale population transfers following World War II brought their social existence to an end. To understand their true nature, one has to recall the complex history of this region.

From 1280 to 1466 the Teutonic Order was the master of Prussia, carrying out a systematic policy of agricultural colonization, and founding cities under German law to replace the markets of the natives. Settlers were recruited from all German stocks. For the colonization of marsh lands requiring experience in dyking and drainage, Flemings, Seelanders and Hollanders, that is, people who today would be identified ethnically with the Dutch and Flemish, were particularly valued.

Under the Polish rule the colonization of the region was resumed with great vigor. Again settlers from German lands were favored as pioneers. In the sixteenth century, homeless Protestants and sectarians fleeing from persecution represented a welcome pool of prospects. Many of them were natives of the Netherlands. Although documents mention Dutch Anabaptists as early as 1540, it is not before 1562 that Mennonite groups are recorded by name as parties to contracts. Most of the "Hollanders," by which all immigrants from the Netherlands, including Flanders, were known throughout Poland, were as a rule engaged in the drainage and cultivation of marshy land. The pattern of colonization in this region fostered group settlement and the formation of ethnic communities. Any attempt to project the national consciousness and nationalistic rivalries of later years to sixteenth-century Poland must give rise to serious misconceptions. Intimate interaction was largely confined to socially and economically self-contained communities, which enjoyed a measure of self-government under elected or hereditary magistrates. New settlements were usually effected by a contract between a landowner and groups of immigrant families who were homogeneous as to place of origin, language, cultural background and particularly religion.

Although the Polish Crown remained faithful to the church of Rome, the reform movement took hold of many parts of the realm. Some local lords embraced the new creed, others were at least tolerant of the Reformers. Under Sigismund II (1548-72) Protestant congregations enjoyed virtual toleration throughout Poland. Shortly after his death, the principle of absolute religious liberty for all religious dissenters was confirmed in the Compact of Cracow. Special privileges were extended to the Mennonites as a distinctive religious body. Although persecutions and infringements upon their civil rights continued in various localities, the Polish kings, as a rule, protected the brethren. Several royal charters were issued guaranteeing them the right to worship in their public buildings, to control their schools and teachers, to baptize their children according to their own rite, and to bury their dead in their own cemeteries.

It is very unlikely that the Mennonite settlements in Poland were solely populated by Mennonite refugees who arrived from the Netherlands in the sixteenth century. Although the ethnic composition of the native population along the lower Vistula at the time of the Reformation cannot be ascertained with any accuracy, it seems pretty certain that the Mennonite immigrants did not come into an entirely alien country where Polish culture and language reigned supreme. Particularly in the north and in the cities, German speech and culture prevailed while cultural and linguistic survivals from Flanders and the Netherlands remained a living memory among the natives. It is also known that Menno Simons himself undertook a missionary journey to the Baltic region between 1546 and 1553, that is, before Mennonite immigrants are at all mentioned in any extant document. Thus it would seem that the early members of the Mennonite church in the Vistula-Nogat Delta were recruited not only from among original Mennonites coming from the Netherlands at the time of the Reformation but comprised also converts from among the older Hollander colonists, as well as other elements, particularly Anabaptists from Middle and Upper Germany. They were equally heterogeneous with regard to their occupational background. In addition to farmers and amber fishers, they included urban dwellers engaged in the manufacture of silk ribbons, the distilling of liquor, in dyeing, banking and commerce.

Despite this variety of backgrounds and occupations, the Mennonite communities in different parts of the country kept in contact with each other and with their mother churches in the Netherlands. Their devotional literature was largely imported from the Netherlands, and printed in literary Dutch. Religious services were, in the beginning at least, conducted in the same language. Common experiences, common interests, particularly in their relations with non-Mennonite neighbours and the public institutions of the country, and a cultural background common to the majority of them, created a bond of cohesion among all Mennonites along the Vistula. Within the larger society of the region they were, in time, clearly perceived as a distinctive social unit. They were differentiated from others primarily by their religious convictions and practices. They were also distinguished by their Germanic speech. In earlier years the Mennonites in Polish Prussia had been equally separated from their German-speaking countrymen with regard to language and culture. But at the time of their migration to Russia, German was largely, if not generally, used in their church services. Over the same period the original Netherland folk dialects had been replaced by the so-called West Prussian Platt. This is a composite Low German folk dialect with Flemish admixtures and is common to all Germans of the Vistula region.

From this brief account it will be seen that at first Mennonitism continued to be primarily a religious movement which spread among the Hollander colonists under the influence of Mennonite immigrants from the Netherlands. Several rural communities became solidly Mennonite, while the more cosmopolitan city populations included Mennonite minorities. The social definition of the group was based primarily on their religion, although their Dutch cultural heritage was a strong supporting factor, to the extent that "Hollander" and "Mennonite" often meant the same thing.

As a consequence of the partitions of Poland, the whole lower Vistula valley was ultimately included in the new administrative unit of the Province of West Prussia. Frederick II, the new ruler, confirmed the Mennonites in their ancient privileges including freedom of worship, control of their own schools, and even exemption from military service. After a few years, however, serious clashes occurred with recruiting officers who were combing the country for soldiers for the Prussian armies. Although Frederick's successor once more confirmed their privilege of military exemption in 1787, he required, nevertheless, the payment of a fine of five thousand dollars a year in support of the Military Academy of Kulm. Shortly afterwards, a royal decree was issued prohibiting any further acquisition of real property by Mennonites, and ordering the payment of tithes to the established Lutheran church on all land purchased from Lutherans. These new restrictions caused considerable concern among the West Prussian Mennonites, all the more since they were prolific and already troubled by a growing landless proletariat. The far-reaching political and economic changes were interpreted by many as a challenge to the integrity of their religious life, and revived memories of the migrations by which, in past centuries, their forefathers had evaded persecutions in the Netherlands. The Tsarina of Russia, engaged in a large-scale colonization project for the newly conquered territory north of the Black Sea, took advantage of this situation.

In the eighteenth century, improvement of farm economy and agrarian reform were high on the agenda of the enlightened monarchs of Eastern Europe, after they had succeeded in wresting vast territories from the Turks and had expanded their domain at the expense of the Polish Crown. Resettlement and colonization of underdeveloped and depopulated provinces was one of the pillars of this broad reform policy. Another was the education of the people to greater economic productivity. In many instances both purposes were combined by creating model colonies with the help of immigrants drawn from economically more advanced countries. Racial or national considerations played hardly any role in the plans of the rulers, although their purely economic and social policies often had the effect of creating large ethnic islands and of strengthening the German element throughout Eastern Europe.

On the other hand, the religion of the immigrants was of greater concern. While the rulers of the day and their advisers were themselves often highly sophisticated in matters of faith, the preservation of religious peace among their subjects, and particularly the uniformity of ecclesiastical institutions under the strict control of the state, appeared as the best guarantee of internal security. Religion was primarily considered as a means of tying the people to the crown, making them law-abiding, industrious and productive, and increasing the prosperity and military strength of the country. The settlement of relatively small groups of foreign dissenters was, nevertheless, frequently encouraged, though with the necessary safeguards against their becoming centers of agitation and unrest. The monarchs of the day were ready and anxious to attract any group of colonists likely to become successful farmers and obedient subjects. Frequently it was precisely sectarians who held out the best promise of answering the demand. The toleration of religious, linguistic, racial and similar differences was all the easier as the empires of the East, unlike the national states of Western Europe, neither required nor aimed at the cultural homogeneity of their populations.

In 1762 and 1763 Catherine II issued two manifestos inviting foreigners from all over Europe, except Jews, to settle in Russia. Free land and many other inducements were offered, together with complete freedom of religion, although any kind of proselytizing, except among her Moslem subjects, was forbidden. A most significant step was the enactment of a special body of laws by which all immigrant settlers were to be kept completely separate from the native population. This legal system was an example of governmental social planning on a broad basis; it regulated not only the flow of immigrants and their support en route and during the first years of settlement at the expense of the treasury, but laid down in great detail the form of economic, political and social organization under which they were expected to live.

The excellent opportunities offered to foreign settlers in New Russia (the present-day Ukraine) attracted the interest of the Prussian Mennonites at a time when prospects in their native country were anything but promising due to the changed political and economic conditions. In 1788 the Mennonites were informed by the Russian Minister to Danzig that special privileges and concessions had been granted to them, as the Russian authorities were very anxious to see them come and settle there. One set of provisions dealt with the conditions of their migration, government subsidies during the trip, and the like. Another section determined matters of taxation and fishing rights, and fixed the size of the family homestead (excluding the use of land held coöperatively by the commune) at a generous 175 acres of *udobnie,* that is, good, arable, productive land. Finally, religious freedom as granted to all foreign colonists, was more clearly specified, particularly regarding the taking of oaths, always a crucial matter with the Mennonites. They were also exempted from all military services for all times. Schools, however, were not mentioned in this document, probably because education was not yet considered a matter of the state but left to the church. These details are of some interest in the present context as they suggest comparisons between the rather liberal conditions granted by Russia toward the end of the eighteenth century and those offered a hundred years later by Canada and the United States—comparisons which were made by the Mennonites themselves and which have frequently influenced their interpretation of certain legal documents.

The first settlement of West Prussian Mennonites was made in 1789 on the Chortitza River, a small creek flowing into the Dnieper just inside the big bend. Both geographically and sociologically, New Russia bore a striking resemblance to the Great Plains of America at the time of their colonization. It was a vast, sparsely populated area of steppe or prairie land where primitive nomadic tribes, such as the Nogaitsi, were being driven from their ancient grazing grounds in order to make room for agricultural settlement. At the time, the war against the Turks was still in progress a short distance to the south.

The flow of Mennonite immigrants continued for several decades. It received a boost when Danzig and Thorn were added to the Hohenzollern possessions in 1792, and again ten years later when negotiations with King Frederick William III failed to bring a redress of Mennonite grievances. A second colony was founded on the Molotschna River,[4] in the Gubernia of Taurida, in 1803. Between 1788 and 1810 an estimated fifteen to eighteen thousand Mennonites reached the Old and the New Colony, the great majority of them coming from the lower Vistula, although groups from East Prussia and the Warthe-Netze district were also among them. Later arrivals included many substantial farmers who were attracted more by economic opportunities than by religious considerations. Although the Russian Government officially halted immigration under the conditions of the Colonial Law in 1833, the introduction of the military draft in Prussia in 1841 induced additional numbers of Mennonites to join their brethren in the Ukraine. Two more colonies were founded on the Volga, namely, Am Trakt, in 1855, and Old Samara, in 1859. Immigration from Prussia, which ultimately reached a total of about 8,000 families,

---

[4] Molotschna is the German transliteration of a Russian word. Although several English transliterations exist, the German version was retained because it has been generally adopted by writers on the Russian Mennonites.

continued until 1870 without, however, leading to the creation of any new colonies.

The Mennonite Commonwealth in Russia[5]

The Mennonite group in Russia was formed in very much the same manner as later the ethnic groups in America were formed: not through the wholesale transfer of entire communities and villages, but through the migration of small bands of individuals who came from different places and had somewhat different backgrounds although common language and traditions helped them to adjust themselves to each other when they met, often for the first time, in the new country. The continued flow of immigrants from Prussia to Russia, old family ties, fond memories, common religious interests, mutual aid, correspondence and travellers—all this generated the feeling that the Mennonite colonies in the two countries belonged together. Yet the unity did not last forever. After some time the Mennonites in West Prussia were differentiated from their German neighbours only through their religion while the emigrants developed into a separate people, clearly distinguished from both the large society and other German-speaking colonists in Russia.

Two factors are responsible for this emergence of a closed Mennonite social system in the new country. On the one hand, the immigrants were motivated not just by a desire to escape a felt threat to their religion and economic well-being, but still more by the hope of finally realizing the utopian community suggested by this same religion, in complete separation from the wicked world. On the other hand, the framework of Russia's Colonial Law fostered the isolation of immigrant groups and protected them in their homogeneity and self-sufficiency. This law was the work of eminent jurists, often Baltic noblemen of German extraction who were entirely familiar with German agrarian institutions. Although it did regulate the life of the Mennonite immigrants in great detail, it was not completely imposed upon them from above. Basically, the Colonial Law of Russia, enacted first on March 19, 1764, and after several amendments incorporated in the Russian Code of Law of 1842, was an adaptation of the traditional

---

[5] For a fuller version see E. K. Francis, "The Mennonite Commonwealth in Russia, 1789-1914: A Sociological Interpretation," *Mennononite Quarterly Review 25* (1951): 173-182, 200.

solidaristic form of settlement and community organization familiar to most immigrants and readily adopted by them. In addition, the authorities were quite flexible in the application of the law. They were anxious to learn by their mistakes, to consult the settlers themselves, and to make adjustments in the legal and administrative practices wherever necessary. In this process of constant readjustment the Mennonite colonies occupied an extraordinary position. A. Klaus, a high Russian official in the colonial administration and a keen student of society, remarked later that the Russian Government, "convinced of the surprisingly quick success of Mennonite economy, took their institutions, up to a certain degree, as a model for the organization of the majority of the other colonies of foreigners in the Ukraine."[6]

The Russian program of colonization was primarily concerned with the type of peasant farmer, at the time still prevalent in Central and Eastern Europe, who, living not only on or from his land but also with his land, is a conserver rather than exploiter of the soil; whose ideas of wealth and well-being cannot be expressed in terms of capital, profit, comfort, and consumption but who draws his satisfaction from pride in work done well, from improvement and increase of his holdings and herds, from the responsible management of a large household, and from the knowledge of having provided for future generations. The social system envisaged by this program was familistic, localistic, and solidaristic; the units of social, as well as economic and political, organizations were accordingly the farm family, the village commune, and the colony. The latter was the basic unit of administration, taxation and the seat of lower courts. Above the district there was the bureaucratic system of the imperial government. On the *volost* level local government elected from below met with the agents of central administration appointed and directed from above: the *Oberschulze* with the council of mayors and other representatives of villages, on the one hand, the inspector or superintendent responsible to the governor on the other. After some experimentation and many mistakes, the foreign colonies in New Russia were completely separated from the jurisdiction of the governors. A special bureau was established, first under the Department of the Interior, later under that of Crown Lands. Its system of administration was a benevolent paternalism in the humane, yet progressive, spirit of the Enlightenment, mainly con-

---

[6] *Unsere Kolonien: Studien und Materialen zur Geschichte und Statistik der ausländischen Kolonisation in Russland*, translated from the Russian edition of 1869 by J. Töws (Odessa, 1887), pp. 163f.

cerned with peace and order, as well as the improvement of industry and economy, but otherwise encouraging initiative and self-government among the settlers without encroaching upon the inner religious and cultural life of the colonies. The authorities dealt rarely with individuals but treated the colonies, and within them the villages, as corporate bodies represented by their own elected officers.

The village commune was the actual owner of all the land within its boundaries. Some of it was parcelled out in holdings of 175 acres each and given to individual families in permanent usufruct. Other tracts of land were reserved for communal pastures, sheep ranges, haylands, roads, churches, schools, mills, distilleries, and other industrial establishments. Small lots were provided for cotters, artisans, and landless folk of all kinds. The village assembly, to which each land-holding family delegated a representative, exercised a large decree of control over the economic, social, and cultural life of all inhabitants. The elected chairman of the assembly, the *Dorfschulze*, acted not only as chief executive officer and mayor but also as tax collector and police judge. Close habitat and the open-field system, which was introduced into the Mennonite settlements shortly after their first immigration, partly as a protection against the as yet insecure conditions in the country and partly in response to a definite government policy, further increased their inner coherence and quickly molded the whole group into a well-integrated social organism.

Both the paternalistic nature of government and the traditions of the Mennonite sect were rather adverse to the cultivation of strong leader personalities. Like the Puritans of New England, the Mennonites constituted a movement of plain folk under elected lay preachers, organized according to democratic, equalitarian, and congregational principles. They were adverse as much to higher learning as to worldly ambitions and conspicuous behaviour among their members. As peasant farmers they had, moreover, little incentive or opportunity to develop an upper class or intelligentsia providing the ground and climate in which ambitions and powerful personalities would thrive. Thus, during their Russian period only one man stands out as a really influential shaper of their destiny, Johann Cornies. And even in his case the resistance of the group and their religious leaders was overcome only through the direct interference of Tsar Alexander I, who not only took interest in the progress of the Mennonite colonies but had great personal confidence in the successful businessman and farmer of the Molotschna colony.

The institution through which Cornies pushed his economic and cultural reforms, with the full backing of an autocratic government, was the *Verein zur Erhöhung von Landwirtschaft und Gewerbe,* a Board of Trade and Agriculture instituted by the Bureau of Colonization in order to supersede the autonomous local authorities wherever their conservatism threatened to stifle economic progress. Through these boards, established in each colony, Cornies was able to force his fellow Mennonites to adopt new farming methods including the use of fertilizers and a four-crop rotation with summerfallow, and to improve buildings, water supply, sanitation, and fire protection. His manifold interests and activities extended, however, also to matters of social welfare and schooling. In particular, he was the instigator of institutions of higher education in the different colonies, forerunners of the *Zentralschulen,* which, in 1859, were recognized as official normal schools for the training of Mennonite teachers.

When Cornies died in 1848, the Mennonite colonies in Russia were on the way to becoming the most prosperous and economically best balanced rural communities in all of Russia, the prize exhibit of the colonization authorities. In 1874 one visitor described the Molotschna colony as follows:

> The dwelling houses were large brick structures with tile roofs, a flower garden between the street and the house, and [a] well-kept vegetable garden and orchard in the rear. The stable with splendid work horses of heavy build, and the shed with vehicles of all descriptions, among them family coaches and all kinds of American farming machinery. They were certainly the best appointed farm communities I had seen anywhere. Scattered over the country were large isolated estates, with buildings reminding one of the feudal baronial castles of Western Europe. Their owners were millionaire Mennonites who had acquired large tracts of land by private purchase. [One of them owned] over half-a-million sheep scattered in flocks all along the coast of the Black Sea.[7]

Amidst all this rapid progress and worldly success the role of religion, once the *raison d'être* of the group, almost receded into the background. It seems that at the moment when the Mennonite utopia, the community of the saints and saved, lay within reach of realization, it became secularized and void of its spiritual content, a commonwealth

---

[7] Quoted by I. I. Friesen, The Mennonites of Western Canada With Special Reference to Education (Master's Thesis, University of Saskatchewan, 1934.)

of ordinary people with the ambitions and motivations of sinners and the fallen nature of man. Religious convictions and interests now were one aspect of everyday life, perhaps still a central but by no means the only aspect. Many concessions had to be made to other conflicting interests which frequently dominated and determined action. Religion, at one time a spiritual power permeating all personal hopes and desires, was institutionalized, and religious institutions were but one factor among many other institutions, often more in the foreground of attention.

As a religious body, the Mennonites were organized into congregations, that is, voluntary associations of believers in a given locality or region. The test of admission consisted in spiritual conversion and high moral conduct. Authority was vested in the *Bruderschaft* (church assembly) presided over by an elder.[8] Elder and other preachers were elected and functioned as teachers of the Gospel and leaders in religious exercises while the deacons took care of works of charity. The *Bruderschaft* watched over the conduct of the members; it could censor them, impose penances, or expel deviants. Mennonites were expected to avoid participation in the affairs of the world, to refuse public offices, and to refrain from any use of force or violence. Intermarriage and intimate social intercourse with non-Mennonites, as well as with excommunicated Mennonites, were forbidden. The unbaptized children of members were to be educated in the faith and treated as novices of a kind. Up to this point the organization of the brotherhood followed familiar lines. It claimed only a segment of the total personality, and its purpose was limited to clearly religious objectives. In addition to being a Mennonite, a member of the brotherhood continued to be part of his local community and of the people into which he was born. Thus the brotherhood presupposes the existence of a large society from whose midst its members are recruited, into which they remain integrated to a considerable extent, and whose economic, political, and in part social benefits they enjoy.

In Russia the Mennonites, defined as such by their membership in the brotherhood, constituted the whole of society, not just a section of it. The law recognized them as a corporate body charged with the satisfaction of all, or almost all, human needs of its members. The

---

[8] The conventional English translation of the German designation "Aeltester" with "bishop" is somewhat misleading, since it suggests an episcopal church organization, and has been avoided in the present context.

individual rights of Mennonites, particularly important property rights, were derived from the corporate rights of the group, membership in which was acquired by birth. Although aided in the beginning by the institutions of the large society, primarily its economy and government, the Mennonites were expected to organize themselves as a self-sufficient, self-regulating, and self-perpetuating social system. Because they were foreigners and heretics they remained sealed off from the rest of the Orthodox and Russian population. Outside contacts were kept at a minimum, above all because of the difference of language. Their prosperity depended primarily on what they were able to achieve with the natural resources put at their exclusive disposal and the opportunities supplied by the economic system of the Russian Empire. The manner in which they would shape their whole way of life, exercise controls, and make social institutions work, was left to their own ingenuity within the rather broad and liberal framework provided by the Colonial Law. If they were not yet a people when they arrived, they were forced into becoming one by the conditions of their settlement.

The novel situation required a redefinition of the relationship between religious and nonreligious interests and institutions. The traditional distinction was made between a sacred (Mennonite) and a secular (non-Mennonite) sphere of life and of social interaction. Now, however, the Mennonite social system viewed as a brotherhood, on the one hand, and the system viewed as a people, as society itself, on the other, became coextensive as to territory and personnel. Yet, a complete identification of both, which could have been achieved through the institution of a theocracy, for instance, was precluded by the Anabaptist teaching on the separation of church and state, brotherhood and society. Accordingly, the autonomous structure of the old sectarian congregation was retained. Parallel to it, a new secular society was organized with its own institutions; that is to say, theoretically at least the Mennonite colony and village community with their local assemblies and elected officers were kept apart from the Mennonite church with its own assembly and functionaries. This subtle division of powers and spheres of influence created new problems and inner contradictions.

Above all, the traditional opposition against participation in worldly affairs became an anachronism; for the "world," at least the immediate little world of the colony, was now a Mennonite world. Nor was there an established church to be protested against in the name of the rigorous spirituality of the brotherhood. Religious freedom did not mean that every individual was free to worship in his own way; it meant the corporate freedom of Mennonites to practice their particular religion according to their own traditions and understanding. Moreover, membership in the secular Mennonite system was defined by membership in the religious congregation. A rapprochement and mutual interpenetration of both systems was thus inevitable, changing the sectarian character of the latter and forcing it into the position of an established territorial or parish church. When faced with the necessity of maintaining peace and order in their own colonies, internal sanctions and the less drastic external sanctions provided by the church assembly proved insufficient. Excommunication as last resort, however, had serious legal implications. For only a Mennonite in good standing and his family could hold land and enjoy the legal privileges extended to the group. Loss of membership in the church meant also loss of civil status amounting in some instances to expulsion from the colony. Because of the socially disruptive consequences of excommunication, often pronounced for petty infractions of church discipline, the practice actually had to be curbed by the Russian authorities. Instead, the Mennonite officer of civil administration was compelled to exercise police power and coercion by force, including corporal punishment, quite contrary to the principles of his religion.

The identification of membership in a parish church and membership in a village and colony also suggested the regional unification of local congregations in conferences of elders and preachers and the establishment of the *Kirchen-Konvent* in 1851. The position of the church officials was thereby greatly strengthened, at times leading to abuse of their spiritual influence for personal ambitions or making religion a means to worldly ends. Particularly in the New Colony, the ministers seem to have sided consistently with the party of proprietors against the growing landless classes. Since the preachers were usually elected from the ranks of wealthy farmers, who wielded influence also in local government, the officially recognized Mennonite church became identified with secular interests and power.

As the religious congregations and preacher conferences, though formally still separate, tended to coöperate ever more closely with the secular administration (at times using the secular power to further religious unity and interests, at times being themselves used to strengthen and support government or economic interests), the old religious forces in the Mennonite heritage were once more set free. Protest movements, essentially sectarian in character, made their appearance, particularly among the lower classes, which claimed that Mennonite principles had been violated by the fusion of religious with nonreligious institutions, even if both were in the hands of Mennonites. This led to the formation of independent brotherhoods of dissenters intent upon restoring the old spirit and religious fervor by withdrawing from their worldly brethren. Although freedom of religious association was entirely in line with Anabaptist and Mennonite traditions, the leaders of the official church did not hesitate to invoke the arm of the secular power and to threaten their opponents with economic ruin in order to enforce religious unity and bring schismatics back into the fold. In some instances, it was actually the Russian authorities who upheld the civil rights of dissenters and religious freedom against the established church in the Mennonite communities.

The Russian period of Mennonite history thus brings clearly to the fore the dilemma and utopian character of a sect. It must either suffer pagans and sinners to run the world, thereby preserving the purity of its ideals without putting them to the test, or it must, like Dostoyevski's Grand Inquisitor, accommodate itself to the stark realities of life in this world, thereby losing its original character. In the period between 1790 and 1870 the Mennonite sectarians in Russia had become a people whose conspicuous secular successes were bought at the price of institutionalization of religion and secularization of the inner life of the group.

CHAPTER II

The Promised Land

The Causes of Emigration

WITHIN less than three generations the Mennonites in New Russia had become a distinctive people with well developed institutions, protected by law and favored by the authorities, thriving by their own industry, and enjoying a full share in the general prosperity of their adopted country. Yet a brief period of five years between 1873 and 1878 witnessed the mass exodus of 15,000, or 30 per cent of the total Mennonite population in the Ukraine to Canada and the United States. The factors responsible can be divided in those of push and pull. Among the factors of push were the inner disturbances on the one hand and the changes brought about by external forces on the other. Among the factors of pull were the lure of better opportunities and more desirable conditions abroad, as well as the intervention of foreign interest groups anxious to attract immigrants.

The religious conflicts within the group have been briefly mentioned. These were closely associated with social problems arising from economic maladjustments. The Mennonite social system in Southern Russia was essentially agrarian, but this does not mean that the whole population was engaged in farming. Particularly among those migrating to the Chortitza River had been many craftsmen and others ill-adapted to becoming homesteaders. Nevertheless the workshops and small industrial enterprises, such as mills or distilleries primarily supplied the wants of the settlers. In the course of time Mennonite farmers as well as manufacturers began to produce for Russia's expanding domestic and export markets. Among the goods sold outside the colonies were farm implements (many of them invented or improved by Mennonites), wool, and livestock for breeding purposes. When the Ukraine became one of the world's great granaries in the latter part of the nineteenth century, Mennonite farm economy shifted from animal husbandry to crop farming, with small grain an important export article shipped via Black Sea ports. Simultaneously, the trade in processed and manufactured goods increased greatly in volume, adding to their prosperity and sustaining an ever-growing population.

This limited commercialization of agriculture, and partial industrialization, absorbed some of the population surplus, but it did not solve all the social problems caused by a high natural increase. Economy and demography were only in part responsible for the difficulties arising in the 1860's. As in every agrarian society, the values of the group were those typical of the peasant farmer; social prestige and personal satisfaction were based on the possession and successful use of land. This standard was supported by the fact that only *Wirte* had the right to participate in public affairs. A *Wirt* was one who held the standard share of 175 acres of arable land in a colony, by virtue of which all other rights in communal property and enterprises accrued to him. Since the holdings were indivisible, the number of *Wirte* in each village remained constant. Thus there arose the problem of what to do about the ever increasing landless population, including not only the descendants of original immigrants who never had acquired land and those who had lost their land through mismanagement or misfortune, but also the non-inheriting children of the *Wirte* themselves.

Several avenues were open to these people. They could work as laborers on farms, in workshops, and in local industries; they could establish themselves in various trades or services; or they could seek employment outside the colonies, for instance in near-by Russian cities, although the authorities discouraged mobility among the peasants. Whatever they chose, their social status remained inferior and they were practically disfranchized. Thus there existed great social and psychological pressure toward the acquisition of farm land, particularly of a holding within the village commune under the provisions of the Colonial Law. The demand for land could be satisfied in a number of ways. One consisted in the foundation of new village communes on land held in reserve within the colonies precisely for that purpose. Yet these reserves were soon exhausted. The partition of surplus land used for grazing, or leased to wealthy farmers and manufacturers, was resisted by the *Wirte* as the original shareholders, because they jointly enjoyed the usufruct of such communal property. Moreover, the farmers were obviously interested in preserving the pool of tractable native labor from among the landless Mennonites.

Another possibility for increasing the number or size of individual land holdings was the acquisition of either small parcels or whole estates outside the colonies. Such land was available from various sources: the Crown, private land owners (particularly the nobility), and the Nogaitsi, a tribe of Tartaric nomads whose reservation contained more land than they possibly could use. Land holdings bought or rented by individuals, although often large and increasing in numbers over the years, contributed to the prosperity of some families without, however, solving the problem of the landless proletariat. Moreover, the *khutors* (private estates) of Mennonites did not fall under the provisions of the Colonial Law. More important was the collective acquisition of land by the colonies, which could be either attached to the original territory or organized into daughter colonies after the traditional model.

A promising beginning had thus been made to solve the pressing land problem although the systematic establishment of new colonies, particularly its financial side, was as yet largely in the blueprint stage. At the same time, however, land immediately adjacent to the original settlements, especially in the fertile Molotschna region, became increasingly scarce. For when the Nogaitsi suddenly emigrated to Turkey, the region was quickly settled by non-Mennonite farmers. The machinations of the *Wirte* party, staunchly supported by the established church and its preachers, an overcrowding of the trades, and a general depression in Southern Russia due to crop failures, brought the fight over the land question to a climax. This conflict and the protracted negotiations between the landless, the land owners, and the Bureau of Colonization dominated the public scene throughout the 1860's, particularly in the Molotschna colony. The land quarrel was finally settled in favour of the landless through a series of imperial decrees issued prior to 1871. But at the time when the emigration began to crystallize, the wounds inflicted during this conflict were still fresh, while the beneficial consequences of the settlement were not yet clearly perceptible. There was a general unrest and ferment which only needed an added spark to activate a large-scale social movement.

This spark was provided by the liberation of the Russian peasants in 1861. Its significance for the Mennonites (and other foreign colonists) became apparent as the principles of the reform were gradually translated into administrative and legal practice. The immediate nexus between the liberation of the peasants and the status of the Mennoites in Russia (who like all foreign colonists were treated as Crown peasants) can be fully appreciated only against the background of the profound changes in the political philosophy by which the country was governed. It was this ideological development rather than the legal measures which most affected the Mennonite position.

The Russian version of agrarian reform followed a pattern which became generally accepted in the nineteenth century in the Western civilized world. Elsewhere economic and political reforms had been the end result of the interplay between a multitude of social forces and intellectual movements affecting the structure of society. In the great empire of the East, however, the new pattern was imposed from above and supported by a rather small élite, while the great masses of the people remained politically inarticulate. To them, government and large-scale social planning was something that happened like rain or hail; it could be influenced, and perhaps prevented, by intercession with the great and powerful but not by popular demand or opposition. New philosophies affected only those who were in contact and communication with the important events of the time, not the illiterate "folk," moving silently in the small world of local communities and within the orbit of values typical of peasant cultures.

Two intellectual movements were shaping thought and action among the educated and influential strata of Russia's society. One followed Western liberal and democratic ideals about the rights of man to individual freedom, equality before the law, and participation in the affairs of state. These were branded as "Westerners" by another group, the Slavophils, who wished to preserve traditional values and institutions and to purge the Russian soul of all foreign influences. Both movements were nationalistic, aiming at the integration of all the subjects of the Tsar in one culturally, economically, and socially unified, cohesive, and powerful social system after the image of the modern nation.

Neither National Liberalism nor political Romanticism were favorable to corporate rights granted to segregated groups in the spirit of an obsolescent political order and philosophy. To the party of Westerners, the little self-contained and localistic colonies under separate law and administration were an anachronism. While the Mennonites were not precisely a privileged estate like church or nobility, they were still privileged as a group. Moreover, their abstinence from public affairs outside their settlements was contrary to the ideals of democratic government. Their schools were particularistic and church-controlled. Still worse, they refused to share in the burden of national defence, considered as both a civic duty and right by the Liberals in their opposition to standing armies, recruitment by fraud and violence, and a military caste system.

The latter argument was understood also by the Slavophils, though for different reasons. Exemption from military service was not only unjust, it was outrightly subversive. To this powerful party the presence of an unassimilated group of sectarians and foreigners, with living standards far above that of the native Russian peasant, was still more distasteful. Like the German ministers and officers of the Tsar, these colonies of pampered German settlers in the nation's richest region appeared as dangerous sources of contamination which no "Russia First" movement could countenance. That this double onslaught on their position did not destroy the separate existence of the Mennonite ethnic system in Russia is largely due to the fact that the reform inaugurated by such hostile ideologies soon bogged down in the quagmire of reaction. The forces which blocked Liberalism and Romanticism inadvertently saved the Mennonite community. As long as the Tsar continued to rule autocratically, he could honor the word of the Tsar, or at least mitigate the threat immanent in the spirit of the new era and its reform legislation.

Although accompanied by much public discussion and attacks in the Russian press, the implications of the liberation of the peasants were not felt by the Mennonites until a decade later when they were applied to the foreign colonists. The Council of State finally decided to dissolve the separate administration under the Department of Crown Lands and to make the Mennonite colonies a part of the ordinary administrative divisions, the *uiezd* (county) and the *gubernia* (province). This meant that the Mennonites now became a rather insignificant minority in the *zemstvos*, the major bodies of local self-government, although the functions of village commune and *volost*[1]

---

[1] The original Russian term for village commune was "colony" and for what we have consistently called a colony, "colonists' district." In 1871 both terms were abolished and the district was now called a "volost."

with their assemblies and lower courts remained unchanged. The landless were given the right to elect representatives who voted together with the landowners on all matters affecting them, including the election of officers. All former Crown land held under the provisions of the Colonial Law became personal property in fee simple. The remaining surplus land in the colonies was to be divided into individual holdings, either of standard size or of half and quarter standard size, and to be distributed among the landless. At the same time the consolidation of scattered strips of land belonging to the same holding was facilitated. The settler-proprietors, as the colonists were now called, were required to pay the regular provincial and state taxes and to contribute to the upkeep of local institutions such as schools and hospitals. Finally, all official records, correspondence or other documents had to be made out in the Russian language. At about the same time the Mennonites were compelled to teach Russian in their schools on all levels, for which purpose Russian teachers were appointed.[2]

Such were the changes brought about in the conditions of the Mennonites in Southern Russia as an aftermath of the liberation of the peasants. Together with a changing climate of public opinion they were danger signals threatening an ultimate breakdown of the coherence, independence and self-sufficiency of the ethnic system. Yet, the reaction to this challenge was formulated primarily in religious terms, not in terms of the new national ideology in whose name the threat was actually made. In Eastern Europe the national minorities had as yet not been fully awakened. Most of the ethnic groups and islands remained in a pre-nationalistic stage of religious culture. To be sure some of the Mennonite opposition against the new situation found its expression in arguments reminiscent of true national conflicts. P. M. Friesen, a prominent Mennonite preacher opposing the emigration, quotes one of its principal promoters, Elder Leonhard Sudermann, of Berdiansk, as saying: "Those of our young people who enter Russian high schools are lost." To this Friesen comments that people like Sudermann apparently thought that Mennonite and German was the same thing. He goes on complaining that such men lacked under-

---

[2] It does not seem that any effective attempt was made by the Russian authorities to assume the direction of the Mennonite schools before 1881, although this is frequently mentioned as one cause of the emigration. At the time, there was apparently much talk about such a step which greatly disturbed the Mennonites, but decisive action was taken only when school supervision was shifted from the Department of Crown Lands to that of Education.

standing and love for Russia which, according to him, was perfectly compatible with loyalty to the Mennonite faith. They obtained, the author continues, their ideas from German history books and from contact with certain half-educated Russians who were narrowly nationalistic, modernistic in their religious belief or even outright anti-religious.[3]

It is very doubtful whether such considerations alone could ever have provided sufficient motivation for the emigration movement. This required an event which could be interpreted as a direct and obvious threat to Mennonite religious principles, so that the general dissatisfaction could be rationalized and the drastic reaction justified. Such an event was the abrogation of the privilege of military exemption for all former foreign colonists. From the Russian standpoint the move was the logical consequence of their new status as free citizens. Military exemptions had been granted originally as an inducement to foreigners to settle in New Russia. Now that the colonial policy had been abandoned, it was but one of many other privileges which had lost their meaning. Yet, to the Mennonites the solemn promise that they would never be called upon to bear arms had been not only a practical advantage but a matter of conscience and trust. Now this trust in the word of Caesar had been broken by unilateral action, while the divine command, as they understood it, required firm resistance and, if need be, martyrdom. In the light of their sacred traditions the situation was absolutely clear on this point. They could not accommodate themselves to the unjust demands of the secular authorities without abandoning the very *raison d'être* of their group.

The responsible Mennonite functionaries approached the authorities in charge. Public meetings were held to discuss the question of military service, as indeed attention was centred on it for a whole decade beginning late in 1870. Petitions were drafted and several delegations were dispatched to lobby in St. Petersburg and the summer headquarters of the Tsar at Yalta. When the new military law was finally promulgated in 1874, making personal service compulsory for the whole population of Russia, its section 157 provided that Mennonites were not to bear arms but to serve as stretcher bearers and medical corps men or in workshops. Yet even these conditions seemed unacceptable to them.

---

[3] P. M. Friesen, *Die alt-evangelische Mennonitische Brüderschaft in Russland (1789-1910) im Rahmen der mennonitischen Gesamtgeschichte* (Halbstadt, 1911), p. 500f.

The agitation for emigration began almost as soon as the plans of the Government became known, and continued during the whole period of protracted negotiations when there was no certainty whatever as to their final outcome. In part, of course, mass emigration was used as a threat to influence the decision of the legislature that not only a few individuals but the whole group would leave. In 1872 the threat to emigrate actually moved the Tsar to dispatch Adjutant-General Count Todtleben to the Mennonite colonies with the mission of convincing the agitated population that the door to further adjustments was by no means closed. Since the new regulations did not become effective before 1880, the intervening time was used to work out a compromise. In the end, the Mennonites were permitted to substitute service in the army with a non-military form of forest service in separate units.

Since the conciliatory attitude of the highest authorities had been evident from the beginning, the extent to which large sections of the Mennonite population began almost at once to prepare for emigration can be explained only by the pre-existing general restlessness and widespread dissatisfaction. There were several public issues around which collective behaviour could crystallize: the conflict with the Mennonite established church; the land question; legal and administrative changes attending the liberation of the peasants; and above all, the deliberations concerning the new draft law.

The form under which relief of tensions was finally found, and the common orientation underlying the ensuing social movement, were determined not by new cultural trends but by the revival of a mental pattern deeply embedded in the sectarian Anabaptist tradition of the group. Withdrawal, flight, emigration—this was by now their institutionalized reaction to any major threat to the dogmas of their faith, particularly to principles which distinguished them from other Christian persuasions. With every repetition of the same reaction pattern, first in Switzerland, then in the Netherlands, in Prussia, and now again in Russia, the release mechanism became more automatic.

The human, all too human, element which played its role in the Mennonite migration from Russia, is reflected in a letter, reproduced by P. M. Friesen, in which a Mennonite elder in the Crimea laments:

In the beginning religious scruples may have played a role, but now this is no more the case. Now friends [relatives who have already emigrated], the expected golden mountains, and curiosity attract them, at best the fear of having to give their sons away to the forest service. Mostly go those who have no idea of non-resistance or Christianity. Then also vanity plays a role, this above all among the richer people. 'Now [they say], the Russians serve us [as farm hands, etc.], later we are supposed to serve them . . .'[4]

Among all the motives mentioned, the lure of the "golden mountains" awaiting them in the New World was undoubtedly the most powerful and decisive. This was the day when America stood before the eyes of Europe's crowded and underprivileged masses as the land of freedom, the land of unlimited opportunities, Utopia become true, where people could hope to find relief from an oppressive present. To the Mennonites it had the added attraction of having been in the past the refuge of many non-resistant groups like themselves, including some of their own brethren. State governments as well as private interests in the United States, with Canada as yet trailing behind, were busy spreading the legend into every town and village. Even in Russia, despite censorship and police supervision, it certainly was not difficult for anyone interested in more concrete information to get hold of one of the thousands of folders and pamphlets describing the country and its cheap fertile land in the most glowing colors.

Yet the Mennonites were a sober and cautious people, well aware of the complex financial and political implications of their undertaking. As a whole they were prosperous and had much to lose. They were not ready to catch at every straw. Moreover, they knew precisely what they wanted, and that was by no means little. Above all, they wanted to be absolutely assured that the experiences which now drove them from Russia would never be repeated again. Only if one realizes that this was the one motive for the migration openly admitted can one hope to interpret subsequent events in Manitoba correctly. The points raised by them in their negotiations from the very beginning indicate that the conditions which they wished to avoid were precisely the ones which had been in the foreground of their quarrel with the Russian authorities.

The Negotiations

Possibilities for emigration to the United States and Canada were investigated simultaneously. As far as the United States was concerned, negotiations proved unsuccessful. It was not the policy of the Federal

---

[4] *Ibid.*, p. 512.

Government to do business or enter into contracts with whole groups of immigrants, or even to make propaganda abroad. This was left to private interests, and, if they so wished, to the state governments. A liberal naturalization law, the Homestead Act, and the protection of individual immigrants from exploitation through the Federal Bureau of Immigration were considered sufficient inducement to come to the United States. With regard to Canada, the situation was entirely different. The Dominion Government considered the colonization of the Western plains as one of its most urgent concerns, not to be left to private business or accident. Although the older Provinces of Quebec and Ontario were free to deal with their own immigration problems, the Province of Manitoba was in its infancy and unable to take care of land settlement involving matters of foreign policy. Immigration and colonization were handled by the Canadians in a manner much more resembling the methods used by the Russians than by the Americans, a fact which also made the Mennonites at once feel more at home. At the same time this very resemblance, which in the end proved more apparent than real, led to many misunderstandings on their part.

The British authorities proceeded somewhat perfunctorily with their role in these transactions, keeping an anxious eye upon the reactions of the Russian Government. Nevertheless, they did transmit several letters from John Lowe, Secretary in the Dominion Department of Agriculture, to the Mennonite leaders giving the desired information about the conditions under which settlement in Canada could be effected. Finally, Ottawa ordered its special immigration agent, William Hespeler, at the time stationed in Western Germany, to proceed forthwith to Berdiansk and investigate the matter on the spot. Hespeler was a colourful personality, whose personal fortunes remained closely connected with those of the Manitoba Mennonites almost thoughout the rest of his long life. A German by birth, and a businessman of Waterloo County, Ontario, while not a Mennonite, he played a role comparable to that of native Mennonite leaders. Although held up by British "red tape" in Vienna, and warned upon arriving at Berdiansk by the British consul of his impending arrest by the Russian police unless he left the Empire immediately, Hespeler managed to establish contact with all the key men in the different colonies. He also held secret meetings in which he offered first-hand information, clarification of doubtful questions, and practical advice.

The Mennonite delegates who in 1873 visited the United States and Canada came as the representatives of definite groups which apparently had already made up their minds to emigrate. They simply acted as "locators" after the traditional pattern of colonization in Eastern Europe. Their mission was the location of suitable tracts of land and the negotiation of satisfactory conditions. Of the four delegates who eventually concluded the agreement with the Canadian Government, two were representatives of the Bergthal colony in the Mariupol *uiezd,* namely, its *Oberschulze,* Jacob Peters, and its elder, Heinrich Wiebe. The other two, Elder Cornelius Toews and David Klassen, represented the Kleine Gemeinde in the Borsenko colony; at the same time they acted as plenipotentiaries of the Fürstenland settlement which sent no delegates.[5] In addition, the delegation included Elder Leonhard Sudermann, of Berdiansk, their leader, the elders of the Alexanderwohl congregation, and of the Swiss and the Prussian Mennonites in Volynia, and Paul and Lorenz Tschetter of the Hutterite brotherhood in the Molotschna colony. They were joined en route by Wilhelm Ewert, a preacher of Thorn in West Prussia. The twelfth man, a wealthy Mennonite land owner, travelled as a private individual and at his own expense with the Bergthal delegates.

The composition of the delegation reflects the selectivity of the movement. Those who wanted to emigrate belonged to sectarian or local sub-groups which for one reason or another had separated from the main body of Mennonites and were dissatisfied with existing conditions. The Kleine Gemeinde (literally: Little Congregation) was the earliest of the many sectarian groups which developed among the Mennonites in Russia in protest against the "worldliness" of the majority and the institutionalization of religion. At first threatened with excommunication, expulsion and loss of their civil status, they were, upon intervention by the Russian authorities, finally recognized as a separate church and permitted to live with the rest. In 1865-66 they left the Molotschna colony for the new Borsenko and Fürstenland colonies, seeking association with Mennonite settlers from the Chortitza colony who were equally conservative, and thus more friendly toward them. Migration to Canada offered them an opportunity to settle separately and to form independent communities.

---

[5] The official petition to the Canadian Government of 1873 was signed by Wiebe and Klassen "for the Colonies of Grünfeld and Heuboden." The term "colony" is used here in its older connotation of village commune without referring to a whole settlement. Both Grünfeld and Heuboden were villages in the Borsenko colony, but Wiebe and Klassen acted as joint delegates of the whole Kleine Gemeinde, some of whose members lived in the Fürstenland settlement.

The Bergthal colony had been founded, between 1836 and 1852, by 145 families of young landless people from the Chortitza colony. As in other settlements created under the provisions of the Colonial Law, the number of farmsteads remained constant. At the time of the emigration, however, there were 500 families living in the five villages of the Bergthal *volost*. The colony was an economic failure so that the majority of the people, mostly landless laborers, were poor. After they went to Canada, the villages abandoned by them were not taken over by other Mennonites but bought by their Russian neighbours or by German Lutherans and Catholics; this indicates that, from the Mennonite point of view, the location was in general undesirable. To a group like this, emigration obviously had a strong economic appeal.

The Fürstenland settlement finally was founded in 1869 from the Chortitza colony on a tract of land rented from Grand-Prince Michael Nikolaievich. Hence its popular name, signifying "Land of the Prince." Since the colony was not on Crown lands, it could not officially be organized as a separate Mennonite *volost* under the Colonial Law. It possessed, nevertheless, its own district office which was legally considered a part of the near-by Chortitza *volost*. Yet their situation was far from secure. Although these villages were located in a fertile region where plenty of fruit was growing, their holdings were only about 140 to 157 acres. Moreover, their tenure had to be renewed in 1879, and they had reason to fear that the new contract would be far less favorable. Again we find a group in unsettled conditions willing to prepare for a radical change once the religious conflict provided a convenient rationalization for such a step.

Having discussed at length the intentions with which the Mennonite delegates undertook their journey to America, the role played by the Canadian Government and its agents may be considered. The settlement of the plains between the Pre-Cambrian Shield and the Rocky Mountains was an absolute necessity to the young confederation of British colonies in North America. At least its narrow fertile belt had to be populated with the greatest speed to forestall invasion by American pioneers across the controversial forty-ninth parallel; this might have easily created political implications similar to those which led to the annexation of Texas. Furthermore, in order to make the transcontinental railroad—which was to link British Columbia with the rest of Canada—economically possible, an adequate revenue had to be guaranteed by attracting settlers. Finally, industrial expansion in the St. Lawrence valley and intercontinental trade depended largely on a substantial agricultural hinterland which, however, could not be built with Canada's own population alone, nor with what immigration could be expected from the British Isles. Not even the United States could have succeeded in doing this without the large influx of immigrants from Continental Europe. It was thus the Dominion's most urgent task to divert some of this stream to its own territory. The way was paved by the Dominion Lands Act of 1872, which followed the example of Lincoln's Homestead Act of 1862. A network of agents was stationed at strategic points abroad and at home, and funds were set aside to pay for the transportation of immigrants and their maintenance en route.

At the time when the first contacts were made with the Mennonites in Russia, policies had been drafted only in the most general manner, the bureaucratic apparatus was undeveloped, and few prospects were as yet in sight. In its keen competition with the United States, Canada as a whole had little to offer except cheaper land, and perhaps better protection against lawlessness and troubles with the Indians. On the other hand, the agricultural potential of the Canadian West was as yet untested, and many doubted indeed that it could ever support a large farming population. To the Mennonites, however, certain added inducements could be offered which in their eyes were more important than economic advantages. All this explains why the Government went to such great lengths to attract the attention of the Mennonite scouts visiting the North American continent. For this was not only the first, largest, and most promising, but also the only tangible immigration scheme with which Canada could seriously reckon at the moment.

It was a common practice of the time to subsidize exploratory expeditions to the West by farmers, businessmen and scientists, and to publish their impressions. Thus, the Canadian authorities persuaded a local Mennonite, Jacob Y. Shantz, to make such a trip. Shantz' coöperation appeared particularly valuable as it was hoped that the opinion of an influential and respected native Mennonite would carry weight not only with his coreligionists in Russia, but also with other German-speaking emigrants. For Shantz, then fifty years old, was a prominent figure in the economic and social life of Waterloo County, Ontario, where he owned as much as 1000 acres of land and several businesses. When he indicated that he had become convinced Manitoba had at least as much to offer as the widely advertised plains of the

American Middle West, Ottawa was most anxious to have his report prepared "with as much detail as possible in a form for publication." It was printed in the spring of 1873 as an official propaganda pamphlet and subsequently re-published in many editions and in several different languages. With this, however, Shantz' work for the Department of Agriculture and the Manitoba Mennonites was by no means completed. Together with Hespeler, he continued to act as a middle-man between them and Ottawa. Moreover, it was to his credit that the young colony was soon put on a sound financial basis with the help of his brethren in Ontario. Two Mennonite villages in Manitoba were later named in his honor, namely, Schanzenberg, near Niverville, and Schanzenfeld, near Winkler. In later years he took an active part also in the opening up of the Didsbury district in Alberta in connection with the Canadian Pacific Railway.

The twelve delegates from Russia arrived in the spring of 1873. After having visited several places in the Eastern United States and in Ontario, they met in June in Fargo, North Dakota, with Shantz and Hespeler for an inspection tour of Manitoba. Although they were formally received by a member of the Provincial Cabinet, and given every facility to get acquainted with the country, most of them turned their backs on Canada. Paul Tschetter summed up his impressions in a few telling sentences:

. . . . the mosquitoes were so bad that one could hardly defend himself . . . the mosquitoes were terribly bad. . . . At some places the land is good, but railroad facilities are poor. . . . The lumber for building purposes must be shipped by way of the Red River from Minnesota. . . . Grasshoppers are very plentiful. The price of stock and agricultural implements is more reasonable in the United States than in Manitoba, and if the same is shipped across the boundary a duty must be paid on it.

In some spots they found the land marshy, in others subject to drought. Then there was the climate, and finally the half-breeds who did not impress them as particularly desirable neighbours. "The people are lazy farmers of mixed Indian blood," writes Tschetter, adding laconically: "The half-breed Indians live on this land and it belongs to them."[6]

[6] J. M. Hofer (ed.), "The Diary of Paul Tschetter, 1873," *Mennonite Quarterly Review* 5 (1931): 112-128, 198-219.

The last remark may conceivably refer to the Riel movement and the manner in which the métis were made to give room to immigrants. Although they had been indemnified for the losses which they had suffered in the course of the land survey, and whenever reservations were made for some specific purpose such as land grants to the Hudson's Bay Company or the Mennonites, they were rather unfriendly toward both government officials and foreigners exploring the country. On one occasion the Mennonite delegates, accompanied by Hespeler, were involved in a brawl resulting from an insulting gesture by one of their Canadian drivers toward some half-breeds. The travellers had to barricade themselves in their room until they were rescued by a special detachment of soldiers from Fort Garry. Although a Winnipeg English newspaper brought the incident into connection with the Riel movement, this was emphatically, and probably correctly, rejected by the French paper *Le Métis*. Tschetter's remark seems to indicate that the Mennonites were aware of the moral aspect of the situation. Shantz, however, considered the presence of half-breeds an added advantage, for he believed they would serve the Mennonites as cheap farmhands, an expectation which did not materialize.

A letter written by John F. Funk, who accompanied the delegates to Manitoba, supplements Tschetter's diary. He, too, complains of mosquitoes, bad roads and swampy land in Manitoba, and adds:

". . . . five of the deputation determined to accompany me to Dakota, as we were fully satisfied with our experience there. Manitoba has a good soil—and good water at some places, but it has not much facilities for transportation to or from—and the inhabitants are nearly all half-breeds, Indians, a poor, shiftless race of people, and I can not recommend it as a good place for settlement."[7]

If Manitoba appeared so unattractive to most of their comrades, the question arises why any four of the delegates, nevertheless, proceeded to Ottawa to conclude the deal for the three groups represented by them. A passage in Tschetter's diary offers a clue. It refers to a conversation with Heinrich Wiebe, of the Bergthal colony, even before they had set foot on Manitoba soil. Wiebe had said he did not like the country they had seen so far in the United States and, what was more important in his eyes, he did not expect that total military

---

[7] Unpublished letter to Funk's wife, dated on board a Red River Steamer, June 27, 1873 (in the Mennonite Archives at Goshen, Ind.). See also Kempes Schnell (ed.) "John F. Funk's Land Inspection Trips as Recorded in His Diaries, 1872 and 1873," *Mennonite Quarterly Review 24* (1950): 295-311.

exemption could be secured there.[8] On the other hand, he believed a "British" government would be more liberal in this respect and able to "grant a charter" guaranteeing such an exemption.[9] In concluding this conversation, Wiebe, according to Tschetter, had maintained that "one should not only consider the land question but also not to forget the matter of freedom, for that is the reason why we came to this country and were making this long journey . . ."[10] An almost identical explanation was offered by the *St. Paul Daily Press*, of January 26, 1873. Under the heading "Immense Immigration Eruption" its correspondent reported that the Mennonite Board of Immigration was more in favor of Canada than of Minnesota because there it had received more positive assurances with regard to freedom of conscience. "But more important," he wrote, "than the pecuniary advantages is the warranted privilege of special laws in Canada to live according to the principles of their faith which are now endangered in Russia by radical changes in all state matters . . ."

This evidence indicates a frame of mind which was more typical of the strictly orthodox and highly conservative descendants of the Old Colony and the Kleine Gemeinde than of the more liberal New Colony on the Molotschna and of Mennonite colonies in other parts of Russia. Furthermore, those who chose Canada were as a whole poorer than the others who went to the United States; their decision was probably also influenced by the fact that land in the United States, even if it was more desirable, was offered them at three, dollars and

---

[8] That Wiebe was perfectly right in this, is borne out by the subsequent negotiations initiated by the two Hutterite delegates who petitioned President Grant in a personal audience at his summer residence in Long Branch. In an unpublished letter of August 13, 1873, the Secretary of State, Hamilton Fish, had informed the President that "they ask . . . to keep their own schools and to administer them according to their own rules." After their return to Russia they received a reply of the Secretary of State to the effect that their request could not be granted by the Federal Government since this was a matter for the individual States to decide. Although he did not expect a war to come within the next fifty years, he thought there was "little likelihood that Congress would find justification in freeing them from duties which are asked of other citizens," if an emergency should arise. (Letter of Sept. 5, 1873, published by J. M. Hofer, in *Mennonite Quarterly Review* 5 (1931): 217. For the debates in Congress related to this question see George Leibrandt, "The Emigration of the German Mennonites from Russia to the United States and Canada, 1873-1880; II," *Mennonite Quarterly Review* 7 [1933]: 15ff).

[9] The opposite stand was taken by John F. Funk's *Herold der Wahrheit* in February, 1873 (p. 30). The Elkhart, Indiana, Mennonite paper pointed out that royal and imperial governments were apt to withdraw at any time privileges granted earlier, and added: "Under the laws of the United States such cannot easily happen, for it is a principle of the Constitution . . . that to each man must be conceded complete freedom of conscience. Thus we believe that the non-resistant Christian will be much safer in this respect under the United States government than any other."

[10] J. M. Hofer, ed. "The Diary of Paul Tschetter, 1873," *Mennonite Quarterly Review* 5 (1931): 199.

more an acre, while in Manitoba it was either free or could be bought at less than one-third that price.

The Agreement With The Dominion Government

Upon conclusion of their inspection tour, the four delegates of the Kleine Gemeinde and the Bergthal colony went to Ottawa to see whether the final bid of the Dominion Government would satisfy their religious as well as their economic interests. In answer to their petition to the Minister of Agriculture, J. H. Pope, a letter was addressed to them, dated July 25, 1873, and signed by John Lowe, Secretary in the Department of Agriculture.[11] This document is of the greatest significance in two respects. First, viewed against the background of other documents previously issued, it shows precisely which points were stressed throughout the negotiations by the Mennonites, reflecting their intentions and concern. Second, it reveals the full extent of the concessions made by the authorities in charge, their meaning as understood by each party at the time, and the legal framework upon which the organization of the Manitoba colonies was based.

Lowe's letter reads as follows:

DEPARTMENT OF AGRICULTURE

Ottawa, 25th July, 1873.

Gentlemen:

I have the honour, under the instruction of the Hon. the Minister of Agriculture, to state to you in reply to your letter of this day's date the following facts relating to advantages offered to settlers, and to the immunities offered to Mennonites which are established by Statute Law and by orders of his Excellency the Governor-General-in-Council for the information of German Mennonites having intention to emigrate to Canada via Hamburg.

1. An entire exemption from military service is by law and Order-in-Council granted to the Denomination of Christians called Mennonites.

2. An Order-in-Council was passed on the 3rd March last to reserve eight townships in the Province of Manitoba for free grants on the condition of settlement as provided in the Dominion Lands Act, that is to say, "Any person who is head of a family or has obtained the age of 21 years shall be entitled to be entered for ¼ section or a less quantity of unappropriated Dominion lands, for a purpose of securing a homestead right in respect thereof."

3. The said reserve of eight townships is for the exclusive use of the Mennonites, and the said free grants of ¼ section to consist of 160 acres each, as defined by the act.

---

[11] This position corresponded to that of a Deputy Minister under present arrangements.

4. Should the Mennonite Settlement extend beyond the eight townships set aside by the Order-in-Council of March 3rd last, other townships will be in the same way reserved to meet the full requirements of Mennonite immigration.

5. If next spring the Mennonite settlers on viewing the eight townships set aside for their use should decide to exchange them for any other unoccupied eight townships, such exchange will be allowed.

6. In addition to the free grant of ¼ section or 160 acres to every person over 21 years of age on the condition of settlement the right to purchase the remaining ¾ of the section at $1.00 per acre is granted by law so as to complete the whole section of 640 acres which is the largest quantity of land the Government will grant a patent for to one person.

7. The settler will receive a patent for a free grant after three years residence in accordance with the terms of the Dominion Lands Act.

8. In event of the death of the settler, the lawful heirs can claim the patent for the free grant upon proof that settlement duties for three years have been performed.

9. From the moment of occupation the settler acquires a "homestead right" in the land.

10. The fullest privilege of exercising their religious principles is by law afforded to the Mennonites without any kind of molestation or restriction whatever, and the same privilege extends to the education of their children in schools.

11. The privilege of affirming instead of making affidavits is afforded by law.

12. The Government of Canada will undertake to furnish passenger warrants from Hamburg to Fort Garry for Mennonite families of good characters for the sum of $30.00 for adult persons over the age of eight years, for persons under eight years half price or $15.00 and for infants under one year, $3.00.

13. The minister specially authorizes me to state that this arrangement as to price shall not be changed for the seasons of 1874, 1875, or 1876.

14. I am further to state that if it is changed thereafter the price shall not up to the year 1882 exceed $40.00 per adult and children in proportion, subject to the approval of Parliament.

15. The immigrants will be provided with provisions on the portion of the journey between Liverpool and Collingwood but between other portions of the journey they are to find their own provisions.

> I have the honour to be,
> Gentlemen,
> Your obedient servant,
> (Sgd.) John Lowe
> Secretary, Department of Agriculture.

Messrs. David Klassen
        Jacob Peters
        Heinrich Wiebe
        Cornelius Toews
        Mennonite Delegates from Southern Russia.

Behind the brief clause included in section 1 of the statement lies a whole history of negotiations. The question had been first broached by Sudermann in his letter of January 1872 to the British Consul at Berdiansk. It was referred to the Canadian Minister of Militia and Defence, who replied by quoting part of section 17 of the Act Respecting the Militia and Defence of the Dominion of Canada of 1868 (31 *Vic.*, ch. 40).[12] While the Mennonites were explicitly exempted from personal military service either in peace or war, suspicions arose as to the meaning of the clause included in the law saying that the exemption was to be granted "upon such conditions and under such regulations as the Governor-General-in-Council may from time to time prescribe." The Russian Mennonites apparently thought that this implied the arbitrary personal power of the Governor in such matters. Accordingly, a second Order-in-Council was passed on September 25, 1872, quoting the questionable section of the Act in full. It added that the intention of the controversial clause was simply to provide the necessary administrative machinery for the implementation of the provision, and that "the constitution does not confer upon the Governor-General-in-Council any power to override or set aside, under any circumstances, the plain meaning of statute law." What the decree, however, failed to mention was that any statute may be changed in due course by the proper parliamentary procedure.

The following eight paragraphs referring to the acquisition and holding of land are in substance an interpretation of the provisions of the Dominion Lands Act of 1872 (35 *Vic.*, ch. 23). Several exceptions to the common practice were made, however, for the benefit of the Mennonites. One was the reservation of a contiguous tract of land for their exclusive use. Similar grants had been made earlier to individuals or associations planning to bring some particular group of settlers to Manitoba, for instance, to the German Aid Society of Montreal.

The Order-in-Council of March 3, 1873, to which Lowe refers in section 2 had actually mentioned "Germans in Russia, Mennonites and others," but this oversight did not cause any difficulty because the Mennonites, coming first, were never able to occupy the whole area before their rights automatically elapsed. More unusual was the provision that, in the reserved townships, quarter-sections in both even- and uneven-numbered sections could be acquired as free homesteads while ordinarily the even-numbered sections were set aside for sale by the Government. Yet, the Mennonites had insisted on this change in order to make possible compact settlement, village habitat and open-field

---

[12] *Order-in-Council*, April 26, 1872.

system. As a matter of fact, Lowe's statement contained a second error in that he omitted mentioning the fact that every township included sections reserved for the Hudson's Bay Company and school land. A further adjustment to their wishes not mentioned in Lowe's letter was made by waiving the requirement of the Dominion Lands Act according to which homesteaders had to reside on their individual sections for at least part of the year; this would have precluded residence in villages. Sections 4 and 5 were inserted upon the expressed wish of the delegates, who apparently were not entirely satisfied with the area originally set aside for them, and hoped that better land might yet be found elsewhere. Subsidized passage, on the other hand, as laid down in sections 12 through 15 reflected the established policy of assisting immigration from Great Britain and the Continent in a way which would attract settlers even from distant places, and offset the practice of American steamship and railroad companies of granting reduced fares for larger groups of passengers.

The statement included in the tenth section of Lowe's letter contained a definite misrepresentation. In its first part it was, of course, entirely in agreement with the liberal principles of British and Canadian government in matters of religion. At the time, even the reference to schools seemed adequate and in keeping with the general Canadian practice of leaving education to the church. Yet, the Department of Agriculture, whether deliberately or unconsciously, failed to mention the fact that under the provisions of the British North America Act, jurisdiction over schools was reserved to the individual Provinces, and that Manitoba was not a party to the agreement with the Mennonites. Moreover, in their eagerness to attract the emigrants, the officials gave the impression of an indefinite stability of the laws in question although, according to the principles of parliamentary sovereignty, the legislature is at all time legally, though not always morally, entitled to rescind or amend any previous statute or to change administrative practice by the enactment of a new law.

The Mennonites have always referred to Lowe's letter as the "privileges" and regarded it as their Magna Carta defining the rights and conditions under which they eventually agreed to come to Canada. They had in mind the various charters issued by the Tsars which indeed had been solemn declarations of specific privileges granted to them "for all times," and which were incorporated into the Russian code of law. Examination of the Canadian document, however, proves that it was nothing of the kind. All that Mr. Lowe intended to do, in fact, all that he was entitled to do, was to offer them an authoritative interpretation of the existing laws of the Dominion, and to confirm the provisions made for them by the Department of Agriculture within the framework of its general powers to promote immigration. Nevertheless, other official documents show clearly that the Canadian authorities of the time were perfectly aware of the understandings suggested by this letter, and of their full significance for the Mennonites. For instance, the Minister of Agriculture wrote in his annual report for the year 1873 to the Governor-General, Lord Dufferin: "The cause of the new projected exodus . . . is also coupled with a question of schools, a new *ukase* requiring that their children should be instructed in the Russian language, and made to submit to the regulation respecting tuition to which their conscience cannot consent." Under the item of "obligations contracted toward these people," the Minister furthermore quotes briefly: "3. The privileges of religious schools of their own."[13]

The legal inaccuracies in the document issued by John Lowe to the Mennonite delegates together with an official German translation had apparently been quickly discovered. The Minister of Agriculture, J. H. Pope, for whom Lowe had conducted the negotiations with the Mennonite delegates, submitted a report to Lord Dufferin on the content of the Secretary's letter, changing its wording in several instances. Apart from some minor alterations, he pretended that the first section of this letter asserted "that an entire exemption from military service *as is provided by law and order-in-council* will be granted to . . ." In addition, section 10 was represented as reading as follows: "That the Mennonites have the fullest privilege of exercising their religious privileges and educating their children in schools, *as provided by law,* without any molestation or restriction whatever." (Italics supplied.) While the Minister's formulations were undoubtedly more correct from a legal standpoint than those handed to the delegates, the circumstances under which these changes were inserted in the official documents put them in a rather questionable light. For, not only was Pope's report dated just three days after Lowe's letter, but it was made the legal basis of the Order-in-Council of August 13, 1873, by which the action was officially approved. Nevertheless, the second document was marked "secret" and thus remained unknown

---

[13] The report, dated January, 1874, is signed by Letellier who, in November, 1873, succeeded J. H. Pope in the Department of Agriculture, when the Conservative Government of Sir John Macdonald was replaced by Mackenzie's Liberal Government.

to the public for forty-five years, so that the Mennonites were made to believe that Lowe's wording was the official one.[14] This devious procedure was the direct cause of the serious conflicts which later on arose in connection with the Manitoba school question.

---

[14] The originals of the English and the German version of the letter, both of which bear the full signature of Mr. Lowe, have been found in the archives of the *Chortitzer Waisenamt* on a farm northwest of Steinbach. In the German translation, which is in rather poor language, the two controversial sections read as follows:

"1. Eine völlige Befreiung von jedem Militairdienste laut des Gesetzes und der Verordnungen im Ministerialrathe einem jeden der einer christlichen Gemeinde der Mennoniten angehört ist zugesichert.

"10. Den Mennoniten ist die vollste Ausführung ihrer religiösen Grundsätze ohne irgend Belästigung oder Einschränkung gesetzlich gestifted; und dasselbe Vorrecht erstreckt sich auf die Erziehung ihrer Kinder in den Schulen."

There can be no doubt but that the Mennonites themselves used this inadequate German translation rather than the English original as the basis of all further deliberations leading to their decision to emigrate to Canada.

CHAPTER III

The Pioneers

The Migration

IN THE short space of three years, twelve hundred peasant house-holds comprising 6140 souls were transplanted "lock, stock and barrel" from their villages in Southern Russia to the virgin soil of Manitoba without any serious mishap or loss of life. The migration, which fell off sharply after 1876, involved a total of 1336 families with an estimated 7500 members. No large groups of Russian Mennonites came to Canada after 1880, when the compulsory forest service was established and the favorable conditions were withdrawn under which whole families, including members of draft age, were allowed to emigrate. The success of the Mennonite migration was quite an achievement for the Canadian authorities who as yet had nothing to go by except the example of some steamship and American railway companies. The Mennonite reservation was difficult to reach, the surrounding country but sparsely populated, and the economy of the province ill-prepared to supply such a sudden influx of settlers with the immediate necessities of life. Still more, this was not the haphazard movement of individuals and small bands, so characteristic of settlement in the North American plains, but the orderly transfer of whole villages from one continent to another. Such a scheme required complex operations at both ends of the trek.

After crossing northern Europe, the immigrants assembled in Ham-burg, where a Canadian agent handed out warrants for their passage. In Canada each party was taken care of by J. Y. Shantz, who was the recognized organizer of the movement on this side of the ocean, or by

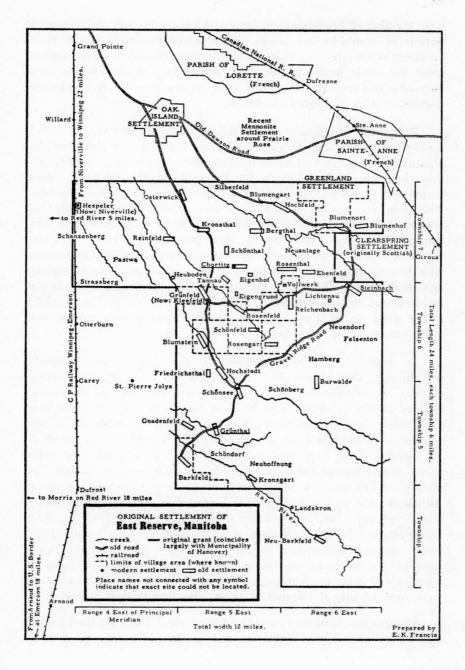

ORIGINAL SETTLEMENT OF
East Reserve, Manitoba

- ———— creek
- ——— old road
- —⊢—⊢— railroad
- ⌐‐‐⌐ limits of village area (where known)
- • modern settlement
- ▭ old settlement
- ———— original grant (coincides largely with Municipality of Hanover)

Place names not connected with any symbol indicate that exact site could not be located.

Prepared by
E. K. Francis

some member of his immediate family. Most of the arrivals proceeded directly to Manitoba but others were received in the homes of their brethren in Ontario to await further transportation. Several families spent the whole winter in the East. By working as farm hands they were able not only to accumulate some money but also to familiarize themselves with Canadian conditions.

Before the completion of the transcontinental railway, the usual route to Manitoba was through the United States, but it had been the plan of the Canadian Government to transport all European immigrants over the Dawson Road, partly for financial reasons, partly in order to prevent American agents from luring settlers away from Canada. This, however, was an ill-considered decision, for the connecting link between Lake Superior and Red River Valley, by wagon-trail and lake transportation, was passable only from June to September, and the trip took at least a week under the most favorable conditions. Shantz, who thought this too hazardous a route for families, protested vigorously against the plan. Thereupon most parties were sent via Duluth, hence to Moorhead on the Red River and by steamboat to Fort Garry, while others went via St. Paul. Even then the trip was cumbersome and often rather full of adventure.

In recognition of the inadequate accommodations then available in Winnipeg, the Department of Agriculture had given Shantz a section of land in township 7-4 East at the western edge of the Mennonite Reserve on the condition that he erect reception halls. At least one party went first to Fort Garry but most others disembarked at the confluence of the Red River and the Rat River in the French parish of St. Agathe. From here they walked or drove to a point four miles inland, where Shantz had prepared sheds and tents for them. Conditions during the first weeks were extremely primitive and life was expensive. Although some settlers had brought huge crates with them containing farm implements and even wagons, most of them had to purchase everything on the spot. Women, children, and old folks remained for some time in the immigration huts while the men set out to locate suitable sites for the future villages, or to buy provisions, oxen, building supplies and tools in Winnipeg. As settlement progressed, newcomers were received into the homes of those who had arrived earlier.

Competition between Canada and the United States for the Mennonite settlers was keen throughout this period. Not only were there many, at times successful, attempts to induce travellers crossing the United States to stay south of the border, and to relieve them of their money on that occasion, but vigorous propaganda was made in Russia itself, impressing upon prospective immigrants the inhospitality of Manitoba and extolling the merits of the American Middle West. They spoke of maltreatment on English steamers, starvation along the Dawson Road, massacre by the Indians, and cast doubt on the sincerity of the Canadian Government in granting religious liberty. One story, apparently originating among the Kansas Mennonites, was carried back to Manitoba from Russia causing great excitement here. According to this information, the Canadian Government had collapsed, Mr. Lowe had died, and there was great danger that the arrangements would be nullified. Still more confusion was created in Russia by letters of disgruntled newcomers who had found conditions in Manitoba, at least in the early years, not much to their liking.

More complex still were the financial arrangements which became necessary with the Mennonite migration and settlement. The sums involved were considerable. Much of the money was, of course, secured through the sale of property in Russia. The sudden desire of whole villages and colonies to dispose of their land, however, caused an over-supply resulting in a real estate slump which affected prices in general. Moreover, possession in Crown lands could be transferred, in the beginning at least, only to other colonists. Where leased land was involved, it was usually held in common and thus could not be sold individually. Since such great numbers were anxious to emigrate at the same time, few could be found who met the legal or contractual requirements for taking over the properties offered. Thus, transactions in connection with the migration tended to involve heavy losses. The need of caring for the less privileged members, particularly among the rather poorer communities like the Bergthal people, meant an added burden. These problems, however, were solved by coöperative effort made possible primarily by the strong solidarity of the religious community.

A rather full account of the financial operations of the Bergthal group is available.[1] The institution through which they were effected was the *Waisenamt*, a trust company managing the property of orphans and widows under the auspices of the church. Both the disposal of

---

[1] Cf. Gerhard Wiebe, *Ursachen und Geschichte der Auswanderung der Mennoniten aus Russland nach Amerika* (Winnipeg, n.d.).

property in Russia and the resettlement in Canada were handled in such a way that the whole congregation became responsible for the transfer of every member, and for the economic security and welfare of all during the difficult years of a new start. This required great sacrifices on the part of the better situated farmers who represented less than 30 per cent of the 500 families comprising this one group. The status of the Bergthal *Waisenamt* at the time of the emigration was quite sound as long as its creditors, who included also people using the trust company as a savings bank, did not recall their deposits. Money deposited with the *Waisenamt* amounted to about $100,000, while claims of about $200,000 were held by it against individual debtors. Under the circumstances, liquidation before the exodus would have resulted in great losses to the investors. Thus it was decided to continue operation of the *Waisenamt* and to transfer it to Canada. Moreover, it was agreed that every creditor could withdraw only as much as was needed for his travelling expenses with the understanding that this money would be returned as soon as possible after the first harvests in order to make it available for other emigrants following at a later date. From all larger bank accounts, 25 per cent was deducted outright as a contribution to be used to help those who were penniless, and to make up for bad debts which, under the circumstances, could not be recovered. Finally, all those who had become surety for others were released from their obligations, while payment of interest was suspended for four or five years. In addition to the funds made available through the *Waisenamt*, many individuals were also able to get private loans from their wealthier brethren. Since the migration was carried out in several stages over a period of three years, it was possible for some to leave the country before all property was sold. Relatives and friends staying behind took care of necessary transactions, so that additional losses were avoided.

The account books of the Bergthal congregation, still preserved in the archives of the Chortitz *Waisenamt* in Manitoba, give evidence of the efficiency, honesty and charity with which debtors, creditors, and church officials coöperated in order to do justice to everybody concerned. The expense of the journey itself was considerable despite the reduced rates arranged for by the Canadian Government. The trip from Russia to Hamburg and the freight expenses for heavy baggage were not included in the price of thirty (later forty) dollars collected from each immigrant for transportation from Hamburg to Quebec. Furthermore, the Russian authorities, though not barring emigration as such, required an advance payment of taxes due for the next several years. To all these expenses must be added heavy fees for exit permits and passports, and the bribes to Russian officials necessary to prevent delay. Despite these handicaps the Mennonites were able to import great sums of money to Canada in addition to their valuable effects. A very conservative estimate would put their total contribution to Manitoba's wealth at over one million dollars, or an average of more than $150 per person. Thus, it can be well understood that all contemporary sources stress the particular importance of this immigration for the as yet undeveloped economy of the young province.

However, the investment in money and other values, necessary to put the Mennonite settlement in Manitoba on a sound economic basis exceeded these imports from Russia. Additional contributions had to be made by the Ontario Mennonites and finally by the Canadian Government, mostly in the form of long-term loans. In the beginning, Shantz coöperated with John F. Funk in establishing a Board of Guardians in the United States, whose main function was the negotiation of reduced passage rates with American steamship companies. Soon, however, he organized a similar association for Canada alone, the *Unterstützungs-Committee von Ontario*.[2] Originally, the function of the Aid Committee was mainly the administration of gifts or loans made available by native Mennonites. Later on, it also undertook management of the $100,000 government loan which was guaranteed by the same persons who had at first privately contributed the funds necessary to assist the immigrants en route and during the first years.

In order to gain an overall picture of the activities of the Ontario group, the government loan of 1875 may be considered first. It was debated in the House of Commons in the spring of 1875.[3] On the Government side, several speakers insisted that the loan was perfectly sound, since it was guaranteed by highly solvent Mennonites in Ontario. It was further revealed that "repayment of debt was a doctrine of the Mennonite faith," that Mennonites were absolutely reliable as debtors,

---

[2] Although various sources mention different names such as "Society," "Aid Committee of Ontario," "Russian Mennonite Aid Committee for . . . County, Ontario," or "Committee of Management of Mennonites in Ontario," all these refer to one and the same organization or group of persons under the leadership of Shantz. The title was apparently chosen in imitation of the German Aid Committee in Montreal which, some time before, had been officially charged with the task of organizing immigration from Germany.

[3] *Debates of the House of Commons 1*, Session 1875, pp. 141, 249-252, 377-291; reproduced by Correll in *Mennonite Quarterly Review 20* (1946): 257-272.

and that they had voiced the intention "that no one should make himself liable for over one-tenth of the value of his property."

The opposition came mainly from Lt. Col. Louis François Roderique Masson, Member for Terrebonne, who urged that such subsidies should be made first and above all to French-Canadians in the United States wishing to return to Canada. Others were opposed to settling people who were not ready to defend the country. The Honorable Charles James Campbell, Member for Victoria, remarked, "it would be better to send to the hills of Scotland and Ireland, and bring out a hardy people who, in time of need, would help to fight the battles of the country." Mr. Acalus Lockwood Palmer, on the other hand, suggested that the money be spent on peaceful settlers rather than used to create military camps which "had demoralized many of our young men."

As a whole the debate in the House of Commons brought out few revealing details, except that Mr. Masson's attack provoked a vivid account of the complete failure which all colonization schemes for Manitoba had met up to the time, with the sole exception of that of the Mennonites. James Trow, the foremost expert of the House in all matters concerning the West, reported that the colony of French-Canadians under the management of a certain Mr. Ralston was a complete failure, and that he had found but seven families instead of the 250-350 persons alleged to have settled there. The French settlement near St. Vincent, Trow added bluntly, was also a failure. Later in the debate he described as "a perfect fraud on the community" the scheme of Mr. Emerson, who was offering one-eighth of an acre in his reservation (the present location of the town of Emerson, Manitoba) for $75. Another scheme inaugurated by the German Aid Society of Montreal had also been unsuccessful. On the other hand, he insisted, "the Mennonite colony . . . was a stern reality. . . . It was the nucleus of a very large settlement, and they were a clan of people who were satisfied with the country." To pacify the French, the following amendment was adopted: "But this House will cheerfully assent to any measure which may be proposed by the Government to encourage the settlement of native Canadians now living in the United States on the waste lands of the Dominion." After this the bill was passed and became part of the budget for 1875-1876.

While the original terms of the Government loan provided for repayment plus six per cent compound interest after ten years, the books were not closed on the matter until 1892. Nevertheless, payments were made to the best ability of the settlers, so that the Government proved lenient in enforcing the letter of the contract. In 1883 a similar loan had been extended to the Icelanders settling on Lake Winnipeg. This loan, however, was soon written off as a complete loss for early disasters prevented the Icelanders from even starting repayments, although in later years the community became one of the most prosperous in Manitoba. This instance moved Mr. Lowe to suggest in 1884 that immigrants should be given free grants rather than interest-bearing loans.[4] In the following year he was able to report that the Mennonite loan "will be an exceptional one among all the advances which the Department had made within the last ten years," since payments had commenced as stipulated and the settlers were now very prosperous.[5]

In April 1889 a new bill was passed, according to which four per cent simple interest was required on the Mennonite loan, and the sum paid to July 1, 1888, namely, $33,986.53, accepted as full payment of interest.[6] The matter is mentioned once more in the annual report by the Minister of the Interior for the year 1892. After declaring, not quite correctly, that the Mennonites had never asked for any relaxation of terms, and that not one of the guarantors and debtors had in any way attempted to escape his obligations, he summed up the whole transaction as follows: "The history of any country does not afford, I undertake to say, a case in which an obligation to the government on the part of any society, company, or individual, has been fulfilled with greater faithfulness than this."[7]

The operations involved in the management of this loan as well as of other funds made available to the Manitoba Mennonites were far more difficult than would appear from the official reports. Very little of this money could actually be used for capital investment. It is true that in the very first year Shantz purchased machinery in the United States, spending at one time $6,000 to buy plows from the Oliver Company, and $12,000 to buy wagons from the Studebaker Company,

---

[4] *Journals*, 1884, appendix 1. The suggestion was not followed since all further assistance to colonists was left to railroad companies and other private organizations, so that the unique experiment with the Mennonites was never again repeated.

[5] *Journals*, 1885.

[6] *Hansard*, 1889, II: 1146.

[7] *Sessional Papers*, 1893, No. 13.

both of South Bend, Indiana.[8] But all extant sources indicate that most of the money had to be used to enable indigent people to reach Canada, and to save the whole Mennonite population in Manitoba from starvation during the early years when grasshoppers and drought destroyed their harvest.[9] It was difficult to collect the installments as they became due from farmers who had started out on a shoestring. That full payment to the Government was at all possible is a result of the charity displayed by the Ontario Mennonites and of the solidarity among the Manitoba group, where the wealthier ones stood up for their poorer brethren.

It appears that all the funds and payments were handled exclusively by Shantz and the central Aid Committee of six members, so that the Manitoba Mennonites were never in direct contact with either individual Mennonite donors or with the Canadian Government. In addition there were subcommittees in each Ontario county having a Mennonite population, namely, in Waterloo, York and Lincoln counties. The Bergthal group received altogether $23,638.52 through the central Aid Committee. This sum was remitted by Shantz in five installments between March, 1874 and June, 1876. In addition to the money raised by the Ontario Mennonites directly, the Bergthal group received $35,329.83 as their share in the 100,000-dollar loan. The sums mentioned in the Bergthal books were for both, the Bergthal and the Kleine Gemeinde people in the East Reserve, including those who later moved to the West side of the Red River. The share of the Fürstenland group in direct contributions by Ontario Mennonites was probably $26,000, and that in the government loan presumably over $60,000.

In Manitoba the money received through Shantz was administered by each of the two groups separately. It is revealing that the name by which it was generally referred to was *Brotschuld* or debt for bread. Apparently, provisions were usually bought collectively through the *Brotkasse* or bread bank. In addition, small loans up to $600 were made to individuals, each of whom had to sign a note endorsed by

---

[8] Cf. Melvin Gingerich, "Jacob Y. Shantz, 1822-1909, Promotor of the Mennonite Settlements in Manitoba," *Mennonite Quarterly Review 24* (1950): 230-247.

[9] In 1876 alone, $25,000 were required to buy provisions for 230 families (*Herold der Wahrheit 13*, Oct. [1876]: 154-185).

the elder and two preachers of his congregation.[10] These had to be repaid in eight years with six per cent interest per annum. Another one per cent was charged on every loan as a contribution for the poor. The Bergthal *Brotkasse* alone was able to collect $1,569.98 in this way.

By 1880 interest accrued over the years on government money amounted to $10,598.95, and on direct loans extended by Ontario Mennonites to $8,037.09. Later the Ontario Aid Committee not only remitted all further interest payments on direct loans, but also reduced the balance of the principal by fully 60 per cent. The total loss suffered by the Ontario Mennonites in principal and interest was probably close to eight thousand dollars. Yet this, together with the loss suffered by the Government in reducing the interest rate on its loan, is a rather small amount if one recalls that a total loan of about $150,000, most of which was repaid with interest, in addition to outright gifts, which probably were never very large, had sufficed to finance the settlement of 1400 farmers and their families, who soon became a great asset to the national economy.[11]

Other government expenditure for the promotion of Mennonite immigration was also moderate. If a rough guess may be ventured, the total cost to the Dominion under this item was about $80,000 or $10.60 per person, which was about $3.25 per person more than the average expended for all immigrants in the fiscal year ending June 30, 1874.[12] Even if one were to concede that—in consideration of probable transportation cost between Quebec and Fort Garry—these expenditures may have been much higher, it should be recalled that the

---

[10] The blank for such a note was worded as follows (in translation):

Waterloo County, Ont.

....187......

I, the undersigned..., member of the Mennonite congregation of..., testify herewith to have received as a loan from the Aid Committee of Ontario the sum of $............................to be repaid within eight years with 6 per cent interest.

....
(Signature)

We as church elders and preachers of the said congregation promise to take care of the repayment of the above sum.

....
(Signature)

[11] During the debate of the government loan in 1875, a member of the House had figured that even if the loans were not repaid at all, the annual loss in interest would amount to only $5,000.

[12] This estimate is based on *Journals*, 1876, appendix 8, p. 13, and on *Sessional Papers*, 1873-1876.

value of the Mennonite settlers to Canada's economy compared with other immigrants was quite out of proportion to their numbers. For many who entered Canada at the time were paupers from the United Kingdom or other persons unfit for farming who only increased unemployment in the cities of Quebec and Ontario. Furthermore, a considerable proportion of those who benefited by reduced passage rates to Canada soon moved on to the United States; for these were no administrative or legal means to check this leakage and its exact extent remained unrecorded. By the time the Mennonites began to arrive en masse, immigration of agricultural settlers as a whole was on a sharp decline, so that in 1875 Mennonite immigration amounted to fully twelve per cent of the total immigration to Canada. Although dropping off in the following year, it still included 34 to 38 per cent of all settlers reaching Manitoba.[13]

The immediate economic contributions of the Mennonites to the province were still more important than mere numbers. Not only did they spend large sums of money, either out of their private means or from loans extended to them, they also imported quantities of farm implements—and later livestock—from the United States.[14] Two eyewitnesses of these events wrote: "The arrival of Mennonites in the province turned out a good thing for the merchants of Winnipeg. . . . As soon as they became settled their trade fell away to nothing."[15] Another witness, G. Bryce, remarked that "their spending made an appreciable difference in the trade of the city."[16] Similarly, the Honourable James Young, Member for South Waterloo, declared in 1876 in the House of Commons, seconded by the Member for Selkirk, that the Mennonites "had done much to relieve the distress prevailing last year by the large expenditures they had made in purchasing the necessities of life."[17]

---

[13] *Journals*, 1877, appendix 6, p. 9. Immigration to Manitoba in 1876 included only three to four thousand settlers, although it rose to 7,000 in 1877, and 11,000 in 1878. Total immigration to the Dominion was 39,373 in 1874, 27,382 in 1875, 25,633 in 1876, 27,082 in 1877, 29,807 in 1878, 40,492 in 1879, 25,504 in 1880, 47,991 in 1881, 112,548 in 1882, 133,304 in 1883, and 103,842 in 1884.

[14] The relative wealth of the Mennonites is constantly mentioned in contemporary sources. For instance, the *New York Sun*, of August 22, 1873, wrote that "they give evidence of being among the most valuable immigrants ever landed at Castle Garden, being among the most intelligent and most moral, and beyond a doubt the wealthiest class who have sought our shores."

[15] Alexander Begg and W. R. Nurey, *Ten Years in Winnipeg* (1879), p. 115.

[16] *History of Manitoba* (1906), p. 181.

[17] *Hansard*, 1876, p. 1173f. American cities, too, benefited from the Mennonite immigration to Manitoba. The editor of the Moorhead *Red River Star*, for instance, after complaining in a jaundiced mood that during the last months one had Mennonites for breakfast, lunch and supper, admitted that there are two things of which they seem to have in plenty: children and money. (July 24, 1875).

Beginnings of the Mennonite Reserves

The term "Reserve" in this context refers to a contiguous tract of land set aside by the Dominion Government for a certain number of years for the exclusive occupation by a homogeneous group of settlers, to be divided according to their own plans. Two different Reserves were provided for the Mennonites in Manitoba. One, the East Reserve, was identical with the land grant of seven townships offered to the delegates in 1873, and coextensive with the present Municipality of Hanover. The West Reserve was established some years later; its boundaries were changed several times but corresponded roughly with those of the present Municipality of Rhineland and portions of adjoining municipalities, particularly Stanley. The names are still locally used to indicate the two major Mennonite settlements in Manitoba, although the old grants cover only the nucleus of the two areas of present-day Mennonite concentration in Manitoba.

The East Reserve had never been meant to accommodate all Mennonite immigrants from Russia, at the time still estimated as 40,000 in number. Doubts as to the desirability of the area offered to them by the Government had already arisen in the minds of the delegates, so that they had requested the privilege of selecting, at a later date, some other portion of the country under the same conditions under which the original grant was made. When the first rather dry year was followed by several unusually wet seasons, it became quite clear that the East Reserve not only had a shallow stony soil texture in many parts, but suffered also from excessive moisture.

The Fürstenland people were expected to arrive in the summer of 1875. Accordingly, Jacob Y. Shantz, with his son Abraham E. Shantz, three earlier immigrants from Russia, a half-breed surveyor and a half-breed driver, set out to explore the plain on the other side of the Red River. At that time the fertile open prairie was consistently by-passed by all settlers.[18] What they wanted were either wooded lands or river lots. Nevertheless, the downs between the Red River and the Pembina Mountains just north of the International Boundary had been well-known from very early times. They had been visited by the Selkirk settlers when, in heavy winters, they used to follow

---

[18] James Trow, probably the greatest expert on conditions in Manitoba during the early period, stated clearly: "Canadians and others, who settled in the province, rejected the lands now occupied by the Mennonites, owing to the scarcity of timber." (*Manitoba and the North-West Territories* [Ottawa, 1878], p. 24).

buffalo and Indian into the sheltered hills to the west. After 1870 they were crossed by a main artery of traffic over which settlers from Eastern Canada and the United States traveled after entering Manitoba by way of the Red River. But all the travelers were headed for the rolling country beyond the marshy plain with its high reeds and grass. In the hills they hoped to find running water and, above all, wood for shelter, timber, fuel and fences. In their search for the choicest land, still to be had for the asking, they did not stop before they had reached Mountain City[19] at the foot of the Pembina Mountains.

While all other early settlers came from woodlands, the Russian Mennonites were adjusted to life in the open steppes. They knew how to strike living water from level ground, how to build comfortable huts and how to heat them, too, without a stick of wood; they also knew how to plant shelter belts for protection against the icy winds of the northern plains. Moreover, the open-field system, unknown among other settlers, did not require any wood for fences at a time when barbed wire had not yet been made available to provide cheap enclosures for the scattered farmsteads of the West. Thus, the West Reserve, laid out between Emerson and Mountain City at a depth of eighteen miles north of the United States boundary, was really the first permanent agricultural settlement ever established in the open prairies of Western Canada without direct access to a major body or current of water. It also turned out to be some of the best farm land in the whole province of Manitoba. When this area was finally set aside "for the exclusive use of Mennonites from Russia" by Order-in-Council of April 25, 1876, both Reserves included twenty-five townships or over half-a-million acres, that is, about six per cent of the total area of Manitoba up to 1881. Other large reservations in the province recorded in 1877 were 1,900,000 acres of railroad land, 430,000 acres of Hudson's Bay land, and 400,000 acres of school land. The Icelander reservation on Lake Winnipeg then remained outside provincial territory, in the District of Keewatin.

Differences between the two Reserves are a result of four factors: the traditional Mennonite habitat, the pattern indicated by the Dominion Lands Act, topography, and effectiveness of social control within

---

19 Mountain City was located on the south-east quarter of section 24 in township 2-6 West. When it was by-passed by the Pembina Mountains branch of the Canadian Pacific Railway, its 200, or so, inhabitants, like those of Nelsonville further north, moved their houses to the present site of the town of Morden.

the various Mennonite groups. The founding of colonies was nothing new to the Mennonites. To their minds, a Reserve in Manitoba was in no way different from a daughter-colony in Russia, or elsewhere in the world. Accordingly, they simply followed a patern which they considered to be the reflection of their own sacred traditions, although in reality it was largely a result of the master plan provided by the Russian Colonial Law. This pattern included 1) village habitat, 2) open-field system, 3) separation between church and civil government, 4) autonomy both on a village and regional level, corresponding to village commune and *volost* in Russia, and 5) a series of subsidiary institutions such as school, *Waisenamt* and fire insurance.

The settlement pattern of the Mennonite village was that of the northeast German colonial *Gewanndorf*[20] characterized by a combination of line village with open-field economy. Each holding included a *Hauskörgl* (messuage, toft) along the village street and one strip in each of the *Gewanne* (open fields) into which the total area belonging to the village was divided. The toft provided space for house and farm buildings, a barn yard, a flower and vegetable garden, an orchard and a small piece of plowland to be used for bulkier crops for home consumption, such as potatoes or cabbage. The fields were larger areas of plowland selected in such a way that the value of all land in each field, as determined by distance, soil quality, moisture, etc., was uniform, providing an equitable share in the available arable land to each villager. The size and number of fields varied greatly according to local conditions. The remaining village territory was set aside for utilization as woodland, hayland and pasture. As the name open-field system indicates, there were no enclosures because all livestock belonging to individual villagers was pastured in common under the care of a herdsman, and in this way prevented from wandering about and damaging the crops. Moreover, after harvest the arable fields themselves were used for stubble pasture. Each homesteader was entitled to send out a definite number of animals with the village herd

---

[20] Cf. Charles P. Loomis and J. Allan Beegle, *Rural Social Systems* (New York, 1950), p. 232. *Gewann* is the German word for an open field. The open-field system is identical with champion husbandry as described by George Caspar Homans, *English Villagers of the Thirteenth Century* (Cambridge, Mass., 1941). There are, however, two differences between the Mennonite village, on the one hand, and the colonial *Gewanndorf* as well as the medieval English champion village, on the other. Champion husbandry in Western Europe has been closely associated with the manorial system, while the estate of the *Erbschulze* (hereditory successor of the original locator of the colony) was typical of its North East German counterpart. The Mennonite villages, however, as all other foreign colonies in Russia, did not include any feudal or other large estate, but only the holdings of individual farmers, each of equal size.

and to take a fixed amount of hay and wood from the common lands. Additional rights in these common lands and services were sometimes granted to either villagers or outsiders; in this case the rent or other payments collected were added to the income of the commune.

The open-field system is closely associated with the practice of crop rotation. A four-crop rotation with summer fallow (called *Schwarzbrache*) had been introduced by Johann Cornies among the Mennonites in Russia, and was brought by them to Canada where fallowing was particularly important in order to preserve moisture in the soil. As a rule, *Flurzwang* is an obvious concomitant of the open-field system, whereby all the owners of individual strips in a given field are compelled to plant the same crop or fallow at the same time. Since headlands and roads were usually kept at a minimum to facilitate weed control and save valuable plowland, all farmers had to agree upon a rigid rhythm in their operations so as to give each one access to his property in season. This frequently required the close coöperation of several farmers or even of the whole village, particularly during harvest when time was at a premium.

The village organization briefly described above may be called the solidaristic type of settlement. For it pre-supposes and fosters strong social coherence, intensive interaction on a face-to-face level, readiness to coöperate and offer mutual aid, and a common value system which leaves few alternatives in one's everyday conduct, and which is enforced by strict social controls based on both inner and external sanctions. In fact, it would appear that it cannot be made to work adequately unless these sanctions have a distinctly religious connotation. For whenever hedonistic and other secular values become dominant, undermining the inner consistency of the total system of constituent group norms perceived in a religious context, the solidaristic type of rural community organization soon tends to collapse, yielding to characteristically individualistic forms of social and economic behavior.

Such was the settlement pattern which the Mennonites intended to reproduce faithfully in Canada's West. Yet, allowance had to be made for the essentially individualistic property system embodied in the Dominion Lands Act. According to it, legal title to land could not be vested in whole village communes as had been the case in Prussia or in Russia, but had to be acquired by each homesteader individually. Moreover, the unit of land measurements was a regular square, nowhere following the natural topography of the country. Planning after the traditional pattern was further restricted through the withdrawal of four sections in every township, sections 8 and 26 being reserved for sale by the Hudson's Bay Company, while sections 11 and 29 were set aside for sale by the Provincial Government for the support of schools.

Accordingly, in selecting the sites of future villages, the Mennonite pioneers had to do some careful surveying and figuring so as to fit the precise number of prospective villagers to the available surrounding area, measured in terms of quarter-sections to be taken up by each of them. They also had to consider the quality of the land, access to water and wood, the location of the village site in relation to its area of land, and its adequacy for building purposes. Once this problem in geometry was solved, however, the individual claims for homesteads were entered haphazardly. For legal ownership in any particular quarter-section had no real significance when the land was finally divided and laid out in common fields with individual strips in each of them, in common pastures, and so on.

While this method of land division, which was actually contrary to the intentions of the Canadian land laws, was made possible by the special concessions granted to the Mennonites by the Dominion Government, it rested on an entirely voluntary basis. Whoever claimed, or would claim in the future, full possession of the particular quarter-section legally entered under his name, could in no way be prevented from doing so. Unlike in Russia, the law of the country did not support the open-field system, so that its institution and maintenance depended entirely on the strength of inner sanctions and social controls among the group itself. Although in the beginning the wishes of most group members favored the establishment of compact villages, there were even then a few who preferred to settle individually on their own piece of land.

A second adjustment was indicated by the topography of the country. Since this was different in the two Reserves, certain definite variations in the over-all settlement pattern resulted. According to the earliest survey maps the East Reserve looked like this: In the north-western corner there was rolling prairie land interspersed with marshy patches, willow brush and undergrowth. To the east, part of a big swamp, most of which lay outside the Reserve, made a dent into otherwise open land. Next to it there was more shrub and bush. In the centre of the Reserve only the environs of the present town of

Steinbach were marked "clear prairie" or at least "prairie with bluffs of poplar and tamarack." From there a high gravel ridge ran southwest to the present site of Grünfeld, and a small ridge just north of it. Most of the centre was broken land marked on the maps as poplar, willow, tamarack, slough, burnt stumps, granite stones, gravel, and lots of weeds as a whole; though drainage seems to have been better here than in townships to the south where numerous sloughs are shown on the maps.

In the beginning, village sites were obviously chosen in natural clearings or on high land. The two gravel ridges alone gave rise to six or seven villages. Several sites chosen in a dry season had to be abandoned afterwards when the water level rose again. The villages founded in wooded land were inevitably strung along the banks of a river or creek; in these cases the village street followed the characteristic slant of the country from southeast to northwest. In open country, however, the rows of houses were parallel to section lines, usually running east and west as a protection against the north winds.

Although the location of some villages was changed in the course of time, while many others have disappeared altogether, an inspection of mounds marking basements and foundations, together with accounts gathered from old-timers, have made it possible to reconstruct the exact location of most of them. In 1877, when population density in the East Reserve was higher than at any other time before 1900, thirty-eight villages were in existence. Five of them, on better soil and larger than the average, were occupied by the Kleine Gemeinde people, while all the others belonged to the Bergthal group. Not all the places mentioned, however, were fully organized village communes. Some were either small hamlets (Schanzenburg, Pastwa, Strassberg, Heuboden, Tannau, Eigengrund, Eigenhof, Ebenfeld, Vollwerk, Lichtenau and Landskron), or incomplete villages planned to accommodate large numbers of later immigrants who never arrived. Most of the settlements laid out in the early years in township 7-4 East, and east and south of the gravel ridge, either on wet or on poor soil, were soon abandoned when better land west of the Red River became available, causing a partial exodus from the East Reserve (Pastwa, Strassberg, Neuendorf, Felsenton, Hamberg, Schönberg, Schönhorst and Neuhorst, somewhat later also Burwalde). On the other hand, a few new hamlets and villages were founded in later years in areas left unoccupied during the first period of settlement (Blumengart, Silberfeld and Neubarkfeld, a daughter colony of [Alt-]Barkfeld).

Generally speaking, the settlement pattern in the East Reserve was more irregular than it had been in Russia. The size of the settlements was much smaller, and the area incorporated in villages was checkered with many patches of unoccupied land. This departure was caused only partly by the more broken topography. In Russia a whole contiguous tract of land had been granted to a colony corporatively, which included not only the arable land belonging to individual homesteads, but also much surplus land for common pastures, haylands, woodlands and so on, in addition to large reserves for future settlement. In Manitoba, however, a village commune could hold only 160 acres for each individual homesteader, so that all land to be used in common had to be cut out from the individual grants, and nothing was left for future occupation after the period for which the reservation was set aside had elapsed. This suggested a very careful choice of village site and territory, besides making unattractive the occupation of less valuable land. Finally, the foundation of the West Reserve in 1875-76, on superior land, prevented later arrivals from joining the village communes which were expecting them, and even caused the depletion of villages already established.

The situation in the West Reserve differed from that in the first colony. Although most of it consisted of open prairie, there also was a huge swamp along Buffalo Creek and Buffalo Lake, so that only the western portion, rising gently toward the Pembina hills, was dry enough for immediate occupation. This area also included a few creeks offering direct access to fresh water and was within easy reach of the wooded slopes of the Pembina hills and of more woods across the border. Thus the first group settling in the West Reserve, namely, the Fürstenland people, were directed to its western and southwestern townships. Since the country offered hardly any natural obstructions, the settlement pattern here was much more regular than in the East Reserve. The villages were usually larger, and the territories occupied by the different villages were contiguous to each other, leaving vacant only the Hudson's Bay and school sections and a small area of low grade soil just east of Neuenburg and Reinland.

The Fürstenland people, arriving between 1875 and 1877, occupied a solid block of land, so that small hamlets, isolated homesteads or new villages could make their appearance only on the fringes of the original Fürstenland colony. In the east it reached to a line running from the present town of Plum Coulee through Kronsthal and thence to Grünthal

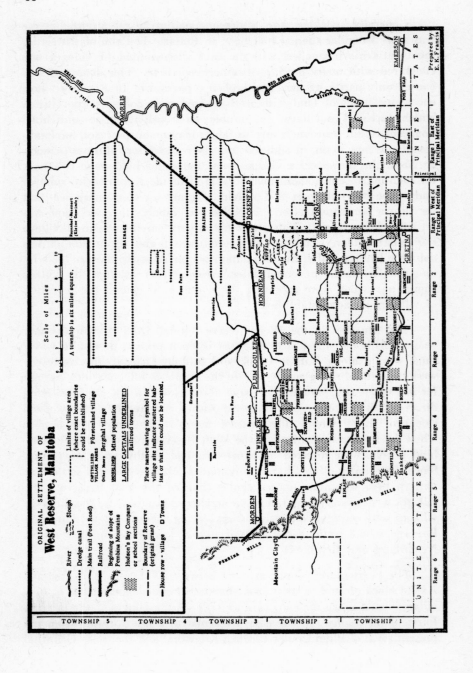

north of Gretna. In the west it was hemmed in by the foothills of the Pembina Mountains and a colony of Ontario settlers northwest of township 2-5 West, as well as by a band of semi-nomad Indians in the extreme southwest corner.[21] Its northern boundary stopped six miles or more short of the extreme limit of the reservation due to wet land encountered there. The southern boundary coincided with the United States border. The villages on the western fringe, for example, Schön-feld, Schöndorf (once a village of some twenty homes) and probably Einlage, either never developed into fully organized villages or soon declined. In the east Gnadenthal was founded in or about 1880, as a daughter colony of Schönwiese to provide for the younger sons of immigrants; two years later Ebenfeld was cut out from marginal land only to be abandoned soon afterwards. Hamburg, too, was probably a late Fürstenland foundation. Neuenburg in the center of the Fürstenland colony, on the other hand, was settled by a group from the Old Colony in Russia who had, for some time, farmed on the so-called *Judenplan* in Pluof, a Jewish colony.

Toward the end of the immigration period a few stragglers from the Bergthal group, anxious to get a share in the superior land of the West Reserve, settled among the Fürstenland people instead of going to the East Reserve. As a result, several mixed villages sprang up along the Plum Coulee-Kronsthal-Grünthal line, namely Grünthal, Eigenhof, Hoffnungsfeld, Reinthal, Rosenbach (a small hamlet), perhaps Krons-thal and Kleefeld, and, far to the northwest, Burwalde. As time went on, many others, who had already acquired a homestead in the East Reserve but had become discouraged, drifted to the other side of the Red River once it became obvious that no further immigration from Russia was to be expected. Eventually half of the Bergthal people settled here.[22]

The first invasion occurred in township 1-1 East, next to the Red River where soil and drainage were excellent, but soon spread to the adjoining parts of the Reserve. Eventually all dry land south and

[21] These Indians came for only part of each year from the old French parish of St. Joseph (now Walhalla, North Dakota). At the turn of the century, about 25 Indian families were still found squatting on sections 4, 5, 8, 9 and 17 in township 1-5 West, but they left soon afterwards and never returned.

[22] According to the Bergthal church books the colony in Russia numbered 540 families, 34 of which remained in the Old Country, while 53 founded the Mountain Lake settlement in Minnesota. The 453 families which immigrated to Manitoba were joined by 9 families from Puchtin and 15 from the Chortitza colony. When the accounts were finally divided in 1887, only 246 families were registered as belonging to the East Reserve, while about 220 families were organized into a new Bergthal congregation of the West Reserve.

east of the big Buffalo marsh, which extended to a line drawn through the villages of Heuboden, Bergfeld, Schönau, and Schönthal, was occupied. During this period of resettlement lasting from 1879 to 1886, the Bergthal people organized village communes after the traditional pattern. But many settlements founded later on the wet lands north of the Heuboden-Schönthal line never attained full village status, while others disintegrated after a short time.[23] Departures from the traditional settlement pattern were more common among the Bergthal people in the West Reserve than among the other groups. Difficult soil conditions calling for more individual initiative were probably one reason, at least in some areas. Another was the weakened social controls which soon were to play havoc with their inner organization as well.

The manner in which the Bergthal migrants from the East Reserve obtained possession of homesteads in the West Reserve was somewhat irregular. At first all the Mennonites here had to settle as squatters, until the survey was completed and the second land grant made. However, while the situation was soon remedied for the original immigrants to the West Reserve, the same could not be done for the Bergthal migrants who already had taken up a homestead in the other colony. It was only under the revised Dominion Lands Act of 1883, (46 *Vic.*, ch. 17, sec. 37), that the right of acquiring a second homestead in another location was granted to all pioneers. This step was taken in view of disappointing immigration figures and the alarming drift of settlers to the United States. Many were selling their free quarter-sections in Canada as quickly as they could in order to start all over again in the Dakotas. This land act provision, however, only increased unsound land speculation and was, therefore, rescinded three years later (49 *Vic.*, ch. 27, sec. 8). By then the movement from the East to the West Reserve had been completed, and all that was left for the migrants to do was to give up their original homesteads.

Relations to the Large Society

The society within whose territory the Mennonite colonies in Manitoba were established, was in a state of flux. Yet, in contrast to

---

[23] The earliest Bergthal villages in the West Reserve were Edenburg, Gnadenfeld, Silberfeld, Schönhorst, Neuanlage and Sommerfeld followed by Halbstadt, Hochstadt, Rosenfeld, Altona (now Alt-Altona), Bergfeld (now: Alt-Bergfeld) and Schönthal, and somewhat later by Schönau and Neubergfeld. Weidenfeld broke up in 1883 shortly after it was founded. Strassberg, Kleinstadt, Eigengrund, Blumenthal, in addition to the wet-land settlements mentioned in the text, were never organized as village communes. Waldheim was founded by Bergthal people far to the west on the other side of the Fürstenland colony.

other parts of the North American plains, the region already possessed a history and a distinctive social organization. It was precisely in recognition of this pre-existing society and because of its antagonism toward the colonization policy of the Dominion Government that the Manitoba Act was passed. But this very same act of political recognition also signalized the end of the old fur trade society, paving the way for agricultural settlers to populate and take over the country.

Small as the total population of the province was at the beginning of its independent history, both the old and the new social systems were much more complex than the short designation of fur trade versus agricultural society might indicate. Besides the outlying posts of the Hudson's Bay Company and a migrant population, both Indian and white, of hunters, traders and trappers widely scattered through an immense hinterland, the old fur trade society also included a permanent settlement at the confluence of the Red River and the Assiniboine River. Here company employees, officials of the quasi-autonomous District of Assiniboia, the garrison, the clergy of several churches and denominations, retired fur traders and sedentary half-breed trappers, boatmen and freighters, mingled with a good number of French and Scottish farmers who were supplying the fur posts and the brigades of traders with provisions. On the other hand, not all of the people who came after 1870 were rugged pioneer settlers of the type that dominated the scene in the Great Plains of the United States. The settlers were accompanied, and in part preceded, by the agents of older institutions of the Canadian East, mainly of government and church, but also of business, transportation, press, and other services. There also was a fair admixture of English gentlemen and urban elements, including a large contingent of speculators and other commercial adventurers who came less to exploit the new country than to exploit the capital and labor of the new immigrants.

This dominance of urban interests and of older social institutions is reflected in the relatively much more rapid growth of Winnipeg from a small crossroad settlement with a population of 240 in 1871, to a thriving political and commercial capital of nearly 8,000 ten years later. At the same time the total population of the province increased from 19,000 to 66,000. The mass of actual settlers thus found themselves at once confronted with a relatively stable institutional framework and with cultural traditions which were not easily dislodged. Nor could they simply overrun the remnants of a preëxisting native society in the same way as their counterparts further south were doing, building their new social order in utter disregard of any Indian or even white societies (such as the Mormon society in Utah, the French society in Louisiana or the Spanish society in Texas, New Mexico and California) which lay in their path. The Canadian pioneers had to respect the protective policy of the Government with regard to the Indians and Métis, and had to accept the full participation of the latter in all public affairs. Accordingly, they were much less free to create new forms of social organization even in the rural hinterland, but had to submit to the dominance of an older society and its agents, reaching out from the East—through the mediation of an incipient metropolitan center—even to the remotest corners of the new West. Wherever the pioneers turned, they were at once followed, and often preceded, by the land survey and the Mounted Police (established in 1874), and by other agents of the law, of civil administration, and of the church. This general tutelage over their social affairs was facilitated by the initial homogenity of most of the colonists themselves. It was further underlined by the fact that the autonomy of the Provincial administration, though in theory far-reaching, was actually superseded by the authority of Dominion agencies precisely in those fields which mattered most in the early years, namely, in the control of immigration and the distribution of land.

Following a suggestion of S. D. Clark,[24] one might distinguish between a pioneer stage as the period of earliest settlement on virgin soil, and a frontier stage as the period when new forms of economic enterprise and exploitation are fully employed, leaving their impact upon the development of social organization. From this perspective, the province of Manitoba during the first decade following its incorporation was largely in the frontier stage, while true pioneer conditions, such as arose in many other parts of the Canadian West, prevailed here only briefly in the more remote new settlements. Since the Red River colony and the French parishes remained the centre of dominance, this period of transition was strikingly short. At the end of it a compromise and equilibrium was reached between the native society, largely half-breed and with a strong French and Catholic component, on the one hand, and the newcomers, predominantly from Ontario and with British and Protestant traditions, on the other.

---

[24] *The Social Development of Canada: An Introductory Study With Select Documents* (Toronto, 1942), p. 1n.

It was in this clash with the French Catholics, essentially a mere replica of the perpetual tension dominating the Eastern Canadian scene, that the Ontario settlers, instead of feeling free to create entirely new forms of social and institutional behavior in the struggle of individuals for favorable positions, were forced to rally collectively around their own traditions. Their initial attempt to make Manitoba a colony of old Upper Canada failed, partly because of their own economic weakness and the successful resistance of the indigenous society, and partly because of political influences and considerations which had their origin outside the province in the composite political order and bi-ethnic social system of the older and dominant parts of the Dominion. Instead, the old and the new societies were integrated into a dualistic system in which the original socio-economic dividing lines were modified according to distinctions expressed more and more exclusively in terms of language and religion.

At the time of the Mennonite immigration, social conditions in Manitoba were still too indefinite and amorphous to permit the crystallization of any determined public opinion on the issue. Whatever articulate reaction was recorded for the first ten years, came from government officials, politicians and the local press, but it is impossible now to gauge the representativeness of their voices. It is probably significant that the French press as well as the clerical and political leaders of the old indigenous society remained consistently silent and aloof, in the face of the vociferous welcome extended to the Mennonites in the English press and the pronouncements of the authorities entrusted with the promotion of immigration. Underneath the sullen silence of the natives, particularly of the half-breeds upon whose very stamping grounds the first Reserve was laid out, one suspects much resentment and apprehension; once it even flared up into open hostility against the party of delegates travelling through the country in search of land suitable for permanent settlement. Yet, since the suppression of the Riel rebellion several years before, the backbone of resistance against agricultural immigration had been broken, and the colonization policy of the Dominion Government and of its local supporters and beneficiaries was accepted as an irrevocable fact. Items on the Mennonite project in the English-language press revealed keen interest and wholehearted approval. In news reports covering the preliminary negotiations and the tours of the delegates, as well as in separate feature stories, the background of the prospective settlers was discussed at length and particular emphasis was given to their honesty, industry, and good reputation as farmers and pioneers.

As early as November 30, 1872, the *Manitoba Free Press* pointed at the wider significance of the project by writing: "The attention which will be drawn to our country by the movement, will have the effect of bringing here a great share of the steady immigration which for years has been filling up the Western States." This puts in a nutshell the attitude toward the Mennonites on the part of the now dominant social strata of the province. Their primary concern was the rapid colonization of the West, and the economic advantages expected from it. The relatively limited population resources of Eastern Canada herself, and the fact that Great Britain was using up all her available human reserves for the expansion of her own industries, combined with the great attraction exercised by the United States not only upon foreign immigrants but even upon Canada's native sons, left large-scale immigration from the European continent as the only hope for rapid colonization of Manitoba and the North West. That the Mennonites were Protestant may have been a factor in overcoming any possible reluctance of Anglo-Saxon Canadians to approve the influx of foreign elements. But if such apprehensions existed, no traces can be found in contemporary documents.

It is much more likely that the thought of cultural and national difficulties which might arise from this policy in afteryears did not even enter the minds of the promoters of colonization. Nationalistic feelings, apart from the conflict between the Anglo-Saxons and French, which, moreover, was perceived primarily in religious rather than in national terms, had little room in a frontier society concerned above all with making a living and with economic advancement. Manitoba, as much as the Canada of the Confederation, was a young country then, with all the optimism and, perhaps, carelessness of youth. Its people were unafraid of foreigners and foreign influences because they were sure of their ability to absorb them in due course, in the same way as the American melting pot had already absorbed millions of non-Anglo-Saxons, and was swallowing many more every year.

Once the Mennonites began to arrive in force, public attention was greatly attracted to their strange appearance and customs; yet, these were viewed with a benevolent curiosity in which any signs of ethnocentrism were conspicuously absent. For the first contact with this foreign folk group was accompanied by the most pleasant experience of a great boost to the local economy. When the buying spree ended, interest in the newcomers subsided; the Mennonites retired to their Reserves where, for some time, they went largely unnoticed by the general public.

Despite this segregation and the almost complete silence on Mennonite affairs after the first few years, a certain amount of intercourse between the Mennonites and their neighbours continued, though limited mostly to the sporadic, superficial and impersonal relations of the market place, of which almost no direct evidence has been preserved. We only know of certain closer business associations between East Reserve Mennonites and Jewish merchants of Winnipeg. Similar connections apparently existed between West Reserve people and their Anglo-Saxon neighbours in the Morden area, and probably in Emerson.

Language, of course, was an effective barrier to intensive social interaction. Another was the almost complete social and economic self-sufficiency of the Mennonite colonies. Other newcomers were too pre-occupied with their own struggle for survival to bother greatly about their strange and retiring neighbours. On the other hand, the reluctance of the Mennonites to associate with non-Mennonites is in part explained by the rough kind of people with whom they came in contact, particularly in the West Reserve which was crossed by a main artery of traffic, the so-called post-road, a trail marked by high posts sticking out above grass or snow.

But the isolation of the Mennonites was not simply an outcome of frontier conditions or of cultural differences. It was deliberate and was enforced by their own leaders and institutions. The idea of withdrawal from the "world" was the very essence of the sectarian basis of the Mennonite group. The Apostle's warning of the "unequal yoke" (II *Cor.* 6:14 and *Eph.* 5:11) was an ever-recurring theme in their religious and social teaching. When the conservative party in the Mennonite colonies of Russia protested against the "worldliness" of their brethren, they deplored as much their social mingling with outsiders as their adoption of the ways and institutions of this world. And when the most conservative of them turned to Canada, they fled from the world's inroad into their life in the Old Country to a place which seemed remote enough and isolated enough, both geographically and socially, to give hope that contact with the world could henceforth be avoided with greater success.

Similarly, the legal safeguards which they stipulated in their negotiations with the Dominion Government were conceived primarily as effective barriers against the "world" encroaching upon their communities. This endeavour to protect the faithful against all influences of infidels and sinners is, of course, a pastoral practice common to all religious bodies of the stricter kind, as exemplified by the widespread prohibition of mixed marriages. In the last analysis, however, this attitude is but one particular expression of the will of all strongly coherent and integrated groups to perpetuate themselves and to protect their social heritage by avoiding the challenge that comes from contact with different cultures.

Even though contacts with the out-group were kept at a minimum, there was no taboo against the learning of another language as a means of communication where it was required for business transactions. Most of the Mennonite men, at least, spoke Russian, and the more adaptable ones did their best to acquire English as fast as they could when they came to Canada. One of the early immigrants, for instance, took an Englishman into his house for a winter so that he might instruct the children in the lingua franca of the country. In other instances, children of earlier immigrants became the language teachers of later arrivals.

As Manitoba's social organization became more settled and the country around the Mennonite Reserves more populated, public interest in the inner affairs of the Mennonites was aroused once more. From the evidence that has been preserved one gathers that the earlier reactions of undisguised curiosity and satisfaction with the economic benefits derived from this immigration were now mingled with expressions of mild apprehension and jealousy. Toward the end of the period under discussion, conditions in these secluded areas of the province were becoming more and more a matter of public concern. The question of assimilation was not posed directly and bluntly. But it was implied in such news reports as that of the Emerson *International*, according to which the Mennonites had ordered home all their young people employed at Emerson, Pembina and environs, after one of their girls had eloped with a soldier and married him in Texas. Still in a vein of good-natured banter, the paper added "for fear of others of the faith becoming similarly demoralized, we presume."[25] But a few years

---

[25] Reprinted in the Manitoba *Daily Free Press*, January 13, 1879.

later the Parliamentary Committee on Immigration at Ottawa took a more serious view of the matter. In one of its sessions in 1886, Shantz was closely questioned as to whether the young people now "mix or move with the other nationalities . . . more than the original settlers did . . . in what way were they mixing—by marriage?"[26]

Nevertheless, the basic problem at issue, which in future years was to dominate relations between Mennonites and the larger society, had not yet become clearly crystallized in the mind of the public, with the exception of a few political leaders in the Dominion Parliament. Criticism, whether implied or overt, against the alien culture in the midst of Manitoba's emerging society remained for some time superficial and peripheral. One matter, widely aired among the Anglo-Saxon section with their self-righteous convictions about morals and propriety, was the treatment of women among the Mennonites; it was discovered that they were doing hard work in the fields. Interviews with several surviving women of the pioneer generation revealed that they had not been forced to do so but had wanted to help as much as possible and to share in all hardships with their men. Since living conditions were very simple, the average mother had time to spare from her household duties, while hygienic arguments against woman labour were as yet unknown. Ignorant of the customary division of labour between the sexes among East European peasants, and with the zeal of antislavery apostles, the Anglo-Saxon critics of Mennonite ways of life in the House of Commons even compelled the Deputy Minister of Agriculture to promise that they certainly would soon conform to the superior moral standards of Canadian society.[27] Behind all this commotion was obviously a certain fear of competition. A farmer from St. Paul's parish, for instance, William A. Loucks by name, testified before the House Committee on Colonization that, due to their frugality and "herd spirit," the Mennonites were under-selling "our people."[28] At a similar occasion, the Honourable Simon James Dawson criticized the Government policy saying that he would have preferred intermingled settlement with English, Scotch and French farmers, as the Mennonites had obtained possession of the best district in the province, the "very garden of the continent where they would prosper and grow rich."[29]

---

[26] To this Shantz answered: "I do not know as for that." (*Report of the Select Standing Committee on Immigration and Colonization of the House of Commons* [1886], p. 27).

[27] *Journals*, 1878, appendix 2, p. 16.

[28] *Journals*, 1879, appendix 1, p. 69.

[29] *Hansard*, 1879, April 25, p. 1549.

Another criticism was expressed by "Outsider," probably a Manitoba contributor, in the Toronto *Globe*: "However pious they may be, they do not carry out the next maxim to godliness."[30] The remark referred to the fact that in the Mennonite house, residence and stable were under the same roof, and that their huge brick stoves were heated either with straw or with a mixture of cow dung, earth and straw. Pressed with special machines, cut into square blocks and left in the yard to dry in the wind and sun, this provided excellent and cheap fuel in the absence of wood or coal, even if its odour was offensive to the Puritanical sensitivities of "Outsider" and others of the same mind.

Despite the dissatisfaction of some with Mennonite ways and habits, public reaction by and large was favorable. In 1876 the Member of Parliament for Selkirk called them "a well conducted people" and declared: "no settlers could be more desirable."[31] In 1881 the same "Outsider" who found so much fault with them had to admit in the Toronto *Globe* that they were intelligent looking, quick to learn, and "as a race . . . thrifty and industrious." Similarly, the *Manitoba Daily Free Press*, of January 11, 1879, wrote that they "have proved themselves to be industrious, hardworking and useful citizens." The same paper observed, in its issue of September 16, 1881, that out of land that at the time was thought to be useless they were making the best of farms. These testimonials have been selected at random from the printed evidence that could be found.

The fullest statement of the same sentiment was, however, made on the occasion of an official visit of the Governor-General, Lord Dufferin, to the East Reserve in August of 1877.[32] In addressing a large crowd of Mennonites he emphasized: "It is with the greatest pleasure that I have passed through your villages, and witnessed your comfortable homesteads, barns and byres, which have arisen like magic upon this fertile plain, for they prove that you are expert in agriculture, and possess a high standard of domestic comfort." Upon his return to Winnipeg, he summed up his impressions of the tour through the province in a public speech, saying:

---

[30] Reprinted in the *Manitoba Free Press* of September 2, 1881, under the heading "Our Mennonite Settlers."

[31] *Hansard*, 1876, April 10, p. 1173f.

[32] Cf. *The Speeches and Addresses of the Rt. Hon. Frederick Temple, Earl of Dufferin*, ed. by Henry Milton London, 1882); also "Ein Besuch des General Gouverneur von Canada unter den Mennoniten." *Herold der Wahrheit 14*, 166; 159-161.

Although I have witnessed many sights to cause me pleasure during my various progresses through the Dominion, seldom have I beheld any spectacle more pregnant with prophecy, more fraught with promise of a successful future than the Mennonite Settlement (Applause). When I visited these interesting people, they had been only two years in the province, and yet in a long ride I took across many miles of prairie, which but yesterday was absolutely bare, desolate, untenanted, the home of the wolf, the badger, and the eagle, I passed village after village, homestead after homestead, furnished with all the conveniences and incidents of European comfort, and of a scientific agriculture; while on either side of the road, cornfields ripe for harvest, and pastures populous with herds of cattle stretched away to the horizon (Great Applause). Even on this continent—the peculiar theatre of rapid change and progress—there has nowhere, I imagine, taken place so marvellous a transformation.

It would be easy to dismiss such oratory as the eulogies of an official charged with the encouragement of immigration and the promotion of good will among all sections of the citizenry. Yet, seen in their context, these passages and the acclaim with which they were received, have the convincing ring of sincerity, besides setting a pattern for public opinion because of the undisputed authority of the representative of the Queen. For Lord Dufferin uttered frank criticism and showed undisguised disappointment in his references to other groups of settlers, particularly to the Icelandic immigrants. This general impression is further strengthened by remarks included in the diary of Lady Dufferin, which was published many years afterwards, such as the following entry under August 21, 1877, the day of the reception in Eigenhof: "The Mennonites are most desirable emigrants: they retain their best German characteristics, are hard working, honest, sober, simple, hardy people; they bring money into the country, and *can settle in a woodless place which no other people will do.*"[33] The last clause is of particular interest; for it was repeated almost in identical words a few years later by a simple farmer, testifying before the House Committee on Immigration. After expressing his resentment against Mennonite competition, the same William Loucks mentioned earlier in these pages paid the greatest tribute to them by adding: "They live where we cannot exist."[34]

---

[33] *My Canadian Journal, 1872-78* (London, 1891), p. 332. (Italics supplied).

[34] *Journals, 1879*, appendix 1, p. 69.

CHAPTER IV

The Challenge To Tradition

Freedom and Social Control

PEOPLE have migrated to North America for two main reasons: economic betterment and freedom. The first was foremost in the minds of most who settled the Canadian West. Although to the Mennonites freedom was the more decisive and overt motive, economic considerations were not entirely absent from their choice. The Canadian authorities and public were sincerely convinced that their country was able to offer full satisfaction of both desires. The speeches made by the Governor-General on the occasion of his visit to the East Reserve were representative of this attitude.

In his address to the Mennonites themselves, his argument ran as follows: They had made great sacrifices in order to alleviate their religious scruples regarding military service. Canada and her neighbour, the United States, were engaged only in a peaceful struggle against the brute forces of nature in which the immigrants were welcome to join: "If you have come hither to seek for peace," Lord Dufferin exclaimed, "— peace at least we can promise you"; never again would they be called upon "to stain their hands with human blood."[1] More important than the material blessings awaiting them in the new country, he added, were the constitutional liberties, municipal privileges and domestic

---

[1] *The Speeches and Addresses of the Rt. Hon. Frederick Temple, Earl of Dufferin* (London, 1882). The same argument reappears in a communication by the United States Secretary of State, Hamilton Fish, to the Mennonite delegates, when he wrote: "It is true however, that for the next fifty years we will not be entangled in another war in which military service will be necessary." Neither statesman could visualize a war between the peaceful nations of this continent, nor did they expect that they would be embroiled in wars beyond the oceans.

freedom which the Canadians were ready to share with them on equal terms.

Several times Lord Dufferin emphasized civil freedom, equality before the law and the blessings of the Constitution, beside the religious liberty and the economic advantages which the Mennonites hoped to gain. He repeated the same thought before an enthusiastic Winnipeg audience a few days later:

> And yet, when in your name, and in the name of the Queen of England, I bade these people welcome to their new homes, it was not the improvement in their material fortunes that preoccupied my thoughts. . . . I felt infinitely prouder in being able to throw over them the aegis of the British Constitution (Loud cheers), . . . We ourselves are so accustomed to breathe the atmosphere of freedom that it scarcely occurs to us to consider and appreciate our advantages in this respect.

Few Canadians realized at the time, or are ready to admit even today, that the freedom offered the Mennonites (and other similar groups of non-Anglo-Saxon immigrants) was in reality a very different kind of freedom than that which they had expected to find in the New World. In order to view, in the proper perspective, the conflict that ensued later between the large society and the Mennonite group, one has to understand these two meanings of freedom. The democratic heritage of England, later extended to the Anglo-Saxon nations of this continent, implied above all the exemption of the individual from governmental control in respect to person and property, religious convictions and institutions, and all matters not plainly affecting the common welfare. It further implied participation in public control through universal suffrage, the equality of all citizens before the law, and social equality, in the sense of no formal distinctions on the basis of birth (including racial and national origin), wealth, occupational status, or religious and political affiliation. It also implied freedom of communication as the principal means through which an enlightened public opinion, and consequently the correct decision about all public issues on the part of the majority, could be safeguarded, resulting in a happier life for all. Finally, it implied the assumption that the institutions of law and government as they had developed in England and among her off-shoots were best suited to realize these basic principles of social organization. To the Mennonites, on the other hand, the idea of the moral autonomy of the individual immanent in democratic philosophy had little appeal. They were not preoccupied with the greatest possible freedom of the individual *from* social controls,

82

but with the freedom of the group as a whole *for* the exercise of strict social controls over each individual member. They wished to be free from all institutional control on the part of the host society in order to preserve and enforce all the more rigidly the constituent norms of their own social system.

In view of this profound difference between the idea of individual freedom underlying Canadian culture, and that of corporate freedom as visualized by the Mennonites, it is not surprising to find that the latter (as did many other groups of foreign immigrants) felt disappointed in their hopes and ambitions, once the full impact of Canada's institutions was brought to bear upon them. They even came to realize that those of their brethren who had remained under the autocratic rule of Tsarist Russia not only reaped aplenty all that the Manitoba group had foregone for freedom's sake: wealth, social prestige, and a flourishing cultural life; they actually enjoyed — at least until the Bolshevist revolution — a much larger degree of corporate freedom and autonomy than democratic Canada, in the long run, was ready to concede to any ethnic group, with the exception of the French. For Mennonite culture and institutions were geared to the political order of Imperial Russia, and were partly a direct result of its ideology and actual functioning, while they were in many respects incompatible with the democratic and liberal premises of the emerging Canadian nation. That the Mennonites succeeded nevertheless in partially realizing their initial program was due to factors operating more in spite of, than because of, the framework of Anglo-Saxon democracy.

One reason for the re-establishment of the traditional pattern of social organization and controls in the Manitoba Reserves, and a very decisive factor, was the absence of any strong political institutions and the general indefiniteness of the social system in the province during the frontier stage. During this time, the Provincial administration followed the policy of leaving intact the institutions of local self-government which, as survivals of the fur trade period, already existed, such as the French parishes, while facilitating the introduction of Ontario institutions where the character of the new settlers promised their ready acceptance. The authorities, too pre-occupied with more pressing problems, were at first not greatly concerned with the inner affairs of the compact colonies of foreigners, both Mennonites and

Icelanders,[2] the more so since these appeared to be self-regulating, giving no cause of complaint. Thus both colonies enjoyed a *de facto* rather than *de jure* autonomy for several years, which the Mennonites used to put their own social system and institutional framework on a solid foundation.

However, to pretend that the agents of Manitoba's larger society permitted the Mennonite autonomy to be established entirely by default would be an exaggeration. They certainly were aware of the contract by which Dominion officials had implicitly conceded to the Mennonites as a group certain functions of self-government. Even if such concessions had been *ultra vires*, the Provincial administrators were not prepared to assert their Constitutional prerogatives before the issue actually arose. It was quite in line with the pragmatie tendencies of British policy to wait and see how things would work out, instead of quibbling over matters of principle. Finally, interference with the inner affairs of the Mennonite settlements did touch upon at least one of the fundamentals of Canadian democracy, namely, religious tolerance. For the Mennonite group was primarily conceived as a religious body both by the Mennonites themselves and by their hosts. Whatever institutions of social control the Mennonites wished to establish could be interpreted, and were interpreted, as expressions of their religious mores rather than as alien methods of secular government.

As a matter of fact, it was extremely difficult to make a clear distinction between those elements of their social organization which were essentially an expression of their religion, and others which pertained to purely secular matters and civil government, and thus were not covered by the principle of religious liberty. Although the separation of church and state was recognized by the Anabaptist creed of the Mennonites, they had come to confuse their strictly religious and their civil institutions when they underwent in Russia their metamorphosis into an independent ethnic system endowed with a large measure of political and cultural autonomy. Upon their arrival in Canada, they insisted in establishing forms of local and ethnic self-government which had no basis whatever in the democratic institutions of the country,

---

[2] The Icelanders established their colony in 1875, in the Interlake region which, until 1881, belonged not to Manitoba but to the District of Keewatin in the North-West Territories. They adopted a republican constitution which did not mention once the name of Canada or the Queen of England but gave the impression that this colony was an independent state built on ancient Icelandic traditions. (Cf. S. J. Sommerville, "Early Icelandic Settlement in Canada," *Papers Read Before the Historical and Scientific Society of Manitoba*, Season 1944-45 [Winnipeg, 1945] pp. 25 ff.)

while giving the impression that these were an integral part of their religious heritage, and a necessary requisite for their existence as a religious community. This was in no way in intentional misrepresentation but rather due to an attitude common to all peoples whose whole social life is permeated with religious ideas and values.

The impression of uninterrupted continuity of their institutions, both civil and ecclesiastical, was further supported by the wholesale transfer of two entire colonies from Russia to Manitoba. The village communes had, of course, to be disbanded, and were reorganized on a smaller scale in Manitoba. But the church government with its elder, preachers and deacons, the *Waisenamt* as the financial backbone of the colony, and the *Gebietsamt* (or local civil government of a district) were simply transplanted. It is certainly significant that Franz Peters, of Vollwerk, the *Oberschulze* of the *Mariupoler Mennoniten Gebietsamt, Kolonie Bergthal,* at once took over the *Gebietsamt* of the *Mennoniten Reserve* east of the Red River. Similarly, Isaak Müller, of Neuhorst, who had been acting as the *Oberschulze* of the Fürstenland colony in Russia, continued in the same capacity among the Fürstenland and Bergthal people in the West Reserve, without any new elections having taken place in either case.

The official business of the Mennonite *Gebietsamt* in a Manitoba Reserve consisted primarily of public works and the taxation necessary for the maintenance of schools, roads, bridges, culverts and ditches. Although the schools were essentially the responsibiltiy of the church, the village commune and the district acted partly as its agents. The same is true of the *Waisenamt,* also a church institution. Whenever a special need arose, the *Oberschulze* would send a written request to the different village mayors within his jurisdiction (the Reserve) stating the amount of money or statute labor required from each commune.

These levies were computed in proportion to the number of households in each village, but it was left to the *Schulze* and the *Schulzenbott* (mayor and village assembly) to divide them equitably among the families. The latter, in turn, designated the person, or persons, who eventually had to perform the required service. Monetary contributions played a small role in these transactions, usually representing payments in lieu of statute labor. As raw material was simply taken from wherever it could be found in the Reserve, regardless of any legal property title a specific individual might hold in such land, taxation consisted essentially in personal service and the supply of draft animals, implements and tools. Self-administration on the village level operated with equal simplicity and efficiency as on the district level, following the pattern customary in Russia.

While routine matters could well be taken care of in this way, the functioning of the local system of government was hampered by the lack of police power and the absence of law enforcement agencies. In Russia, both the mayor's office and the district office had exercised judiciary functions, backed up by the superior courts of the Russian Empire and the full police power of the state. In Manitoba, on the other hand, Mennonite institutions of civil administration lacked any authority other than that voluntarily recognized by the group members. While there was no outside interference with Mennonite civil affairs, the county courts could not be expected to uphold decisions by self-constituted authorities which often were contrary to Canadian customs and laws.

Well aware of the anomalous situation, the Mennonites avoided any contact with the public agencies of law and law enforcement. They were so successful in this that in the early years their criminal record appeared impeccable, while civil law suits involving Mennonites were almost unheard of. Even the press, then as now relishing a crime story or a shocking scandal, had nothing of the kind to report about the Reserves. This, of course, is not to say that the Mennonites lived in a utopian state of peaceful anarchy. The problem of social controls and external sanctions was a crucial one for them, but they solved it in a peculiar manner. First, any appeal to the courts or other authorities of the country was declared a grave sin. If a Mennonite was perchance summoned before a judge or magistrate, he had to submit to indictment and fine without the slightest attempt to defend himself. In this way, they avoided conflict between their own interpretation of right and wrong and that of agents of the Canadian legal order; for such a conflict could have led to disastrous consequences for the stability of their socio-economic system.

In addition, their own ecclesiastical authorities had jurisdiction over any act that implied an infringement of Mennonite mores, including even matters of purely secular concern. While in Russia the officers of civil administration on the district level were appointed by the Russian authorities following public elections, they were now nominated by the *Kirchendienst* (elder and preachers) and elected by acclamation in the *Bruderschaft* (church assembly). This led, of course, to a form of

86

theocracy which was actually contrary to their Anabaptist creed. Yet, the breach of principle was concealed by the fact that the elders and preachers of the different congregations had acted side by side with the civil functionaries of the colonies in the organization of the migration to Canada, and thus were recognized in the New Country as the natural leaders in all affairs affecting the common welfare.

As it turned out, the authority of the ecclesiastical leaders and the sanctions they could invoke proved so effective that the civil officials of the Mennonite colonies came to rely entirely on them whenever the need arose of forcing a recalcitrant member of the community to abide by the customary law and the decisions of the majority.[3] Whenever a Mennonite was reported to the preachers by a mayor or *Oberschulze*, they would go, one by one, to his house to talk to him. They would play upon his conscience to make him see his sin. If this did not help, he was summoned before the *Bruderschaft*, the general meeting of all adult male members of the church presided over by the elder. As a rule the questioning to which he was subjected, the accusations hurled against him, the admonitions couched in biblical language, the public sentiment expressed by this assembly, which functioned as a supreme court of justice and at the same time as a tribunal acting under the law of God—all this sufficed to bring the sinner to reason. He recanted, submitted to public censure, confessed his guilt, and amended his ways. If he didn't, as a last resort the grand ban could be imposed upon him.

An excommunicated person was an outcast, shunned and avoided as a publican. No church member, not even a member of his own family, was permitted to speak to him or to approach him in any way, though he was housed and fed as long as he chose to remain in his village. To leave the community was no solution for his problem, although Canadian courts would protect him in his civil and property

---

[3] In this connection it is highly significant to read that even in this day and age the Mennonites in Paraguay are regulating their affairs without any recourse to written laws, courts or prisons. In his recent book *Pilgrims in Paraguay: The Story of Mennonite Colonization in South America* (Scottdale, Penn., 1953) Professor Joseph Winfield Fretz reports that at present criminal offenses are effectively dealt with by either the church elders or the colony office. The Bible is considered the only law, and offenders are treated "in the light of Scriptural teaching and Christian common sense." Ecclesiastical punishment consists in excommunication, punishment by the civil authorities, money fines, forced labor, and in extreme instances in corporal punishment or banishment from the colony. "It is significant," the author adds, "that most of the social offenders are again reinstated into full community membership. Most of those punished corporally as young men are today good citizens, active church members, and looked upon as well-integrated members of the community. . . . Very few of the past social offenders left the community after punishment" (p. 110f.).

rights. Even if he was able to make his way into the large society, he found himself among strangers speaking an alien tongue, of whose manners and ways he knew nothing and cared less. Thus the church ban was an almost omnipotent means of social control, a sanction whose impact was more painful than jail or fine.

Disruptions of the Social Fabric

In this way the traditional political order within the Mennonite colonies was for a while maintained by the church despite the lack of support by the organized power of the state. Its collapse was due as much to the challenge implied in the legal order of the country, as to inner cleavages which soon appeared within the Mennonite social system itself. The weak point was the seam, as it were, at which originally different Mennonite communities were superficially welded together into administrative units. For, as was indicated before, each Reserve included two distinct social subsystems: the East Reserve was settled by Bergthal and Kleine Gemeinde people, the West Reserve by Fürstenland and Bergthal people. Each of these three groups arrived with their own religious leaders and institutions. But in Russia only the Bergthal and Fürstenland people had possessed their own political administration which could be transferred to Manitoba. By previous agreement the Bergthal district office continued to function in the East Reserve, while that of the Fürstenland group took control in the West Reserve.

This arrangement met with little difficulty in the East Reserve. The Kleine Gemeinde people, having functioned in Russia as a purely religious brotherhood within an institutional framework dominated by the members of the local established churches, were satisfied with organizing homogeneous village communes in Manitoba and submitted on the district level to the rule of the Bergthal group. The fact that they had no influence upon the election of the *Oberschulze,* which took place in the *Bruderschaft* of a church other than their own, does not seem to have bothered them. They had no political traditions or aspirations, and gladly left the government of the district to their more experienced neighbours. Meanwhile they were able to concentrate on the quiet development of their own little economic empire around Steinbach. Serious conflicts between the two groups settling in the East Reserve were avoided primarily because the Bergthal people who remained in this area were the more conservative elements and of one mind with the Kleine Gemeinde people in regard to the strict enforcement of religious principles.

In the second Reserve on the west side of the Red River harmony between the Fürstenland group and those of the Bergthal people who later joined them there lasted only a short time. The Fürstenland people had entrusted the Bergthal delegates of 1873 with all the necessary arrangements preliminary to their own emigration; both groups stemmed from the Old or Chortitza colony, speaking the same dialect, having the same religious and cultural traditions and being bound together by many kinship ties; moreover a formal agreement had been reached while still in Russia providing for a peaceful division of functions, and full coöperation in all public affairs. It had been arranged, in particular, that members of one group settling within the jurisdiction of the other would submit to the local authorities in a spirit of brotherly love.

Nevertheless, difficulties and frictions soon arose. Since the Fürstenland group occupied the West Reserve en bloc, their *Oberschulze* was recognized as the supreme civil authority in that region. The relatively few Bergthal people residing there in the beginning were quickly absorbed into the local village communes. They made common cause with their Fürstenland neighbours in all secular matters, and even participated in their religious meetings. It was only with the rapid increase of the Bergthal population in the West Reserve in and after 1879, following the haphazard and unplanned movement of large numbers of them from the East to the West Reserve, and after the foundation of solid Bergthal villages in the latter area, that any organized resistance against the Fürstenland hegemony made itself felt.

A Fürstenland member complained in his diary that the spirit of solidarity which had at first existed between the Bergthal and the Fürstenland people was beginning to show signs of serious strain.[4] According to him and other sources, too, the cause of dissension lay primarily in the rigid enforcement of social controls by the religious

---

[4] Unpublished diary of P. Elias. See also the discussion on p. 1 of *Mennonitische Rundschau,* February 22, 1888.

leaders and functionaries of the Fürstenland church,[5] which was not to the taste of the Bergthal people. As in the East Reserve, the enforcement of law and order became more and more dependent on religious sanctions and on the authority of the church; without these the *Oberschulze* could achieve little. However, the West Reserve *Oberschulze,* himself a member of the Fürstenland group, could rely only on the support of Elder Johann Wiebe and the Fürstenland church, while his Bergthal subjects professed allegiance to Elder Gerhard Wiebe, of the Bergthal church, who resided in the East Reserve, then several days of car-ride away from the scene.

This obviously was a convenient rationalization on the part of those unwilling to submit to the rigid controls enforced by the Fürstenland leaders, which indeed became more and more oppressive. For the Fürstenland church made lavish and indiscriminate use of excommunication not only for serious offenses threatening the social existence of the Mennonite group as a whole, but also for partisan reasons and minor infractions of old customs. Among the many "sins" and "crimes" which were punished in this drastic manner, the following have been mentioned: sending children to a public school, seeking employment with Anglo-Saxons, selling land to outsiders (even to Mennonites of other churches), mortgaging one's property, insuring it with the mutual fire insurance associations established by the Bergthal people, adopting such novelties as bicycles, buggies,[6] musical boxes or sleigh bells.

Some of these taboos were apparently imposed as a reaction to the modernistic attitudes and ideas which were prevalent among the Bergthal group, at least those of them who had left the East Reserve to settle on the other side of the river. Whether there was any initial difference in the orthodoxy and conservatism of the two congregations

---

[5] The church of the Fürstenland group is generally referred to as *Altkolonie* or Old Colony Church, and the group itself as *Altkoloniers.* Apart from the fact that its official title was actually Reinland Mennonite Church in Manitoba, this terminology is also misleading because both the Fürstenland and the Bergthal people came from daughter colonies of the Old or Chortitza colony in Russia, while actually a small group of immigrants from the Old Colony properly speaking joined the Bergthal rather than the Fürstenland group when settling in Manitoba. Accordingly, the more descriptive designation of Fürstenland group (and Fürstenland church) has been adopted so as to avoid the confusion which would have arisen by applying first the name used in Russia and later the new name adopted in Canada in referring to one and the same group of people. A similar terminological confusion arose later as a result of the split that occurred within the Bergthal group whereby the dissident faction in the West Reserve retained the traditional name for their church organization, while the successors to the original Bergthal church changed their names into Sommerfeld church in the West Reserve and Chortitz church in the East Reserve.

[6] While today the buggy is considered the symbol of the most conservative Amish people in the United States, the Russian Mennonites of the early days actually used the heavy farm wagon rather than the buggy for the transportation of persons, and most of the time simply walked on foot.

is not clear, though to some degree the Bergthal colony in Russia seems to have shown signs of social disorganization even before it arrived in Manitoba. While the Fürstenland people followed to a man their leaders to Canada, several of the Bergthal group, for instance, broke away to remain in the United States, and many others separated from their own colony in the East Reserve either to join the Fürstenland people or to form, in rather an irregular manner, a new settlement on better land. It may be safely assumed that those of them who filtered gradually from the East to the West Reserve, and began to farm their own land instead of establishing village communes, were of a more individualistic and adventurous frame of mind. By so doing, they not only attained great economic advantages but also escaped the effective control of their own church whose center remained for some time to come in the distant East Reserve. Thus, by and large, church discipline among the Bergthal people in the West Reserve was weak, and led to a general softening and final breakdown of the traditional social fabric among them. Their very presence in this region was also a threat to the effectiveness of the social controls in the Fürstenland colony itself, since any one excommunicated by the established church there could simply join the Bergthal church next door and carry on as before, often even without moving to another village.

This situation led to such a rapid deterioration in the relations between the two groups settling in the West Reserve, that at times intermarriages between them were forbidden, and the two churches barely recognized each other as stemming from the same Anabaptist and Mennonite root. While the Fürstenland people isolated themselves more and more from the outside world, even from Mennonites of different religious observances and political convictions, the Bergthal people began to cast their lot with the Provincial authorities in order to free themselves of the control of their brethren. This was the weak spot through which Anglo-Saxon institutions first penetrated the Mennonite colonies. The old Mennonite institutional fabric eventually collapsed over the inner cleavage.

From Volost to Municipality

During the first years after the creation of the Province, little was done to introduce institutions of local self-government into the new settlements, while the old ones were carried on under the traditional form of the parish. Although the Province was organized into five counties for both judicial and administrative purposes as early as

1871,[7] this set-up remained largely on paper except for the establishment of county courts. The Mennonite colonies, at least, were not affected by these early attempts at providing administrative units since they possessed their own administrative machinery in the *Gebietsamt,* and as non-citizens the redistribution of the Provincial constituencies in 1873[8] did not concern them either. While other officials, such as justices of the peace, commissioners for taking affidavits, county constables, county clerks, coroners and so on, were appointed elsewhere in due course, they do not seem to have functioned to any extent within the Mennonite settlements.

Beginning with 1873, almost every year some law or ammendment was passed by the Provincial Legislature providing this or that form of local administration, none of which seemed to work out satisfactorily. The most important feature of these experiments was the introduction of municipalities as units of local self-administration below the county level, resembling the townships of New England States. In the beginning, the incorporation of some settlement as municipality was optional and by petition only. While the Mennonites never made any use of this opportunity, even Anglo-Saxon settlements were slow in applying for incorporation. Finally a drastic step was taken in 1883, when the Municipal Law was once more revised, dividing the enlarged Province into three judicial districts and twenty-six counties, each of the latter comprising a number of municipalities whose boundaries were legislated without much consultation with the local population.[9] If no petition was made for the incorporation of a municipality, the Lieutenant Governor was now empowered to appoint a commissioner who was to set up the necessary machinery of assessment and taxation.

The new regulations put the Mennonites on the spot. Yet, in the East Reserve the transformation from a *de facto* autonomy, after the pattern of the Russian volost, to a *de jure* local self-government according to the traditions of the Anglo-Saxon majority, was effected with little difficulty. The first municipal elections were held on December 27, 1882, even before the law making incorporation mandatory was actually passed. It seems that the step was well prepared by Hespeler who was able to point out that compliance with the wishes of

---

[7] *Statutes of Manitoba,* 1871, chs. 2 and 34.

[8] *Ibid.,* 1873, ch. 10.

[9] Cf. A. C. Ewart, "Municipal History of Manitoba," *University of Toronto Studies, History and Economics,* Vol. II, no. 3 (1904).

Legislature and Government would make the Mennonites eligible for Provincial subsidies and public works. The Mennonites themselves recognized that the functioning of self-government in the colony, particularly tax collection, would be facilitated if their own officers enjoyed official status instead of having to rely exclusively on their personal authority and that of the church. While the Kleine Gemeinde abstained from voting, a member of the Bergthal group, Gerhard Kliewer, of Hespeler (now: Niverville), was elected first reeve of the Municipality of Hanover and confirmed in his office by the Provincial authorities for the year 1884. However, the Municipal Law divided the territory covered by the East Reserve into two municipalities: Hespeler including the more densely populated townships 7-4, 7-5, and 7-6 East, and Hanover comprising the remaining five townships. This division was entirely arbitrary and never really enforced. From the very beginning, the reeve of Hanover, actually a resident of Hespeler, acted for both areas, while the letterhead of his bureau for some time read "Municipalities of Hespeler and Hanover." At once the Government was petitioned to grant "a change of the borders," upon which the whole Mennonite colony was reunited as the Municipality of Hanover.

At first the office of the municipality was in the residence of the secretary treasurer. Council meetings, too, took place in private homes, the next meeting place being determined at the end of each session. A separate building was eventually put up near Schönfeld, which in 1905 was moved to Chortitz, both villages of the Bergthal people. When Steinbach, a Kleine Gemeinde village, became the undisputed commercial center of the region, the seat of the Municipality was transferred there.

Although the incorporation of the Municipality of Hanover satisfied the letter of the Provincial law, at first it meant a change in name only. For reeve and Municipality carried on their business for many years to come in precisely the same manner as the *Oberschulze* and *Gebietsamt* had done before. Although unincorporated villages and hamlets had no official status under the administrative set-up of Manitoba, the traditional hierarchical organization by family, village commune and district was fully maintained. Taxes were still assessed and collected not by individual farm holdings as was customary in Canada, but by villages organized as self-governing units. The Municipality acted primarily as a territorial moderator and a go-between for village commune and higher authorities. Even the statistical records kept by the secretary-treasurer in accordance with the provisions of the law were consistently computed by villages instead of townships and wards. Only gradually did the old customs fall into disuse and Canadian practices became generally acepted, without any pressure being exerted upon the Mennonite office holders from above.

In sharp contrast to the East Reserve, the matter of incorporation under the Provincial laws became an explosive issue in the other colony. At first little trouble was anticipated. The Bergthal group welcomed the new system as a means of freeing themselves both from the Fürstenland hegemony and from a pattern of social organization which they considered an obstruction to individual economic advancement. They had already begun to deviate from the traditional system of field community and village habitat, some taking up residence in the little commercial towns established in the Reserve along the railroad lines by outsiders, mainly Anglo-Saxons. Thus they saw in the new order not only the chance of legalizing such progressive tendencies but also a moral justification for their modernistic attitudes. As P. Elias wrote in his diary: ". . . und als unser Volk erst dahinterkam, so gefiel es einem manchen besser nach amerikanischer Art" (and after our people found out, many of them preferred the American way). The Fürstenland people, on the other hand, like the Bergthal people in the East Reserve, were persuaded by Hespeler of the many advantages to be expected if they would nominally comply with the wishes of the authorities, thus avoiding unnecessary frictions. He also promised (whether authorized to do so or not is not shown) that the Fürstenland Oberschulze would be appointed reeve and nothing would be changed in the inner functioning of the local administration.

About 1881 the West Reserve was unofficially constituted as Municipality of Rhineland,[10] the Oberschulze acting as reeve. Thus the ground was prepared for a peaceful settlement similar to that achieved in the East Reserve. Yet, in December 1883 and January 1884, a small clique of Fürstenland dissenters joined with the Bergthal group to elect Jakob Giesbrecht as reeve. Giesbrecht had been village mayor of Reinland but had fallen out with his elder and had been excom-

---

[10] The name Rhineland seems to be derived from the village of Reinland, which in the early years was a kind of capital of the Fürstenland settlement. In the German spelling Rhine reads Rhein (referring to the river in Germany) while "Rein" in the name of the village of Reinland has an entirely different etymology, meaning clean. As most Mennonite place names, this one belongs in the class of so-called wish names, widely spread among the German colonists in Eastern Europe. Thus Reinland means clean land, Grünthal, green valley, Rosenfeld, field of roses, Blumenort, place of flowers, and so on.

municated by the Fürstenland church. The church countered this coup d'état by forbidding its members under penalty of excommunication to do any business with the Municipality, while *Oberschulze* Isaak Müller was recognized as the sole and legitimate civil authority.

At about the same time the Provincial Government divided the Mennonite reservation west of the Red River, or at least that portion of it which, by then, had been solidly populated by Mennonites, in such a way that the Municipality of Rhineland comprised only Fürstenland villages, while Douglas included the whole Bergthal group in addition to two or three Fürstenland villages such as Blumenort. The incorporation of Douglas was effected without any great difficulty, as the Bergthal people were favorably disposed to it and in the overwhelming majority.[11]

In the Municipality of Rhineland, however, an anomalous situation arose since the Fürstenland majority refused to coöperate. It seems that some sort of municipal elections took place in a meeting, or several meetings, under the chairmanship of a Provincial representative, as a result of which the machine dealer Javis Matt was appointed first reeve serving for 1884. Matt was an Anglo-Saxon Baptist, although not more than a handful of non-Mennonites lived in the area at the time. Afterwards the Bergthal minority, supported by Fürstenland dissenters, obtained full control of municipal affairs in Rhineland until the reunion of Rhineland and Douglas, in 1891, under the common name of Rhineland.

In the eyes of faithful members of the Fürstenland group, this arrangement was in no way better than if the Government had appointed an Anglo-Saxon commissioner. They wished to have no part in it, and withdrew completely from public affairs, renouncing all solidarity

---

11 To avoid confusion, one should keep in mind that the general area which was first known as Municipality of Rhineland now belongs to the Municipality of Stanley, while the original Municipality of Douglas became extinct, being succeeded by the present Municipality of Rhineland.

In 1884, Rhineland included townships 1-3, 2-3, 3-3, 1-4, 2-4, 3-4 West, and the easternmost two miles of townships 1-5, 2-5, and 3-5 West, and Douglas: townships 1-1, 1-2, 2-1, 2-2, 3-1, and 3-2 West, while 1-1 East was added later. In 1891, however, both municipalities were merged under the name of Rhineland, covering townships 1-1 East, and townships 1-1, 1-2, 1-3, 2-1, 2-2, 2-3, 3-1, 3-2, 3-3 West (with the exception of the incorporated villages of Gretna and Plum Coulee). From 1886 onward, the adjoining area in the west belonged to the Municipality of South Dufferin. In 1901, however, the Municipality of Stanley was incorporated with townships 4-5, 1-4, 2-4, 3-4, 4-4, in addition to townships 1-5, 2-5, 3-5, 4-5, 1-6, 2-6, 3-6, 4-6, all west of the Principal Meridian (with the exception of the town of Nelson, now extinct). After a redivision in 1908, Stanley included townships 1-5, 2-5, 3-5, 1-6, 2-6, 3-6, and township 3-5 West (excepting Morden and Winkler) to which were added on December 1, 1916, townships 1-4 and 2-4 West, originally belonging to the Municipality of Rhineland.

with other Mennonites in the colony. Henceforth they formed, as it were, an ethnic group within an ethnic group, and since they maintained their own *Gebietsamt* unofficially, even a state within a state within a state. This odd situation continued unchanged until their exodus after World War I. There always was a Fürstenland *Oberschulze* officiating independently from the reeves of Douglas, Rhineland or Stanley. An *Oberschulze* led his people to Latin America where to this day an *Oberschulze* presides over their communal affairs.

Because of the abstention of the Fürstenland majority, the original Municipality of Rhineland did not function very effectively, which apparently led to its merger with Douglas. From then on, the records of the (larger) Municipality of Rhineland, including, until 1901, prac- tically the whole Mennonite settlement west of the Red River, show that the dual administration of the unofficial Fürstenland *Oberschulze* and the official reeve did not seriously hamper the functioning of local self-government. The *modus vivendi* that was eventually reached is reflected in an item found in the records of the Municipality. According to this information, dated 1913, the secretary-treasurer requested the Fürstenland *Oberschulze* to instruct all village mayors under his juris- diction about the filing of death certificates. The significance of this small incident is that the local authority, properly instituted under the laws of the country, recognized the *de facto* jurisdiction of the Fürsten- land *Oberschulze* over village communes which continued to function without any legal basis. On the other hand, the *Oberschulze* dealt with higher authorities through the mediation of municipal officers in whose election none of the persons represented by himself had taken any part. Even outside the Fürstenland settlements, the rural municip- ality, all of whose officers were Mennonites, for a long time used the surviving smaller units of local self-government as its agents. It had direct contact with individual ratepayers, as provided by the law of the Province, only in as far as the old village communes had ceased to function.

Before Douglas was incorporated, its boundaries had been laid down in the Municipal Act of 1883, without consulting the local population. Thus a whole township (1-1 East), which sociologically was part of the compact Mennonite settlement, was added to the French Municipality of Montcalm. Although there obviously was as yet no intention of disregarding ethnic boundary lines, the decision may have been suggested by public criticism of the concept of ethnically homogeneous reservations in general, and of the preferential treatment of the Mennonites in particular. In its very first meeting of January 8, 1884, the Municipal Council of Douglas protested unsuccessfully against this arrangement. But the residents of the township created a *fait accompli* by paying taxes to the municipality of their own choice. On July 8, 1891, the authorities finally made the desired boundary revisions. The Municipality of Douglas received township 1-1 East, but had to pay Montcalm $39,000 for taxes levied unlawfully.[12]

One of the principal responsibilities of a municipality in Manitoba is the creation of school districts and the maintenance of public schools. As a matter of fact, Legislature and Government had been motivated in their insistence upon incorporation of municipalities largely by their desire to bring some order into the Provincial school system. Similar motives lay also behind the support given to incorporation by the West Reserve Bergthal group. Thus Douglas, the municipality controlled by them, at once set about issuing two by-laws, both dated August 19, 1884, which provided for the creation of nine public school districts, namely Gretna, Edenburg, Grünthal, Kronsthal, Rudnerweide, Bergthal, Altona, and Rosenfeld; Schönthal was added in 1889. On the other hand, the Fürstenland people, and the groups residing in the East Reserve, objected to public schools for a long time, so that municipal functions in the Mennonite settlements were greatly limited in this respect.

By and large the substitution of Anglo-Saxon Canadian for old Mennonite institutions of local administration was less fraught with conflict than other institutional changes. This may have been due in part to the lesser importance attached by the Mennonites to self-government on the district level as distinguished from village self-government. Another reason may be seen in the difficulties encountered in maintaining an office which had lost its legal authority, once it was removed from the Russian framework. Last, but not least, change in this respect was brought about not so much by the superior power of the state as in later instances, but by a diplomacy using trends and dissensions within the group itself as levers. And this change came early, that is, before the institutional framework of the group had had the time to become solidified.

---

12 Cf. [H. H. Hamm], *Sixty Years of Progress, 1884-1944: Diamond Jubilee of the Rural Municipality of Rhineland* (Altona, 1944).

The Village Commune and its Breakdown

More consequential than the transition from *volost* to municipality, though in a way related to it, was disorganization on the village level. As was indicated earlier, the Mennonite village consisted of a number of homesteads built closely together, and of a given area of land belonging to them. It was a tightly-knit community held together by common interests, and in a great measure self-regulating and self-sufficient. Its solid subsistence basis was the open-field system requiring coöperation, strict social controls, and a considerable amount of collective management.

The functions of the village commune were vested in the *Schulzenbott*[13] (village assembly) and the *Schulzenamt* (mayor's office). The *Schulzenbott* consisted of the *Wirte* (owners of homesteads), although also older sons of owners seem to have attended meetings. The elected officers included the *Dorfschulze* (short: *Schulze*) or mayor, the *Hirtenschulze* who was in charge of pasture and herd, and the *Brandschulze* or fire marshall. Meetings were called as the need arose, often several times a week. The frequency of summons reported by old-timers suggests that the *Schulzenbott* had also an important social function for adult males in a community which had neither an inn nor a beer parlor. Official business mainly included the following: 1) Matters related to the open-field system; that is the lay-out and the cultivation of the fields, weed control, the timing of farm operations, arrangement of headlands, the share of individual farmers in communal haylands and woods, above all the care of live-stock. 2) Building and maintenance of roads, ditches, bridges, culverts, and care of the graveyard. 3) Frequently a threshing machine was owned and operated by the village commune. 4) Fire protection. 5) Coöperation with the church in the upkeep of the school, in the care for the aged and disabled, and in the functioning of the Waisenamt. 6) Taxes and statute labor.

The old records and account books of various villages indicate the nature and character of their functions. The items shown in these accounts may be divided under six general headings on the debit side: expenses for the village administration itself, transmission of official mail, public works, school administration, village herd and pasture, insurance premiums on public property. On the credit side we find

---

[13] The first part of the term refers to the *Schulze* or mayor, its second element is derived from the verb *bieten*, to summon. Thus the Schulzenbott is the mayor's summons. A village by-law was called a *Schulzenspruch*.

the monetary equivalents for statute labor rendered, money paid in lieu of statute labor, rent on public land, fees for the use of the pasture, school tax, tuition fees, proceeds from sales of public property, and finally the land tax. The form of tax levies and the manner in which taxes were assessed, however, seem to have varied from place to place, and time to time.

Expenses for village administration included mainly the salaries of officers. The *Dorfschulze* of Steinbach, for instance, drew, in the early years, ten dollars per annum plus one dollar for keeping the accounts. *Hirtenschulze* and *Brandschulze* received five dollars each. These salaries were doubled in 1893. Each member of the assembly received a per-diem pay for attendance at meetings, amounting to twenty-five cents for each of eleven meetings in 1892. Since assembly members and ratepayers were actually the same people, this was apparently a device to stimulate participation. In the records of Neubergthal for 1909, an item of three dollars for brandy is entered which, it would seem, was consumed while making the final accounts for the fiscal year.

At first Winnipeg was the post office for the East Reserve; later a separate post office was opened at Hochstadt. In the West Reserve, Emerson was the closest post office with Blumenort as a sub-station. All mail had to be transported by carrier. Anybody who happened to travel one way or the other on foot, horseback, or by cart, would call at the mayor's office to take along letters, tax receipts, or fire insurance premia. For this service a definite tariff was set up, known as *Wegegeld* (road money). For a distance of about four or five miles it amounted to ten cents, for about ten miles, to one dollar.

The building and maintenance of roads and ditches, the cutting of weeds on public lands, and the upkeep of the graveyard were carried out by unpaid statute labor. Every family was credited in the account books with a certain amount of money for services rendered. The working day was then ten hours, a dollar a day being the customary wage throughout Canada's West. While one man-hour was valued at 10 cents, a man with a team of horses received $1.70 a day, according to the Steinbach accounts of the 1880's. At the end of the year, the total amount credited to each family was divided by the total number of families in the village. Those who had worked less than the average had to pay the difference in money which was distributed among those who had done more than their share.

Statute labor was also used for the construction and maintenance of school houses, which often served also as religious meeting places, the commune contributing the timber. The transportation of the school inspector from one place to another was also a form of statute labor. Cash expenses, however, had to be covered by the school tax which, for instance, amounted to $281.85 in 1910 for 19 families in Neubergthal. A year earlier, $45 were spent on scribblers, chalk, light, fuel, cleaning and repairs. The largest item under the title "school" was the salary for the teacher, who was an employee of the village commune. The money for this did not come from the general revenue, however, but from a special tuition fee, called *Kindergeld* (children money), collected for each child sent to school. While at first the teacher was paid in kind rather than in cash, his salary is listed as $210 in the Neubergthal accounts of 1909. In 1923, the teacher of the Blumenort private school received as much as $65 a month, a hay lot and free lodging in the school house.

The only other public employee was the village herdsman. According to the early Steinbach records, he was hired at $60 for the warm season only. He also had the use of a special lot and house. In another case, twenty dollars were paid for herding the livestock of the village during one month; in addition the family which undertook the job was granted the right of pasturing ten head of cattle free of charge. In another year, Steinbach's schoolmaster received four dollars a month for tending the herd, but in later times the herdsman's wages run as high as $115 per annum in Neubergthal. The Blumenort herder, on the other hand, in 1923 was paid exclusively in kind, namely, in the form of 28 acres of plowed farm land, some hay land, seed grain and the use of a house which was repaired at village expense. In 1925 he received $15 for the months when the livestock was confined to the communal pasture, and $45 for each month of stubble pasture, in addition to two bushels of wheat and the same amount of barley from every neighbor.

The village bull had to be stabled from October to May 15, for which one Steinbach farmer received $20 and 20 bushels of oats, while $9.50 were paid for the bull's upkeep during the warm season. Once a sum of one dollar was paid for bringing back a run-away bull, and another small sum is recorded for chasing cattle out of the grain fields. Other expenses for the pasture included fencing, cutting a path through the bush, and digging a well. Every homesteader, excluding *Anwohner* or cotters (landless people owning only a house lot and garden), had the right to send a certain number of cattle to the common pasture free of charge. As expenses increased, or when the number was exceeded, a special levy was computed according to the *Viehliste* showing the head of live-stock pastured by each family. In 1892 a cotter was charged $2.50 per cow for the summer. At times, cattle might be pastured by outsiders for a fee, for instance, in one case by an Emerson butcher at Neubergthal.

General revenue was derived from the *Stellengeld* or land tax, amounting to $1.50 per acre in Neubergthal in 1909. Other income came from rent collected on public lands. For instance, one Klaas W. Reimer had to pay $2.50 rent per year for his cheese factory built in Steinbach in or about the year 1891. One *Holzlos* (wood lot), that is, the right to cut a certain amount of timber in the village forest, was valued at 48 cents per annum in Steinbach. In Neubergthal a portion of the communal property was parcelled out as hayland, while another tract was leased to a wealthy Mennonite farmer. When the field community was abandoned in 1910, the pasture fence sold for between four and eight cents per pole, and the herdsman's house with stable was purchased by a private individual for $285.10. According to the Blumenort records of 1923, three parcels of land in different locations were rented for 43, 27½ and 28 per cent of the crop respectively. In 1924, the rental for three other fields was 30, 31 and 33 per cent of the crop while smaller plots were often rented for certain services and statute labor. Despite this wide scope of village activities, the actual cash turnover was small. In 1885 it was only $122.50 for Steinbach with a population of 18 families. In the year 1909, the last in which the Neubergthal village commune was still in full operation, the total turnover was close to $700, including $210 for the teacher's salary, and $115 for the herdsman's wages.

Fire protection was only in part a responsibility of the village as it was organized on a district basis. It was combined with an insurance system whereby the *Brandschulze* acted both as local fire chief under district supervision and as insurance agent. A similar relationship existed between the *Schulzenamt* and the *Waisenamt* which was under the sponsorship of the churches. The operation of both institutions will be discussed later.

The disorganization of the local community followed quite a different pattern in the two Reserves and among the sub-groups settled in each. It involved three distinct processes. The first was the dissolution of the field community under the open-field system, referred to as *auseinanderreissen* or *zerreissen* (pulling or tearing apart). The second affected close village habitat and was called *aufs Land ziehen* (to move onto one's own land). Thirdly, local self-government was given up, even where the village survived physically. The first step did not necessarily lead to the other two, so that some villages have been preserved to the present day though without open-field system or local government. The field community began to disintegrate at an early date, particularly among the Bergthal people of the West Reserve, and disappeared completely with the Fürstenland exodus to Mexico shortly after World War I.

In assessing the causes and consequences of this breakdown of the traditional Mennonite communal organization, the advantages and disadvantages inherent in the open-field system and in the solidaristic form of settlement must be considered. This form of socio-economic organization provides the individual with a maximum of both psychological and economic security, and with an incessant stimulus to observe accepted standards of work. Like a convoy, such a farming community can progress only as fast as its weakest member. Thus the efficiency of each is the vital concern of all. Even if charity did not demand it, sheer self-interest would require that neighbours do the planting and harvesting of a disabled member of the community at the proper time. Close habitat relieved the Mennonites of the great hardships suffered by other pioneers during the long Manitoba winters when communications were slow and roads often impassable. It also facilitated neighbouring and borrowing from home to home, making it easy to find a helping hand in raising a roof or repairing a machine, and to get an extra team or a suddenly needed tool.

Finally, the most effective teacher of the farmer is observation of the success or failure of others. The concept of "patent" has no meaning in agriculture where one's workshop lies wide open to the eyes of all, and where competition for markets is usually insignificant. Thus one learns from the experiences of others, exchanges views, and asks for advice which is gladly given. For efficiency is measured in terms of effort and hard work rather than of inventiveness or ingenuity. Many of the common worries of the farmer such as weed and pest control can be resolved only by concerted effort and they are more easily dealt with in a solidaristic community.[14] The justice of land distribution removes causes of jealousy and conflicts. Economic benefits accrue from the common use of roads, headlands, wells, watering places, ditches, saw and flour mills, and threshing machines, from the elimination of enclosures and from coöperative utilization of animals for breeding purposes.

On the other hand, all the elements of the system are so closely interrelated that the omission or decay of any one element soon brings down the whole structure. For instance, the fact that the Mennonites never adopted *Flurzwang* in Manitoba, leaving every farmer free to use, or misuse, his strips of land in the common fields at his own discretion, was evidently one reason for the early abolition of the whole solidaristic system of farming. The numerous roads and headlands, created as a consequence of this individualistic practice, gathered drifting soil to such a degree that their height was sometimes increased, it is said, to as much as seven feet above the plowland.

Innovations and improvements in farming techniques are difficult to introduce when the consent of a whole community is required even to test them. This is true not only for better utilization of land or superior forms of crop rotation but also for improvement of livestock. Such considerations, however, seem to have had little influence upon the Manitoba Mennonites who, as a group, have remained rather mediocre dairy farmers to this very day. In fact, voluntary pasture coöperatives have been retained by them much longer than other aspects of the open-field system. The high quality of land in the West Reserve and some parts of the East Reserve probably were of greater importance for their choice; for this made the exclusion of large areas from cultivation as permanent pastures appear wasteful. Finally, the traditional narrow field strips were unsuitable for the American type of farm machinery.

Few of these economic difficulties were beyond the control of the Mennonites. The disadvantages usually mentioned by Mennonite sources as having led to the abolition of the open-field system appear rather as convenient rationalizations for a trend initiated much less by economic necessity than by sociological and psychological factors. Everywhere the movement apparently started with individuals becoming disgruntled with the state of affairs in their communities. Frequently those who

---

[14] The Blumenort village assembly, for instance, ordered in 1923 all villagers to clean the fields, to seed the fallow land (apparently with a cover crop) and to cultivate it.

held property title to superior land within the village commune disliked sharing good and bad fields with their neighbours. Tensions and petty quarrels will, of course, never fail to make their appearance in any community. The decisive point is whether group pressures and the authority of the leaders can succeed in preventing group members from making the final break. Although in the beginning only a few requested the full possession of their individual quarter-sections, the withdrawal of property by one member was often sufficient to cause the collapse of the whole delicate system.

The manner in which the problem was handled by the different groups proves that the attraction of some individuals to the Canadian type of individual farming and the benefits of commercial agriculture by themselves could not have led to the collapse. For the Fürstenland people retained the field community until their exodus, while the Kleine Gemeinde group did not abandon it until shortly before World War I. At first the movement affected only the Bergthal group in the West Reserve, who were followed by their brethren in the East Reserve, both being groups where weaknesses of the whole social structure were previously noticed. There is no indication that the more conservative groups were economically less successful than those who more readily imitated the Anglo-Saxon model, particularly in cases where topography and soil conditions permit a comparison, as between the West Reserve Bergthal people, on the one hand, and the Fürstenland people, or the Kleine Gemeinde people in the Scratching River colony, on the other.

The challenge was, of course, felt in all settlements and among all groups. But the Fürstenland people and their church met it with the liberal use of excommunication. Where the mere threat of ecclesiastical censure failed to impress a dissenting member, his farm and house were usually bought by neighbours and resold to one who would abide by the law. Elsewhere, however, abolition of the field community became a social epidemic. Even some Fürstenland settlements fell victim to it, significantly enough only those located on the fringes such as Blumstein (1883), Burwalde (1884), or Blumenhof (1895). The greatest losses were suffered by the Bergthal communities in the West Reserve, most of which gave up the field community within ten or fifteen years after immigration. Among the last to do so were Alt-Altona, which lost the old socio-economic organization in 1896, Grünthal (1894), Sommerfeld (1912), and Neubergthal (1912).

In the East Reserve similar changes took place among the Bergthal group quite early, while the Kleine Gemeinde people retained the field

104

community many years longer. Economic reasons had little to do with this. For grain farming and the use of large-scale machinery were of little importance here, land was cheap and plentiful, while livestock was generally pastured among trees and on wild grass lands. It seems that the exodus of many Bergthal people to the west side of the Red River had made it difficult in many places to continue the open-field system even though the desire to do so may have been present. As scores of village lots and farm holdings were abandoned, those who remained behind were unable to reorganize functioning communes. Some settlements had been laid out on a large scale in expectation of many more immigrants but they could not be completed when de-population set in. As time went on, the grown-up children of the pioneers could have filled the gaps. But by then, the chance to organize new villages under the open-field system had passed. Specu-lators and non-Mennonites had acquired many vacant sections, so that contiguous tracts of land for settlement were no longer available. Yet, wherever village habitat could be preserved on a scale making field community at all possible, this was retained until about 1905, and in two instances at least (Barkfeld and its daughter settlement Neu-Bark-feld) until the emigration to Latin America after World War I.

Among the Kleine Gemeinde group, abolition of the field com-munity seems to have been partly the result of a religious schism. Some time during the 1890's, a Mennonite evangelist from Indiana, Johannes Holdemann, was invited to preach in the East Reserve and the Scratching River colony. He found many followers who eventually separated from the Kleine Gemeinde to form the Church of God in Christ. For a while, the dissenters continued to participate in the communal life of the villages in which they resided, just as the Kleine Gemeinde members had done in Russia for more than eighty years. After some time, however, a peaceful separation took place in the village of Blumenort. Approximately one section in the northwest corner of the village territory was set aside for Holdemann's followers to start a colony of their own. Under the name of Greenland it became the center of the sect and attracted many of its members from other villages also. The exodus to Greenland, as well as to other places of Holdemanite concentration, tended to weaken the open-field system in all Kleine Gemeinde villages. It was generally abandoned by 1912 or 1913.

While economic factors had some influence, the abolition of the open-field system was essentially part of a much more inclusive process of social change. The sequence in which the field community was given up by the different Mennonite sub-groups varies directly with their susceptibility to innovations in other respects. The trend was initiated by the West Reserve Bergthal group in 1879, where several factors had led to a lack of social coherence and the prevalence of individualistic over group values. Next, the East Reserve Bergthal group was affected by circumstances beyond its control. Shortly before World War I, the open-field system had been relinquished by all except the Fürstenland group and a few die-hards among the Bergthal people in the East Reserve. With their emigration to Latin America these remnants disappeared also.

With the removal of its economic foundation, the organization of the village itself, that is, the institutions of self-government and, ultimately, village habitat, disintegrated. Whenever the legal proprietor of the quarter section on which the village site happened to be located demanded unrestricted use of his land and expelled those who had their houses built on it, the village had to be disbanded. In this way many of the original villages disappeared completely as soon as the field community was relinquished. More often than not, however, some compromise was reached. Only the most recalcitrant and disgruntled moved onto their own land in the Anglo-Saxon manner, while the majority tried to save as much of their traditional community life as they could by voluntary coöperation. Sometimes the legal owner of the village site simply allowed his neighbors to stay where they were. Frequently, however, the villagers purchased their lots from him without bothering about having the sale duly registered. Only in later years were these transfers legalized in the form of so-called village plans entered with different land titles offices. These resemble the general lay-out of incorporated villages and towns in Manitoba but are not administrative units under the law of the country.

The ideal of the Western pioneer was the scattered homestead; close habitat was reserved for trade centers and commercial towns, which were located primarily along the railroads at a rather regular distance from each other.[15] Accordingly, the municipal laws of Manitoba did not provide for the recognition of genuine farm-operator villages of small size, usually referred to in official documents as "hamlets." The

---

[15] Cf. the study by N. L. Whetten, *The Social and Economic Structure of the Trade Centers in the Canadian Prairie Provinces with Special Reference to its Change, 1910-1930* (Harvard Ph.D. thesis, 1932), reported on by C. C. Zimmerman, *The Changing Community* (New York, 1938), pp. 30 ff.

incorporation of places was made dependent on conditions which were inapplicable to farm settlements with close habitat, with the sole exception of the French parishes originating in the fur trade period. Not only was a relatively large number of residents required, but the functions attributed to incorporated places, including methods of taxation, were appropriate for rural trade centers rather than for farm villages. Accordingly, communities with a predominantly Mennonite population, even if they could fulfill the requirements of the law as to minimum size, usually found it more advantageous not to apply for incorporation. Thus relatively large towns like Steinbach or Altona were incorporated only since the second World War.

Unofficially, however, successful attempts were made to continue the traditional form of self-administration in the old Mennonite villages where close habitat was at all preserved, even after the field community was abandoned. But its functions were considerably reduced, being limited mainly to the maintenance of the private school and the administration of the system of fire protection. When, however, the private school was generally replaced by the public school, administered for the Provincial Department of Education by the rural municipality, even this shadow of local self-government disappeared, though village habitat has survived in many places, and has in some instances even been revived in recent years.

Where the field community was given up, local self-government also declined, and, as social controls weakened, village habitat itself lost its attractiveness. Since no one was bound any longer by the decision of the commune, a degree of mobility became possible which was unheard-of under the old regime. Villagers freely sold their property, while outsiders moved in. Although non-Mennonites rarely tried to buy a lot in a Mennonite village, except in one giving promise of developing into a rural trade center, members of different and often hostile churches began to settle side by side. Once, the school house in the middle of the village served as a social and religious center; a separate church building was sometimes added later. As the village population decreased while that of the surrounding countryside increased correspondingly, the school, particularly the public school (which replaced the private school altogether in later years), moved to the outskirts of the village or even to a crossroad somewhere in the fields. Moreover, each congregation with members in and around a village tended to build its own church. Thus the local community was deprived of a common meeting place;

it became ever more heterogeneous and segmentalized, losing the intimacy whih had been its greatest charm. While under the open-field system a rather even distribution of wealth had been maintained, gossip and public opinion checking the display of greater wealth and social stratification, the social pyramid, too, tended to grow somewhat steeper with the breakdown of solidaristic community organization. The further decrease in homogenity induced people who would have preferred village habitat to lose interest in communal life and to retire to their own farms. It was a vicious circle through which the old local community among the Mennonites was undermined.

It has been possible to gather proof of the existence, at one time or another, of no less than 110 Mennonite villages in Manitoba. According to a map of the West Reserve compiled by C. A. Dawson, 63 of them were still in existence in 1890.[16] This does not necessarily imply that all of them continued under the open-field system or even functioned as self-governing village communes, but it only indicates distinct village sites with close habitat. Between 1890 and 1922, 33, and between 1922 and 1936, 11 more of these 63 villages also disappeared.[17] While Dawson's record includes several minor mistakes, it clearly reveals the general trend. By 1922 all but 5 of the original Bergthal villages had been disbanded, while only a few Fürstenland villages had been affected, all of them in a fringe area west of range 4 and north of township 2. The exodus to Latin America led to the dissolution of many more former Fürstenland and of a few surviving Bergthal villages. That the effect was not greater was due primarily to the Russländer immigration which quickly filled most of the vacancies left by the emigrants.

At the time our own survey was undertaken, over twenty of the original West Reserve villages had survived. Several of them had retained the traditional lay-out and architecture. Of others, only a few houses were left, with many vacant lots in between, but the rows of cotton - wood trees planted by the pioneers remained and had grown to majestic heights. In some of these villages secondary additions had been made,

---

[16] Cf. C. A. Dawson, *Group Settlement*, p. 116.

[17] A record book of the Municipality of Hanover for the year 1889 names 35 separate places, but the size of 14 of them did not exceed five families. The largest villages were Steinbach (47 families), Blumenort (23), and Hochfeld (20 families); ten villages included between 11 and 19 families, while the rest were made up of between 6 and 10 families. Corresponding figures are not available for the West Reserve villages, as statistics in the Municipalities of Rhineland and Douglas were computed by school districts. As a rule, however, their size was apparently less variable, and generally somewhat larger, than in the East Reserve.

such as new streets or new houses. New buildings, erected since the close of the pioneer period, were as a rule modeled by local craftsmen after neighbouring non-Mennonite farmsteads or some catalogue of American or Canadian contracting companies. In the lay-out of the farm buildings, now generally separated from the residence, they mostly followed the suggestions of certain government agencies.

Once a village had been dissolved in the West Reserve, no attempt was ever made to revive it. In the other colony, however, changes followed a much less regular pattern. In some instances the site of villages was shifted, usually nearer to an artery of communication, so that close habitat, though not conforming to the original lay-out, was preserved. Almost always the name was retained. Only the old open-field village of Grünfeld was superseded by the nearby new crossroad settlement of Kleefeld. In many other cases there was a tendency for people to cluster together in secondary settlements having no basis in any one of the original pioneer villages. The old name of Hochfeld was applied to a new cluster of houses along the road, one mile west of the original site where only two farm houses now remain. By 1946, 4 of the 21 open-field villages listed in 1889 had survived in the East Reserve as against 20 out of 63 in the West Reserve. None of the former bears any formal resemblance to their originals. One has grown into a teeming town, another is straining every effort to follow suit. In most other cases, young growth of birch and poplar has overrun the abandoned sites. On the other hand, four new villages had sprung up in the East Reserve, two of them since 1930. Ten new settlements, all of them trade centers along the railroad, had appeared in the West Reserve, in addition to Hildebrandsdorf, a family settlement founded in 1890. Wherever old pioneer villages have survived, or new settlements have been formed, there is probably little danger that they will disappear in the near future; close habitat is still valued by the Mennonites so that there even is a tendency to enlarge existing villages. (See Table 11.)

To sum up, the challenge to tradition which followed contact with the dominant Anglo-Canadian society and its institutions, brought about fundamental changes in the organization of the Mennonite group. The incorporation of the rural municipalities interfered directly with the traditional institutions of self-government and eventually led to their collapse. More decisive than the imposition of Canadian institutions of local government, however, was the kind of legal and political freedom permitted to the individual, fostering dissension within the group itself and resistance against social controls. Yet the challenge did not result in a complete surrender to the competitive individualism of Anglo-Saxon Canada, or in the disintegration of the Mennonite social system. Social disorganization involved in the loss of certain functions of self-government, in the dissolution of the field community, and in the partial abolition of village habitat, was followed by social reorganization on a new basis. The changed institutional and social framework soon became the accepted standard of the group. As some sub-groups lagged behind, rifts in the total structure became apparent and deepened, but at first only where a distinction between various sub-groups had existed before. It did not lead to assimilation and the drifting away of individuals into the large society, but caused occasional shifts from one Mennonite sub-group to another. In fact, the core of the common culture was preserved and continued to differ from that of the large society.

CHAPTER V

Prosperity

From Subsistence to Commercial Farming

THE Mennonites had come to Manitoba with the firm resolution
to restore and continue a way of life which they considered the sacred
expression of their religion. To this end they had made great economic
sacrifices without expecting to gain any material rewards. All that they
hoped and worked for was to find a modest living for every member
of the group and to keep intact their culture. As it turned out, they
were more successful in advancing economically than in preserving
their social institutions. While they have been blamed for their
struggle to save the integrity of the group, they have been admired
for their industry, thrift, skill and business acumen, qualities which
were soon rewarded by the outward signs of prosperity. All contemporary sources are unanimous in stressing the impressive economic
progress made by the group.

In searching for reasons of this favorable reaction, one might
think of the rapid colonization and cultivation of land thought almost
worthless by others. Or one might recall the famous words spoken by
one of their neighbours: "They make a living where we cannot exist."
The substantial homes and granaries, and the orderly looking Mennonite villages suggested invidious comparisons, while rural slums or any
other signs of poverty were almost completely absent in their settlements. Then there was the apparently more even distribution of wealth
and income; and the greater resilience of the Mennonites not only to
the natural catastrophies of the mid-seventies—grasshopper plagues,

floods and crop failures—but also the aftermath of the man-made crisis of 1882. To this may be added the expansion of their land holdings in Manitoba, often at the expense of non-Mennonites; the establishment of thriving rural trade centers; and their more efficient utilization of land and human resources, permitting a greater population density without seemingly lowering the level of living.

Between 1870 and 1890, Manitoba's economy as a whole underwent a rapid transformation from the original fur trade economy, through the pioneer and frontier stages, into a system of high capitalism. As applied to agriculture, high capitalism was characterized by the cultivation of cash crops, extensive and largely exploitive farming methods, new technical inventions, and a struggle for money and profit. Mennonite culture, on the other hand, resembled, in the beginning at least, more that of a simple folk society. It is true that agriculture was valued by the Mennonites primarily as a way of life, and felt to be in conformity with the social principles of their religion. Even in Russia, however, they had not been confined by any means to primitive subsistence farming and to a self-sufficient, closed, village economy. On the contrary, for several decades prior to their emigration, they had been competing successfully for a share in the expanding markets of the Russian Empire, had freely adopted technical inventions, and had become familiar with capitalistic finance operations and a market economy. In Canada, too, they tended to orient economic action according to competitive capitalistic standards. But in other spheres of their culture they emphasized sacred traditions and the welfare of the group as a whole, so that the rate of social change was slowed down.

A better understanding of the seeming contradiction between their tenacious adherence to traditional institutions and values, on the one hand, and their readiness to adapt themselves to production for capitalistic markets and to technological progress, on the other, may be achieved if one realizes that the value systems of most societies are far less monolithic than they are frequently thought to be. In addition to action patterns which are rigidly regulated by the dominant profile of cultural orientations, there are in almost every culture certain areas permitting several alternatives, and occasionally complete freedom of choice. What is still more important, different types of orientations which seem to go together and to be consistent with each other frequently vary independently. It is quite possible, for instance, that individual achievement may be emphasized in one sphere of activity, such as in economic action, while in other spheres collective values, aiming at the integrity of the social system, remain paramount in the total cultural profile of a given group.[1]

Mennonite culture not only permitted alternative orientations, but the dominant culture profile itself was far from purely traditionalistic, sacred, solidaristic and static. During the earlier period it included a holy sphere of group-centered values and institutional patterns which was extended to aspects considered typically secular in Canadian culture. But at the same time there was an area of action where the individual was free to pursue ego-centered interests, and to play the game of those from whom the satisfaction of these values was to be derived. One has to distinguish, however, between the type of economic action where adaptation was permitted and another type where it remained controlled by superior group-centered values. For instance, actions threatening the open-field system were objectionable because the traditional institutions of village economy were felt to be an essential factor in the maintenance of group coherence and solidarity even though, under Canadian conditions, they might have had definite economic disadvantages. The cultivation of wheat for sale or the adoption of more efficient farm machinery, on the other hand, did not have similar social implications. This was considered permissible according to the maxim that individual material gain was desirable in competition with members of the outgroup, and that the economic advancement of each in-group member in this competition was actually conducive to the welfare of the group as a whole.

The degree to which the Mennonites submitted to the change from pre-capitalistic subsistence farming to the more capitalistic practices of a commercial farm economy depended largely on opportunities, and above all on markets and on soil conditions. At the time of their emigration a mixed type economy had prevailed in their Russian colonies with much of the livelihood derived from the farm itself, but with a certain amount of local and regional exchange of goods and services, and some production for a wider market. The situation in Manitoba actually compelled them at first to revert to a more primitive form of economy. Before even the self-sufficiency of the individual homestead

---

[1] Cf. Florence R. Kluckhohn, "Dominant and Substitute Profiles of Cultural Orientations: Their Significance for the Analysis of Social Stratification." *Social Forces 28* (1945: 376-393.

could be established, they had to go through a pioneer stage which required the expenditure of considerable capital, derived either from the sale of their property in the Old Country, from loans, or from outside work. Yet this stage was relatively short. Crop failures and inferior soil somewhat retarded progress among the earliest immigrants, but the process was speeded up in better locations and among later arrivals.

The transition to commercial farming, too, was quite irregular. It depended mainly on the means of transportation provided by the new railroads, on markets, but also on the topography. The latter is responsible for the great difference in the progress made by different colonies, the East Reserve generally trailing far behind the West Reserve. For several years after the first immigration to the East Reserve, new land was constantly being put under the plow and new settlements were being made to accommodate the growing second generation. While at a given time subsistence farming may have been the prevailing form in one place, another area would be far advanced on the road toward commercial farming, and a third one just starting out under conditions more or less typical of pioneers.

During the earlier pioneer period two types of activities were prevalent: the breaking and cultivation of new ground, and construction. The first primitive shelters were gradually replaced by quite substantial buildings, and construction work was brisk for several years. While much timber had to be imported from the United States, some was found locally, particularly in the East Reserve. The solidaristic form of socio-economic organization made possible a pooling of natural resources. Building material was taken from wherever it could be found within a village area or even a whole colony, without any need for market transactions. Other supplies, however, had to be bought, for instance, window panes, sashes, frames and doors, while iron nails were used sparingly. Lumber was supplied by William Hespeler, who had acquired timber rights on Dominion lands east of the Reserve in the present Municipality of La Broquerie. Such rights were also obtained by individual Mennonite village communes in the East Reserve. West Reserve villages hauled much of their timber from nearby woodlands in North Dakota. Fuel was obtained in much the same way as building materials although, as a rule, it was more readily available.

During the winter months, logging became the principal occupation of the male population, including very small boys. Some logging and hauling by means of home-made sledges was also done under contract, particularly for Hespeler, who was building a town on the new railroad; it was first named after him, but later renamed Niverville. Buildings included a grain elevator said to have been the first one built west of the Great Lakes. This provided some badly needed outside income; more could be earned by road and drainage work for the Province and particularly by work on the first Manitoba railroad which skirted the East Reserve, linking Emerson and the American railway system with St. Boniface and Winnipeg by 1879. Many Mennonites were thus able to save from $30 to $50 a year.

Although in Russia the Mennonites had been accustomed to working with horses, they were now forced to adopt the ox as the principal draft animal; eows were used for lighter work. An early attempt by Shantz to import a carload of horses from Ontario proved a failure. The animals arrived in poor condition and did not become acclimatized. Only much later did more adaptable breeds become available. With a team of oxen and a 12-inch wallowing plow having a fixed mould-board, a farmer was able to break about 6 acres of virgin land a year; with horses and more modern machinery about 20 acres of new land could be cultivated. Seed was broadcast by hand and covered with a wooden or a brush harrow. At first hay and grain were cut with a scythe or sickle, but soon grass mowers were introduced. These were so heavy, however, that the oxen had to be changed every 2 to 2½ hours. The first reaper made its appearance in 1878, in Grünfeld (East Reserve). Threshing machines, which were driven by two pairs of oxen, began to replace threshing flails as early as 1876.[2]

Under the open field system, farm operations on arable land were exclusively left to the individual homesteader, but hay lands were often utilized in common. During the hay harvest a whole village would set out to gather the swaths in small heaps, 4 to 6 of which made a load. It was then determined by lot which of the heaps were to be hauled away individually by different homesteaders.[3] Such coöperation, however, seems to have been typical only during the pioneer period. Implements such as mowers and reapers were frequently bought by a group of farmers and used coöperatively, each supplying

---

[2] Cf. P. P. Epp, "Aus meinen Erinnerungen," *Mennonitische Rundschau*, July 4, 1934. 8f.

[3] Cf. [Joh. R. Dück], "Aus den Pionierjahren der mennonitischen Siedlung in Manitoba," *Mennonitische Volkswarte 1* (1935): 139f.

one or two draft animals in turn. When working for others, the owners of a reaper received one bushel of grain for each acre cut. The expensive steam threshing machines introduced later were more often communally owned and operated.

The first seed grain was brought along in bags by the immigrants. Even as late as 1882, quantities of it were still imported from the Old Country.[4] As a whole, Russian winter wheat proved a failure. The settlers were thus forced to switch to spring varieties either procured by Shantz from the United States, or provided by the Provincial Government, which in the lean 1870's distributed seed grain free of charge to be returned in kind after the following harvest. Besides spring wheat, oats and barley also became staple crops, while rye, highly valued in Central and Eastern Europe as bread grain, remained of little importance. It appears that the Mennonites were the first to introduce flax to Manitoba. Vegetables and fruit were also cultivated; in 1876, as an example, Shantz provided $50 worth of vegetable and fruit seeds. While they failed in raising trees from seed, four-year-old apple trees sent by Shantz from Ontario were successfully transplanted.[5] In later years, however, Shantz had to admit that, "it was pretty hard to raise fruit there." Yet he added hopefully, "they raise plums and all kinds of wild fruit, strawberries, raspberries, etc. I have the opinion that some fruit can be raised", mentioning particularly the Siberian crab apple.[6] Most of the produce was for domestic consumption; still some of it found its way to local markets. With the steady stream of immigrants and an increasing urban population both in Winnipeg and some smaller centers such as Emerson, there was enough demand though prices remained unattractive. The scarcity of fresh fruit and vegetables in the Province created a ready market for watermelons, called *Arbusen* after a Russian word, which along with sunflower seeds were always a culinary favorite with the Mennonites.

Another important aspect of early Mennonite economy was the introduction of shelterbelts and of methods of dry farming. Being among the first to settle in Manitoba's open prairie, the Mennonites were also among the first to adopt these practices with which they had

---

[4] *Journals*, 1883, appendix 6, p. 82. The Russian thistle seems to have been introduced to the Canadian West with the Mennonite seed grain.

[5] Weekly *Manitoba Free Press*, November 8, 1879.

[6] *Report of the Standing Committee on Immigration*, 1886, pp. 39f. J. H. Ellis, C. B. Gill and F. W. Brodrick (*Farm Forestry and Tree Culture Projects for the Non-Forested Region of Manitoba* [Winnipeg, 1945]), mention that the wild cherries and plums now growing in the West Reserve came either from seedlings carried by the wind from the Pembina hills, or had been transplanted by the early settlers.

been familiar in their native country. Whenever a village was laid out, rows of trees were planted along the road and around each homestead. Similarly, isolated farms were always protected by windbreaks. Native trees such as balsam, white and black poplar, ash, maple and oak were used for the purpose, while box elders were planted as garden hedges. Most common, however, was cottonwood which at the time was not growing in the Province but could be found at a short distance across the border along the Pembina River. From shoots these poplars grew rather rapidly until they reached a maximum height of about 80 feet with a diameter of 4 feet. At the present time, many of the cottonwood trees planted by the pioneers have already reached their natural age limit and are gradually being replaced, in recent years largely by evergreens. Professor Ellis pays high tribute to the farm forestry practiced by the earliest settlers of Southern Manitoba, who included many Mennonites. He writes:

> The physical need to ameliorate the bleak environment of the dwellings and the aesthetic desire for more attractive home sites were primarily responsible for the early practice of planting shelterbelts or windbreaks around farm homes, building sites and gardens. . . . The citizens of Manitoba owe a debt of gratitude to those who . . . demonstrated in a measure what may be accomplished and what should be avoided. The point to be emphasized is that the pioneer experiments in tree culture on prairie farms were undertaken because of recognized human needs.[7]

Dry farming, aimed at the preservation of moisture in more arid prairie soils through intensive summerfallowing, is generally believed to have been brought to Canada's West by immigrants from the United States. It had its forerunner, however, in the *Schwarzbrache* (summerfallow with repeated cultivation) as it had been practiced by the Mennonites in Russia since the time of Johann Cornies together with a four-crop rotation. It was certainly used by them also in their Manitoba settlements. Its importance was less obvious in Southern Manitoba, and during the early years of settlement when lack of moisture was not a problem.

The earliest major crop cultivated commercially by the Manitoba Mennonites seems to have been flax. Seven carloads were shipped from Emerson to Minneapolis in 1878. Waterloo County in Ontario became the chief consumer of Manitoba flax. Manitoba's total production was over 60,000 bushels in 1886, most of it grown by Mennonites.

---

[7] *Farm Forestry*, p. 1.

In 1893 it amounted to 116,454 bushels, or almost half of Canada's total crop. Lack of man power and early snowfall made it impractical to cure flax fibre at the height of the harvest season, so that the plants were always cut and used for seed only. Until the turn of the century the Mennonites, both in Manitoba and in Ontario, had a kind of monopoly of Canada's flax production.

TABLE 1—WHEAT PRODUCTION AND LAND UTILIZATION IN THE MENNONITE RESERVES, 1886 and 1921*

	WEST RESERVE			EAST RESERVE		
	1886 Rhineland and Douglas	1921 Rhineland	p.c. increase† 1921 over 1886	1886 Hanover and Hespeler	1921 Hanover	p.c. increase† 1921 over 1886
Number of farm units	1,105	1,125		365	629	
Wheat produced (bushels)	443,007	1,036,980	134	61,105	144,886	137
Wheat produced per farm unit (bushels)	401	922	130	167	230	38
Wheat planted (acres)	30,143	83,937	178	4,866	15,298	214
Wheat yield per acre	13.3	12.3	—7	12.6	9.5	—24
Wheat acreage per farm unit	27	75	177	13	9	—30
Percentage of average farm area planted in wheat	17	38	124	7	4	—43
Occupied land (acres)	117,857	220,598	87	72,063	147,436	104
Occupied land per farm unit	161	196	22	197	234	18
Improved land (acres)	59,255	187,105	215	10,333	54,977	432
Improved land per farm unit	54	166	207	28	87	211
Percentage of area of average farm improved	33	85	157	14	37	164

* Unless otherwise indicated, all the tables are based on data published by the Dominion Bureau of Statistics.
† Decrease is indicated by a minus in front of figure.

The rapid progress made by the Manitoba Mennonites in land utilization and wheat production is borne out by census figures for representative areas in the West Reserve. The wheat acreage per farm unit in 1921, for instance, was nearly 3 times as much as in 1886, resulting in a 130 per cent increase in the wheat production of that period. Much of the 924 bushels of wheat produced by the average farmer in 1921 was sold. In 1886 only one-third of an average farm was improved, leaving the rest mostly for natural pasture. Yet within 5 years, the area of improved land in the combined Municipalities of Rhineland and Douglas increased by 60 per cent, although at the same time almost 65 per cent more land was occupied. After 30 years, that is in 1921, practically all available land in the West Reserve was fully utilized for agricultural purposes. In the Municipality of Rhineland only about 30,000 acres, or 15 per cent of all occupied farm land, were then recorded as "natural pasture," while 85 per cent of an average farm consisted of improved land, mostly planted in wheat or other small grain, with 13 per cent fallow and 6 per cent improved pasture. At about the same time, namely between 1886 and 1916, the number of cattle per farm unit decreased from 7.6 to 6.5, although the average farm size increased by approximately 20 per cent. The sharp increase from 3 horses per farm unit in 1886 to 7.9 in 1916 indicates the

TABLE 2—LAND UTILIZATION IN AREAS OF MENNONITE CONCENTRATION, 1881-1921

Year	Census Subdivision	Occupied Land (Acres)	Unimproved Land	
			Acres	As a p.c. of occupied land
1881	Morris West	62,640	55,471	89
1886	Douglas and Rhineland	177,857	118,602	67
	Hespeler and Hanover	72,063	61,721	86
1891	Douglas and Rhineland	274,509	176,303	64
	Hespeler and Hanover	81,884	68,435	84
1921	Rhineland	220,598	33,493	15
	Hanover	147,436	92,459	63

replacement of oxen as draft animals and a much greater use of farm machinery.

The successful cultivation of cash crops was largely dependent on the introduction of improved farm machinery, which was readily adopted by the Mennonites.[8] On the other hand, Shantz and other responsible leaders were anxious to protect their brethren from falling victim to "agents and horse jockeys." The purchase of implements on all sorts of "easy payment" plans often led to the loss not only of the down payment and initial installments, but of the buyer's land and property as well. In testifying before the Standing Committee on Immigration of the House of Commons, Shantz gave the following vivid account: "The agent will come along and say, 'you must have a machine.' And the farmer will reply, 'I am too poor.' The agent will then say, 'You must have a horse and a machine, then you will be able to pay for them out of the land'."

Besides the disapproval of credit buying, other social checks were imposed upon the adoption of new machines and innovations. Greater efficiency alone was by no means a valid criterion of whether a labor-saving device was acceptable. Mennonite mores insisted upon a frugal mode of living, and set definite standards as to the amount of human effort to be expended on the working of a farm by its owner and his family. Machines and gadgets designed only to increase personal comfort or to reduce labor without increasing total output and profit were therefore rejected.

Along with farm implements, small saw and grist mills were of considerable importance. However, while the number of implements tended to increase with commercialization, that of mills decreased proportionally. In early Manitoba subsistence economy on a local level was quite common also among the non-Mennonite settlers. Since scattered habitat prevailed outside of the river settlements and French parishes, small rural trade centers took over the function of providing the hinterland with commercial milling facilities. The general trend in early Manitoba was for mills to be located wherever settlers were concentrated in sufficient numbers to make their commercial operation economical. While at first mills were numerous and small, later larger plants tended to draw business toward a few focal points throughout the province. The Mennonites made use of milling facilities wherever they were provided commercially by outsiders, and built their own mills only where such services were not available. Most West Reserve Mennonites went to West Lynn, Emerson, Nelson, Morden, Morris or

---

[8] Cf. G. G. Kornelson, "Aus deutschen Siedlungen," *Der Nordwesten-Kalender* ([Winnipeg], 1945); the unpublished papers of his father, G. S. Kornelson, of Steinbach, contain a wealth of historical information.

Walhalla, North Dakota, to have their grain ground for feed and flour.

Windmills were located in several Mennonite villages such as Rosengart, Neuhorst and Reinfeld; the one at Rosenhof (Scratching River colony) served for many decades as a well-known landmark in Southern Manitoba. One of the earliest steam mills in the West Reserve was installed by Johann Wall, of Blumenort, before 1878. Others were established in Altona and Gretna, the new railroad towns. In custom milling, which was most common, 1 out of 8 bushels went to the miller, and 1 out of 6 bushels was paid for sifting. The construction of mills was of greater urgency in the East Reserve, for the region was more isolated and removed from trade centers. Even Niverville, though located on a railroad, was far away from the center of the colony and difficult to reach with the available means of transportation. As early as 1876, windmills are known to have existed in Tannau, Eigenhof, Reinfeld and Steinbach. They had been built and were operated by millwrights who had learned their trade in Russia. The total cost of a windmill at the time was $2,000.

In the woodland of the East Reserve wind was an inadequate source of power. Moreover, intensive building activities in the colony soon created a demand for more efficient power plants and the combination of grist with saw mills. Since the Mennonites were not as dexterous in handling an axe as the pioneers from Eastern Canada, they depended on prepared boards for the construction of permanent homes. At first all timber was sawed domestically and by hand. The logs were laid on high wooden racks; one man pulled the saw blade downward, while another, standing on top of the rack, pulled it up. In 1878 A. S. Friesen, of Steinbach, supplemented his windmill with a steam engine at a cost of $1,300, thus providing sufficient power for both milling and sawing on a commercial basis. At about the same time a smaller steam plant was installed by Wiens and Braun at Schönwiese. Other plants were operated in Blumenort (since 1878), Grünthal (1892-1909), Hochstadt and Rosengart. They usually were owned by companies of Mennonite farmers, although Anglo-Saxon names are also found among those early mill operators in Mennonite colonies.

When the Steinbach windmill was sold in 1879 for $1,550, to a company of three men from Rosenhof, Scratching River colony, local farmers put up a subscription for the purchase of a steam flour mill. Individual pledges ran from $25 to $50. Peter K. Barkmann, the best millwright in the colony, was chosen manager and sent to Waterloo

County, Ontario. There he bought a second-hand mill for $2,500, borrowed from Ontario Mennonites, but before operation began in August 1880 the mill had cost twice as much. A company was formed, with Barkmann and his sons holding half the shares, Klaas Reimer, the wealthiest local business man, three eighths, and the former mill owner, A. S. Friesen, the rest. After the mill burned down in 1892, Klaas Reimer built a roller steam mill with 75 barrels. This plant, a 5-storey building, about 50 feet high, changed hands in 1918 at a price of $12,500, but burned down in 1920.

Cheese making was another industry which gained some importance among the Mennonites. In 1888 there were 24 cheese factories in the province, none of them in a Mennonite settlement.[9] The first Mennonite cheese factory is recorded for Steinbach in the year 1889. It was managed by Klaas W. Reimer, who built two more plants, one in Blumenort in 1892, the other in Hochfeld. During 6 months of operation in 1897, he produced a total of 150,000 pounds of cheese in all 3 plants. In the same year he also won a first prize for cheese at the Toronto Exhibition, the first national dairy prize which ever went to the province. Jacob T. Regehr started a cheese factory at Hochstadt, and had one of his sons, who later became mayor of Steinbach, trained as cheese maker at the Manitoba Agricultural College. Between 1897 and 1907 the elder Regehr served no less than eight times on the board of directors of the Manitoba Dairy Association. Other cheese factories, all operated on a coöperative basis, existed in the East Reserve at one time or another in Grünthal (since 1893), Greenland, and perhaps three or four more places.[10] In the West Reserve, dairying was of little importance, although one creamery is recorded for Morden prior to World War I. In 1885 a cheese plant was installed at Reinland but went bankrupt after a few months operation. All of these early Mennonite cheese factories disappeared when the fresh milk and cream market of Winnipeg brought better prices and communication was improved.

The differences in the economic behavior of the various Mennonite settlements can be explained almost wholly by geographical factors. On the favorable soil of the West Reserve wheat and cash crop farming soon became prevalent, while most of the East Reserve with

---

[9] Cf. *Fifty Years of Dairying in Manitoba: Memorial Souvenir presented by the Manitoba Dairy Association on the Occasion of its 50th Annual Convention* (Winnipeg, 1935).

[10] Cf. *Das 60-jährige Jubiläum der mennonitischen Einwanderung in Manitoba, Canada* (Steinbach, 1935), report by Klaas W. Reimer, pp. 25-29.

its inferior soil was for many decades confined to subsistence farming. Since land was plentiful and cheap, much of it was left uncultivated and used as natural pasture. At the same time when in the West Reserve more and more land was taken up, the area of occupied land in the Municipality of Hanover increased by only 8.8 per cent between 1886 and 1891, and by 55 per cent in the following 30 years. In 1886 about 86 per cent of all occupied land was classified as unimproved, while as late as 1921, 32 per cent was still described as natural pasture (as against 14 per cent in the West Reserve). Field crops were raised on a much smaller scale in the East Reserve, mainly for domestic consumption and feed for livestock. Whatever cash income was derived from the farm came primarily from dairy products, some beef cattle and small farm animals. In the earlier years sheep breeding was of some importance here, but herds declined from 3.4 head per average farm in 1886, to 2 head per farm in 1916. At the same time, even the cattle population decreased from 13.3 to 12.8 per farm, although remaining about twice as large as that in the West Reserve. Similar trends can be observed with regard to wheat production. In 1921 only 4 per cent of the total acreage of an average farm in the East Reserve was planted in wheat (as against 38 per cent in the West Reserve) while the wheat yield per farm unit increased by 38 per cent (against 130 per cent in the West Reserve) between 1886 and 1921.

Farm size was another significant difference between the two areas. Of course, originally all farms were of almost equal size according to the standard of 160 acres set by the Dominion policy. In the East Reserve the tendency over the years was to increase farm size, the average in 1921 being as high as 234 acres as against 196 acres in the West Reserve. More revealing are the differences in the distribution of farms by size groups. In 1881, 89 per cent of all farms in a representative Mennonite district were of standard (or near-standard) size, while 3 per cent were below, and 8 per cent above standard. Five years later, 11 per cent of the farms in the Municipalities of Rhineland and Douglas were below, and 8 per cent above standard (1 per cent over 320 acres) while the corresponding figures for the Municipalities of Hespeler and Hanover were 5 and 22 per cent respectively with 6 per cent above 320 acres. Until 1921 there were more large farms in the East Reserve, and relatively more very small as well as standard-size holdings in the West Reserve.

TABLE 3—FARM SIZE IN AREAS OF MENNONITE
CONCENTRATION, 1891-1946

HANOVER

	1891 No.	1891 %	1921 No.	1921 %	1936 No.	1936 %	1941 No.	1941 %	1946 No.	1946 %
All Size Groups ..	201	100.0	629	100.0	883	100.0	1,088	100.0	1,113	100.0
1-10 acres	13	6.5	5	0.8	133	15.1	147	13.5	220	19.8
11-50 acres	3	1.5	11	1.7			114	10.5		
51-100 acres	6	3.0	61	9.7	138	15.6	170	15.6	202	18.1
101-200 acres	120	59.7	281	44.7	348	39.4	378	34.7	422	37.9
201-299 acres	59	29.3	83	13.2	97	11.0	127	11.7	133	11.9
300-479 acres					136	15.4	127	11.7	117	10.5
480-639 acres			188	29.9	20	2.3	16	1.5	13	1.2
640 acres & over					11	1.2	9	0.8	6	0.5

RHINELAND

	1891 No.	1891 %	1921 No.	1921 %	1936 No.	1936 %	1941 No.	1941 %	1946 No.	1946 %
All Size Groups ..	866	100.0	1,125	100.0	1,240	100.0	1,249	100.0	1,221	100.0
1-10 acres	16	1.8	36	3.2	200	16.1	71	5.7	237	19.4
11-50 acres	75	8.7	49	4.4			173	13.8		
51-100 acres	113	13.0	109	9.7	148	11.9	139	11.1	145	12.0
101-200 acres	500	57.8	551	48.9	480	38.8	441	35.4	417	34.1
201-299 acres	162	18.7	177	15.7	199	16.0	195	15.6	193	15.8
300-479 acres					179	14.4	184	14.7	176	14.4
480-639 acres			203	18.1	24	1.9	34	2.7	43	3.5
640 acres & over					10	0.8	12	1.0	10	0.8

STANLEY / MORRIS

	STANLEY 1941 No.	STANLEY 1941 %	STANLEY 1946 No.	STANLEY 1946 %	MORRIS 1941 No.	MORRIS 1941 %	MORRIS 1946 No.	MORRIS 1946 %
All Size Groups	896	100.0	984	100.0	757	100.0	784	100.0
1-10 acres	37	4.1	203	20.6	31	4.1	36	4.6
11-50 acres	91	10.2						
51-100 acres	75	8.4	99	10.1	37	4.8	63	8.0
101-200 acres	302	33.7	270	27.4	200	26.4	211	26.9
201-299 acres	106	11.8	122	12.4	112	14.8	103	13.1
300-479 acres	192	21.4	219	22.3	213	28.1	216	27.5
480-639 acres	60	6.7	45	4.6	80	10.6	76	9.7
640 acres & over	33	3.7	26	2.6	84	11.1	79	10.1

In view of the fact that the general trend in wheat growing areas
has been toward increased farm size and more extensive cultivation,
the pulverization of farm holdings among the West Reserve Mennonites
requires some explanation. Social factors seem to have been mainly
responsible. The decrease in farm size was more pronounced in the
census subdistrict which included the Fürstenland settlement than in
that mostly inhabited by the more adaptable Bergthal people. Unlike
the underpopulated East Reserve, the whole West Reserve soon began

to suffer from overpopulation. Not that reasonably good land was unavailable elsewhere or that the Mennonites could not have afforded to pay for it; but they insisted on group settlement and kept their young people close to home until an opportunity arose to found daughter colonies in Saskatchewan. Due to the rapid natural increase of the Mennonite population, all available land within or adjacent to the West Reserve was soon exhausted. Their system of inheritance forced them to divide the existing standard-size homesteads, although in many cases ownership of small parcels of the original paternal farm, distributed among several children, was largely nominal.

While all immigrant-settlers had been owners, by 1891 the ratio of tenants in the West Reserve, primarily in the part including the compact Fürstenland settlement, had increased far above the Provincial average. This was largely a result of the practice by which retiring farmers leased their farms to one of their sons. Of the rent paid, a certain amount was reserved for the father to provide a living for himself, his wife and possibly minor children. The balance was credited

TABLE 4—FARM OWNERSHIP, FOR MANITOBA AND AREAS OF MENNONITE CONCENTRATION, 1881-1921

Year	Census Subdivision	Total Population	Mennonite Population	Mennonite population as a per cent of total population	Owners	Tenants	No. of tenants per 100 owners
1881	Manitoba	65,954	7,776	12	8,776	301	3
	Morris West	1,947	1,946	100	338	—	0
1886	Manitoba	108,640	9,112	8	16,401	1,170	7
	Douglas and Rhineland	6,645	6,404	97	1,023	82	8
	Hanover and Hespeler	2,107	2,045	97	355	10	3
1891	Manitoba	152,506	°	°	20,319	2,252	11
	Rhineland } Douglas }	9,560	8,837	92 {	729 637	137 } 64 }	15
	Hanover and Hespeler	2,300	2,175	95	360	24	7
1921	Rhineland	8,400	7,924	94	741	184	25[1]
	Hanover	4,907	3,040	61	554	42	8[1]

° Not available.
[1] Does not include part-owners and part-tenants. Their number in 1921 was for Rhineland 200, and for Hanover 33.

to the account of the tenant-son. After the owner's death the regulations of the *Waisenamt* required that each child receive an equal share in the estate. Accordingly, the young farm operator now had to buy up the shares of the other heirs in order to obtain full ownership in the farm. To this he could apply the portions of rent paid over the years to the father which had been credited to his account. If he was still unable to indemnify the other heirs, primarily his mother and siblings, the farm was nominally divided among all of them though it remained under the management of the one son. Until he was able to buy back all the land, he continued to figure in the census as tenant. Tenancy among Mennonites was thus a device to prevent public auction and to keep homesteads in the family, while at the same time complying with the traditional rule of equal inheritance. This system of succession was supported by a special institution, the *Waisenamt*.

Supporting Institutions

The *Waisenamt* was a church institution managed by two elected officers whose title was *Waisenmann* or *Waisenvorsteher*. Each of the original groups settling in Manitoba transferred its own *Waisenamt* from the Old to the New Country. After the Bergthal church was divided into three separate congregations, there existed at the same time five institutions of this type: the *Altkolonier Waisenamt* of the Fürstenland group, the *Kleine Gemeinde Waisenamt,* the *Chortitzer Waisenamt* of the Bergthal group in the East Reserve, the *Bergthaler Waisenamt* of the liberal Bergthal group in the West Reserve, and the *Sommerfelder Waisenamt* of the conservative faction among the Bergthal people in the West Reserve. As indicated by its name (which means literally "orphans' bureau"), the primary function of this institution was the protection of the interests of orphans and the general management of esates. It was not simply a trust company, but its rules represented a body of laws regulating the transfer of property from one generation to another. Finally, it served as a savings bank and finance institution. Historically the principles under which it operated reflected ancient concepts of farm property and inheritance which once had been wide-spread among the German colonists in Eastern Europe.[11]

---

[11] Cf. E. K. Francis, "Mennonite Institutions in Early Manitoba: A Study on Their Origins," *Agricultural History* 22 (1948): 147f., 150.

The basic ideas underlying the Mennonite system of inheritance were these: An estate was divided in such a way that the surviving parent received one-half of its value, and each of the children, both male and female, equal parts of the other half. At the same time the family homestead was taken over either by the surviving parent or by one of the grown-up sons. Even if the surviving parent married again, which was the rule, the family unit was not necessarily disrupted, for the minor children from the previous marriages remained in the new household. Although eventually a cash settlement was required, great care was taken that this obligation did not encumber the farm excessively. As a rule estates were assessed at a rather low value, while the heirs left their share in the farm as an interest-bearing investment.

A distinction has to be made between children who were of age at the time of the death of a parent, and those who were minors and thus continued to live with the surviving parent and the new spouse. Major heirs, though entitled to ask for cash payment after a certain period of grace, did so only upon marriage. Otherwise the farm remained their real home, and they themselves shareholders, although they might be working at some other place. Minor children were, as a rule, left with the surviving parent, while their inheritance remained an integrated part of the family property without bearing interest. These children had all the rights and duties which would have been their due had both parents been living. Among their duties was the obligation to contribute their customary share of work to the domestic economy until they came of age. If they were working out, their wages were treated as a part of the family or farm income, and administered by the head of the household. Their rights included their proper upbringing and education; both were supervised by the *Waisenamt*. Unless a widow remarried, she was supposed to choose two curators (called *Gute Männer*) but had a right to operate the farm by herself.

In addition to their share, computed on a basis of the total value of an estate, children were also entitled to a special *Zugabe* or "extra." It took the place of the customary dowry which they would have received if both parents had lived at the time when they left the common household to found their own families. The *Zugabe* consisted of specified items which differed for males and females and varied somewhat according to the wealth of the family. They included livestock, clothing and household goods, which were apparently intended to enable grown-up children to get started in life on their own. These items could be converted into cash payments, which were fixed at a surprisingly low rate.

The *Zugabe* gives some insight into the manner by which the foundation of new family units and households was made possible economically, regardless of whether the parents were alive or not. At the time of marriage two dowries (or "extras", as the case may be) were joined together, providing the bare essentials for the young couple. The capital necessary for the purchase of a farm (or the establishment of a business), however, had to be secured in a different way. First, the young people could work for wages after they had come of age and thus accumulate cash savings over the years. Second, they could draw as much as could be spared without endangering farm operations from the parental property. During the life time of both parents such withdrawals were treated as advance payments of the share to which the children would eventually be entitled when the estate was divided among all heirs. Third, if the parental estate had already been divided, then they could claim their share in cash.

The Mennonite system of property transfer from one generation to another is characterized by the principle of equality—equal rights of husband and wife in the family farm, and equal inheritance among all children, male and female. This left nothing to the discretion of a testator although, on occasion, testaments were written out to satisfy the law and to make sure that the continued operation of the Mennonite law of inheritance would not be jeopardized in a common-law country. In such a case the testator simply declared that he left all his property to his wife in trust to be divided and administered in accordance with the rules of the *Waisenamt* of his church. In this way the pulverization of standard holdings was prevented. At the same time, inheriting sons could not accumulate great riches at the expense of non-inheriting siblings. For the shares of the latter had to be redeemed from current farm incomes, often over a great number of years. Every farm actually was supposed to yield enough not only to guarantee a living for the members of the household but also to establish new homesteads as grown-up children married. Only a moderate capital was provided for every new start, so that great pressure was constantly exerted upon the owners of old-established, as much as of newly-founded, homesteads to maintain a very frugal level of living, and to work hard and efficiently with their families during their whole life. The system seemed to be particularly appropriate for the economy of typical colonizers. It required the steady addition of land and included incentives for cultivating new ground even under very hard conditions. In this way it contributed to the success of the Mennonites as pioneers, and to their tendency of founding daughter colonies through migrations.

Among the Mennonites property was not meant to serve a clan as a symbol of status and unity. Transfer of real estate through the male line, though common, was less important than the welfare of every family unit, however it might be composed. Compound families were quite frequent, including half-brothers and half-sisters, both in the paternal and maternal line. Augmented family households, on the other hand, were rare, since only minor children were bound to the homestead, and they usually left upon coming of age. While in Russia a special building was set aside as *Ausgedinge* or *Altenteil* (old part), no such provision is known to have existed in Manitoba. Retired parents either lived with the new farm operator or moved to some town. The structure of the family and the organization of domestic economy were thus essentially functional, favoring relatively small households and medium-sized farms which could be efficiently operated by the owner, his wife and their unmarried children.

The transfer of farm property from generation to generation under the supervision of the *Waisenamt* was neither a private trans- action nor purely a family affair, but a public concern. The settlement of an estate required the presence of all the heirs (or their attorneys), the *Waisenvorsteher* and the village mayor. The final contract became valid only after the church elder himself had signed it. Also, contested cases were submitted to the judgment of the elder whose personal decision could not be appealed. As a rule, inheritances remained invested in the family farm and were paid out gradually and directly. Yet the *Waisenamt* held in trust money of orphans, widows, and absent heirs, particularly in cases where, for one reason or another, the estate had been sold by public auction. In addition, it was widely used as a savings bank since non-Mennonite institutions were often distrusted, and since it seemed desirable to keep investment capital within the colony. Accordingly the institution always had at its disposal consider- able amounts of liquid money which was made available to private individuals in the form of loans.

Transactions were carried out on a business basis. Interest on deposits was 5 per cent and on loans 6 per cent while a 2 per cent commission (called *Auszahlgeld*) was asked for every withdrawal of deposits. Interest rates followed the common practice in Manitoba but other costs were very low, as the overhead of the institution was negligible.[12] No securities were required for loans other than promissory notes countersigned by two church members in good standing. Thus the *Waisenamt* functioned very much like a credit union, acting as a strong regulative and stabilizing factor in the whole Mennonite economic system. While the *Waisenamt* and its regulations had been recognized in Russia by law, no such official backing existed in Canada. Actually, the Mennonite principles of inheritance were contrary to common law and could not have been upheld, had they ever been tested in court. As in the case of the open field system, the Mennonites solved the difficulty by tabooing appeal to Canadian courts, and by putting their system of property transfer from one generation to another under the direct sanction of the church.

The preamble to the regulations of the Chortitzer *Waisenamt* related its basic principles to Bible passages, thus invoking the highest authority recognized by the Mennonites. Furthermore, the regulations stated cautiously and somewhat ambiguously that, if a testament existed, the laws of the country would have to be observed, adding: "These, however, are not known among us." In point of fact, the regulations of the *Waisenamt* as a trust and finance company had to be approved by the Canadian authorities. That no objections are known to have been raised, could be explained in this way: In the eyes of the Canadian officials, these rules did not have the character of a binding public law as they had to the Mennonites, but were voluntary agreements which as such were not contrary to law. Thus it was quite in order that Mennonites had their estates administered by the *Waisenamt* if they wished to do so; but there was no way of compelling any one of them to observe these rules should he decide to use some other form of disposing of his estate which was permitted by the laws of the country. It was the latter case which, if challenged in court, might have led to serious difficulties.

The practice of following the *Waisenamt* rules declined in the course of time even among the Fürstenland people. Settlements made between 1916 and their exodus to Mexico indicate clearly that the

---

[12] According to the Blumenort records of January 3, 1923, interest on sums due to the *Waisenamt* on account of minor or absent heirs was reduced to 4 per cent. In still more recent years, the Chortitzer *Waisenamt* decreased its interest rates to 2 per cent on deposits, 3 per cent on loans to church members, and 4 per cent on loans to non-members.

principle of equal inheritance was no longer strictly adhered to. Contracts made out in the traditional manner in Blumenort, for instance, included complex distinctions and provisions such as were unknown in earlier documents. Yet this change was more gradual and less disruptive than in the case of the other institutions discussed in the preceding chapter. The difference was due to the fact that the *Waisenamt* and the law of inheritance were considered to be directly matters of the church, while the open-field system or the organization of the village commune were essentially secular affairs and thus came under the sanction of the church only indirectly. While in the latter sphere a dissenting Mennonite could easily escape religious censure by joining a more liberal group, at first all the Mennonite churches held strictly to the traditional principles of *Waisenamt* operations.

In connection with the Mennonite credit system another important aspect of the financial structure is of interest. It will be recalled that during the early period substantial sums had been made available to the immigrants in form of loans granted either by the Government or the Ontario Mennonites. All the money, including the Government loan, had been raised collectively, guaranteed collectively, and doled out by the Ontario Aid Committee and managed by Shantz through the "bread banks" in the Manitoba colonies. After the immigrants had weathered the troubles of the pioneer stage and become well-established, the promoters of the whole scheme decided that the recipients of such money should convert their debts into individual mortgages on their farms to which they had by now acquired title. The reasons for this new policy can be conjectured from the testimony of Shantz in 1886 before the Standing Committee on Immigration of the House of Commons.

Shantz had considerable difficulty in explaining to the parliamentary committee why he had forced the Manitoba settlers to convert debts, indirectly owed to the Dominion Government at a low rate of 6 per cent interest, into individual mortgages taken out with private loan companies at rates running as high as 8 and 10 per cent. One contract made out in 1886 with the *London und Ontario Leihgesellschaft*, for instance, contained the following stipulations: From the loan of $300, a commission of $22.80 was deducted at once, leaving $277.20 to the borrower. Beginning with 1888, $25 had to be repaid annually for 3 years, and the balance of $225 had to be refunded in 1891. The interest rate was 9 per cent for the first, and 8 per cent for the following

4 years. What the Members of Parliament overlooked was the fact that Shantz and other Mennonite leaders did not think in terms of cheap or dear money, but were primarily concerned with the economic and social stability of the group as a whole. As it turned out, the loan conversion actually stimulated, first, more responsible farm management on the part of individuals; second, the elimination of unsuccessful farm operators thereby increasing both the local farm labor supply and the supply of land available within the colonies to those who could make the best use of it; and, third, a certain financial self-sufficiency of the Mennonite commonwealth.

As long as the various loans were under the management of the local "bread banks" and the Ontario Aid Committee, individual recipients did not feel the pressure of doing their utmost to meet their obligations, knowing very well that the community would stand up for them if their property were in danger of being lost. The Ontario guarantors had gladly given aid while the immigrants had been in real need of it and could not offer any security of their own. But they were unwilling to carry the burden so that the beneficiaries could squander the easy and cheap money on expensive machines or additional land. In his evidence, Shantz mentioned in particular 25 to 30 families who were shiftless and unable to manage their farms properly. He thought it would be beneficial for the community if such people were forced to sell out, once they had to meet the more rigorous terms of private mortgagers. In fact, he announced that arrangements had been made by which more prosperous Mennonites would buy up run-down and overburdened farms, redeem all debts, and pay small amounts of ready cash to the former owners with which they could start again on a scale more in keeping with their individual abilities.

Shantz implied that those who lost their homesteads in this way might learn a lesson. But even if they did not learn it, the land was at least saved from falling in the hands of non-Mennonites and speculators, and was put to the best possible use by people who had proved their mettle. Shantz was convinced that, apart from these few, other debtors would in the long run profit by being forced to thrift and good management. At first most immigrants were almost destitute and many had small children. In the meantime the children had grown up providing a ready labor supply. As Shantz put it: "They are well fixed . . . and I think they might take their burden on their own shoulders. They obtained a loan, therefore, but their mortgages are not much, only $300, $400 or $500. I think they might look after themselves."

Farsighted leadership did still more to put on a sound basis the economy of the group seen as an integrated whole. One of the great dangers of prosperity and a rapidly expanding economy lay in the overbuying of machines and of land. Individual farm mortgages kept a check on the fever of speculation and credit buying to which, at the time, many other settlers in the West had fallen victims. Other moral checks put on the purchase of farm implements have been discussed earlier in this chapter. They applied in part also to the buying of livestock and land. In addition, a formal agreement was reached by the Manitoba Mennonites according to which, for a certain period of years, no one would add any land to his free homestead even if he was in a financial position to do so. This rule obviously did not apply to the establishment of new farms for grown-up children. Indeed, the measure was taken in view of the constant need of new land for the second generation, after the land reserve of the original colonies was practically exhausted, and the effects of overpopulation became felt.

The prohibition of enlarging farms through the purchase of additional land also affected the financial structure of Mennonite economy. For in this way credit was made available within the colonies at a time when investment capital was in great demand, namely, after the Government and Ontario loans had been repaid. Such credit could either come from commercial banks, loan corporations, and other non-Mennonite investors, or be raised within the group itself. The latter was more desirable for several reasons. Outside loans tended to drain profits away and entailed the danger that foreclosed holdings would be sold to non-Mennonites. Mennonite credit, on the other hand, was inexpensive and, above all, without risk. While the *Waisenamt* required promissory notes, an oral agreement and a pencil note in a ledger sufficed between private parties. Mortgages would have been of little use, for Mennonites were not permitted to go to court. Abuses seem to have been extremely rare even where great sums were involved. It was unheard-of that anyone should ever try to deny the facts even in contested cases. For the content of contracts soon became public knowledge; moreover, the reliability and honesty of the partners were subject to public scrutiny. Thus informal social controls were much more potent in enforcing contracts than any legal action could have been.

As a last resort, the church had to decide a contested case. Since Mennonite churches were unanimous in their interpretation of proper conduct in such matters, there was no loophole through which an individual could escape his obligations. On the other hand, the letter of a contract was always interpreted in the spirit of Christian justice and charity. If a debtor was really unable to meet his obligations, the creditor could not insist upon his rights, but had to make adjustments. He was morally bound to consider the welfare of a tardy debtor, and particularly of his family, to the extent that he was compelled to advise and to guide him in the management of his farm until he was able to repay his debts. There is not one tale known among the Manitoba Mennonites of Shylocks and usurous money lenders, although the folklore of other peasant societies usually abounds in such characters.

The Mennonite economic system was supported by yet another institution, fire insurance.[13] It was known in the Lower Vistula region as early as 1526, and probably was of non-Mennonite origin. In Russia it had been fully incorporated into the autonomous administration of their colonies and village communes, to the extent that the *Brandschulze* acted not only as the local fire marshall but also as insurance agent. With the downfall of village self-administration in Manitoba, the institution first became a responsibility of each church, but was later converted into a mutual insurance association (except among the Fürstenland people). Organized on a regional basis, the insurance was managed by the *Brandältester*, or district fire chief, aided by the local *Brandschulze* and assessors. Although apparently compulsory in earlier years, insurance was by and large voluntary, and extended to private farms as well as communal property; most associations, however, excluded other businesses or insured them only to a limited amount. The value of every property was assessed prediodically according to a different system than that used for tax assessments or assessments of estates. The insurance value was usually two-thirds of the actual market value, and stores of grain or livestock were assessed according to fixed rates. The total value of all property insured at any given period with a fire insurance association was made the basis of any future computation of premia. Any losses suffered by an individual insuree through fire or lightning were at once appraised by the local *Brandschulze* and assessors. Their report was sent to the *Brandältester*,

---

[13] Cf. J. W. Fretz, "Mutual Aid Among Mennonites," *Mennonite Quarterly Review* 13 (1939): 51.

who remitted two-thirds of the amount from current funds. The sum was then collected on a pro-rata basis from all the other insurees and returned to the fund. A fictitious example will clarify this method. If the loss suffered by an individual amounted to 2 per mil of the total value of property insured with the association, each of the other insurees had to pay a premium of 2 per mil of the insured value of his own property. Later records mention rates as low as $\frac{1}{2}$ per mil. The system was thus very simple, efficient and inexpensive, while strict social controls limited the factor of risk to acts of God alone.

As a last type of institutions supporting, or rather supplementing, the socio-economic system of the Manitoba Mennonites, those of public welfare have to be mentioned. As in other familistic societies, the care of those unable to provide for their own subsistence was primarily a function of the kinship group. Where it failed, the local community stepped in either through informal aid from neighbour to neighbour, or through more formal measures such as boarding destitute residents with private families at the expense of the commune or occasionally placing them in separate poor houses. Yet public relief on the village level was never of great importance in Manitoba.

It is necessary to distinguish between formal institutions of public welfare in charge of the civil authorities and works of voluntary charity under the auspices of the church. In Russia, a beginning had been made with the organization of public welfare in a modern sense, such as tax-supported hospitals. In Manitoba, the economic difficulties of the pioneer period and the early disruption of Mennonite self-administration blocked the revival of such practices. In the field of public health the Mennonites became dependent on services provided by the Provincial or Municipal authorities from general tax funds. Poor relief, on the other hand, was blended with the charities organized by the churches. Every one of them had a special officer, called *Diakon* (deacon), who was entrusted with the collection and distribution of funds. At the same time, the *Oberschulze* levied a regular poor tax on the villages under his jurisdiction. Even after the breakdown of territorial autonomy, there remained the moral obligation of contributing a set portion of the harvest to central stores kept in the specially fortified attics of church buildings or, later on, in separate bins.

In addition to these more or less obligatory levies for the poor, a variety of charitable activities were carried out by the churches. Little of what was really done has become known publicly because the

Mennonites were, and still are, rather shy about advertising charity, which they consider primarily as an act of religious worship. All donations remained anonymous; there was no passing around of collection plates during church services, but many a silent offering was slipped unnoticed into the boxes at the back of the churches. Needs were announced from the pulpit and the deacon would inform well-to-do church members privately of some particular emergency. This brought ample response, although a donor could not expect any acknowledgement other than a grave nod and a murmured "Vergelt's Gott" (May God reward you).

Mennonite charity was extended as much to outsiders as to group members. Although few records have been preserved, individual receipts have been found, for instance, of donations made to non-Mennonite Germans in Winnipeg. It is also known that the Manitoba Mennonites participated in a relief action for their brethren in Russia in or around 1910. In 1915 the Municipality of Rhineland raised $1,765.45 to ship a carload of flour to Belgium. A still larger sum was collected by three Mennonite churches for the Manitoba Patriotic Fund, amounting to 5 per cent of the funds raised in the province outside of Winnipeg. On a single page of the Blumenort village records, covering the period from July 26 to December 28, 1923, four charities (in addition to payment for the funeral of an old neighbour recorded on another page) are mentioned including collections for "German Children," "Poland" and "Mexico" (the latter may or may not refer to Mennonites) and the reception of Russländer refugees in homes. These few isolated instances, however, do not present a full picture of the scope of Mennonite charitable contributions made outside their colonies.

On the other hand, the Mennonites were always very reluctant for their own poor to accept any money from public funds. H. H. Hamm reports that, before the Depression, any relief money ever paid out by the Municipality of Douglas-Rhineland had gone exclusively to non-Mennonite residents. Only English names are found among the local recipients of seed-grain which was distributed by the Government in 1889 among indigent farmers in the province. "Unemployment relief as such from public funds," writes Hamm, "was unknown in our community, as the various church congregations took care of their own needy members." But in the Depression "the demand for assistance in charity exceeded the supply of the churches with the result that municipal councils, urban and rural, had to tackle the relief problem under Dominion-Provincial jurisdiction."[14]

The preceding discussion has revealed that economic action among the Mennonites was oriented according to group-centered, and largely non-economic, values. The economy was controlled by specific institutions, and in part deliberately planned by leaders in such a way that the group as such would benefit most. Inter-group contacts were limited to trade, leading to more rapid and more complete acculturation in the economic than in any other sphere of life. Though closely interwoven with the general economy of Canada's West, Mennonite economy in the areas of compact settlement retained a measure of distinctiveness and independence. Differences between the two Reserves were mainly due to the natural environment. Nevertheless, response to the topography followed patterns which differed characteristically from the adjustment made by non-Mennonites to similar environmental conditions. The Mennonites utilized natural resources, technical improvements and markets so successfully that, within a relatively short time, one finds prosperity in the more favored Reserve, and a moderate but still comfortable level of living in the other one. At the same time they maintained an even distribution of wealth and a high degree of social security.

---

14 *Sixty Years of Progress*, p. 16.

CHAPTER VI

Expansion

Invasion of the Reserves

IN STUDYING the development of Mennonite colonies in Manitoba one is struck by the dogged effort of the ethnic group to occupy contiguous tracts of land, to prevent outsiders from settling in its midst, and to expand compact settlements along their fringes rather than permit its members the acquisiton of new land elsewhere. The conscious aim was the preservation of social and cultural homogeneity in the local communities, the formation of ever larger territorial units to resist all the better outside influences, and the maintenance of almost complete isolation from the "world." These objectives were realized by what may be aptly called a deliberate Mennonite land policy initiated by the various branches of their church. The practical arrange-ments, on the other hand, which were necessary to bring such a policy to fruition were left to private individuals, often men of means, or to voluntary action groups formed whenever the need arose.

The generous land grants which had originally been made to the corporate body of Russian Mennonites in Canada have never been fully utilized by them. As early as 1879 it became evident that the immediate occupancy of all this land by them was out of the question.[1] At the same time, Mennonite successes in the plain between the Red River and the Pembina Mountains whetted the appetites of the Ontario settlers who by now began to arrive in ever increasing numbers. Land speculators, too, resented the withdrawal from the market of the choicest morsel of free land in the province. Thus in 1881 the

---

[1] Cf. *Journals*, 1879, appendix 1, p. 17.

Government took notice of the "great pressure . . . brought to bear upon the Minister of the Interior by those desirous of securing" un - occupied land in the West Reserve, which was described as "exceptionally valuable, conveniently situated, very eligible . . . for farming purposes."[2] This, in fact, was only part of a much broader attack by the Conservative Party, returned to power in 1879, upon the Dominion Lands policy of its predecessor. When the original grant was about to expire toward the end of 1881, the Mennonites petitioned for its renewal. Not that they were in any immediate need of all the reserved land, but they were anxious to keep substantial land reserves close to their present settlements for their children. Political reasons compelled the Dominion Government to avoid any clear-cut decision, even though the pressure of public opinion tended to become less urgent with the collapse of the Manitoba land boom in the following year. The authorities issued periodic threats to open one or the other of the Mennonite Reserves to the general public, but nothing came out of it.[3] Nevertheless, considerable changes in land ownership had taken place long before the last period of grace expired at the end of 1896.

In the beginning the Mennonite colonies covered only part of each Reserve and tended to expand within the limits of the liberal grants. In the course of time, however, the Mennonites themselves yielded portions of the reserved lands to non-Mennonites and acquired other parcels outside of their boundaries. Although the Mennonites considered the whole reserved area as theirs, the meaning of the word "Reserve" became eventually attached to the territories actually occupied by them, particularly after the original grants had expired. In order to avoid confusion, the historical term "Reserve" will be used henceforth to indicate the two compact Mennonite settlements, while the territory set aside for their exclusive use by law before 1897 will be referred to for the purpose of the present discussion as reserved lands or reservations. At the time when the Municipalities of Hanover, Douglas and Rhineland were incorporated, only a few non-Mennonite resident farm owners were living within any area of compact Mennonite settlement; most of them were Anglo-Saxons located along the fringes of the Reserves who had squatted there even before the Mennonite reservations had been made. In addition, several sections of land

---

[2] Cf. *Free Press*, August 31, September 3, 15, 29 and October 17, 1881; *Hansard*, 1881, debates of March, 1881.

[3] Cf. *Orders-in-Council* of January 17, 1885, of May 6, 1885, of October 28, 1886, and others.

situated within the Mennonite colonies were owned but not farmed by non-Mennonite individuals. As long as sufficient good land was available elsewhere, few if any of these land owners ever contemplated settling among the Mennonites. They acquired and held such parcels only in the expectation of realizing a good price once the ever land-hungry Mennonites were forced to buy up all property within their reach.

In the Municipality of Rhineland, for instance, only 1,760 acres located within the compact Mennonite settlement were owned by outsiders, among them an Ontario Mennonite and a businessman of Gretna. In the Municipality of Douglas the situation was quite similar at that time but changed substantially within a few years, during which several properties were acquired by outsiders from Mennonite debtors unable to meet their obligations. Thus we find that by 1889, of a total of 97,582 acres of occupied land, as many as 16,139 acres were registered under the names of Gretna burghers, Jacob Y. Shantz (1,200 acres), some other Ontario Mennonites, as well as several English, French, Polish and Jewish investors. Yet, wherever possible, land which for one reason or another came on the market was often bought by Mennonites so that it might not fall into the hands of outsiders, and was resold, possibly without any profit, to one of their brethren. In 1889, for instance, 1,120 acres were entered in the assessment roles under the name of an individual Mennonite who apparently held the land in trust for communal interests, while legal title to another 320 acres was held by a corporation called Mennonite Association of Reinland.

In contrast to the scramble for land on the west side of the Red River, much land in the East Reserve remained unoccupied or was actually abandoned by its original Mennonite owners. Many of those who moved to the West Reserve, or who had failed in their pioneer efforts, were ready to sell their quarter-sections of partly improved land to anyone offering a reasonable price, or any price at all. Investors were little attracted by the conditions in the Municipality of Hanover, although occasionally outside businessmen acquired property rights in lieu of unpaid debts. By the same token, here immigrants with limited means found an opportunity to buy cheap land on the fringes of the compact Mennonite settlement, particularly next to the railroad station of Niverville, and east and south of Steinbach. This situation is clearly reflected in the assessment roles of the Municipality for 1898. There were two blocks of bona-fide farm owners adjacent to the Menno-

140

nite colonies, namely, the Clearspring Settlement in the northwest corner of the Municipality which included close to two dozens Anglo-Saxon proprietors holding title to 5,620 acres, and the Friedensfeld Settlement of German Lutherans with 4,860 acres. The other outsiders were absentee landlords, such as a Jewish merchant owning three quarter-sections of partly improved land, a man from Ontario (two quarter-sections), an Ontario Mennonite (one quarter-section), Shantz (400 acres), Altona and Gretna businessmen (four quarter-sections), an English investor (3,630 acres), and a Winnipeg loan company (four quarter sections).

According to the original land grant, the Clearspring Settlement had comprised nine sections. It had been founded about four years

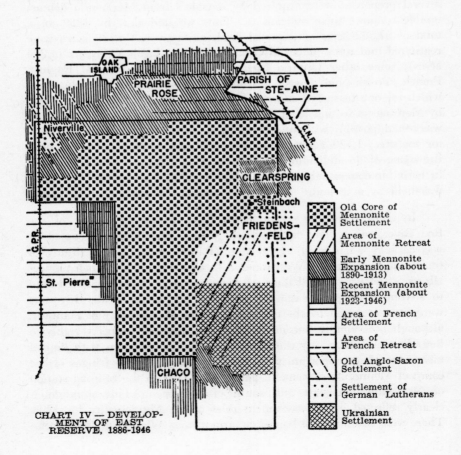

CHART IV — DEVELOP-
MENT OF EAST
RESERVE, 1886-1946

before the first arrival of the Mennonites. At its height, the colony comprised about 30 to 40 families, some from Ontario, others from the Old Country. As these Scotch Presbyterians were otherwise surrounded by French Catholics, they were naturally inclined to associate more closely with their Mennonite neighbours, and to use Steinbach as their trade center. During the years when few Mennonites knew any English, the Clearspring settlers learned to speak Mennonite Platt. Intermarriage was not uncommon and some conversions to the Mennonite faith occurred. The gradual decline of this enclave, which by 1946 comprised only about six families, is due partly to the relatively low fertility of this group, and in part to their tendency to drift away to ethnically and culturally more congenial sections of the country, such as Pilot Mound and Grandview.

The second ethnic group with which the Mennonites came to live in close association were German peasants from Eastern Europe, mainly Lutherans who arrived in Western Canada after about 1890.[4] The background of these people was very similar to that of the Russian Mennonites who had come as an avant-guarde some fifteen to twenty years earlier. But while the Mennonites, at least in Canada, settled as a group, the German Lutherans migrated as individuals and in small bands, usually without institutional backing. Whenever an opportunity presented itself they associated with fellow-countrymen and coreligionists, forming derivative ethnic groups. Many of the German Lutheran immigrants came from the Ukraine, where they had lived under the same colonial law as their Mennonite neighbours. Others arrived from Volynia, and much smaller numbers of them from Galicia and Southern Hungary; that is, parts of the Austro-Hungarian rather than the Russian Empire. The success of the Mennonites in Manitoba, well advertised by press and grape-vine all over Eastern Europe, influenced not only their decision to emigrate but also their choice of a new country.

Some of the German Lutherans coming to Canada turned first to the Mennonite Reserves in Manitoba and worked there for a while as hired help. According to the census of 1891, there were 50 Germans in the East Reserve and over 200 in the West Reserve; ten years later, the figures were 1,000, and 200 to 300 respectively. The Germans were well received by the Mennonites, who called them *Hochdeutsche*

---

[4] Cf. H. Lehmann, *Das Deutschtum in Westkanada* (Berlin, 1939), particularly chapter 4.

to distinguish them from German-speaking Mennonites.[5] While a clear sociological distinction was thus maintained between the Mennonite in-group and the "High German" out-group, it was not quite as emphasized as the distinction between the Mennonites and their French-Catholic or Anglo-Saxon neighbours, or the non-German immigrant groups arriving later.

Many of the German Lutherans soon moved on to Saskatchewan, but others indicated the desire of acquiring land near their Mennonite employers. In this they were actively aided, through credit and advice, and in some instances even through deliberate arrangements facilitating the foundation of compact colonies. It would appear that in the largely depopulated area south and east of Steinbach the few remaining Mennonite farmers left voluntarily to make room for the German Lutherans who established the Friedensfeld settlement there. In the West Reserve, on the other hand, Lutheran colonies sprang up in areas which, though once included in the Mennonite reservation and now incorporated in predominantly Mennonite municipalities, had never been actually occupied by Mennonite farm operators. West and north of the railroad station of Rosenfeld, close to an old Mennonite village of the same name, the German Lutherans took over some wet lands which, just then, were being drained. Other tracts of land, though less compact, were bought by them north of Winkler.

Besides German-speaking Lutherans and Catholics, still other groups of East European immigrants were drawn to the Mennonite colonies in Manitoba, above all Ruthenians[6] and later Jews. While most of the Ruthenians started out as railroad workers and farm hands, the Jews settled in the rural trade centers. Some of the Ukrainians were directly influenced in their choice of Canada by what had become known of it through the Mennonite grapevine. Others sought employment on Mennonite farms because there they met with less suspicion and hostility than among Anglo-Saxons, and had less difficulty of communication. Not only were most of the older Mennonites familiar with their language, but many of the Austrian Ruthenians had picked up

---

[5] The reason for the designation, meaning High Germans, is not quite clear, as most of the non-Mennonite German immigrants spoke Low German dialects related to Mennonite Platt, though not identical with it. In Russia, apparently all non-Mennonite Germans were referred to by this term, many of whom spoke indeed High German dialects. Moreover, due to the great dialectical differences which prevail between German-speakers, the lingua franca among Mennonites and non-Mennonite Germans was literary German, also called High German.

[6] Cf. Paul Yuzik, *The Ukrainians in Manitoba: A Social History* (Toronto, 1953).

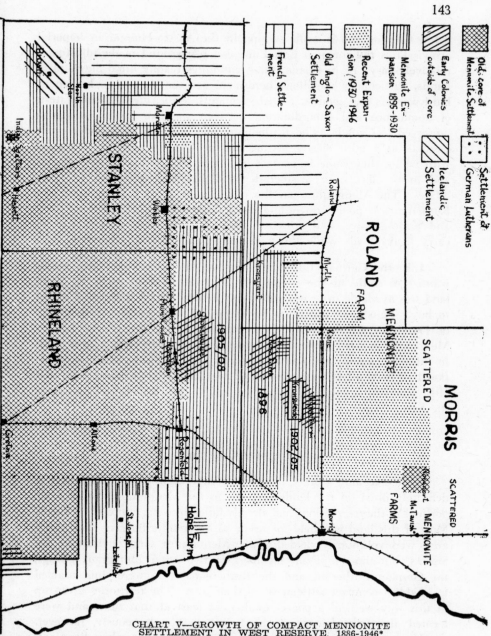

CHART V—GROWTH OF COMPACT MENNONITE
SETTLEMENT IN WEST RESERVE, 1886-1946*

* This simplified sketch is based on a variety of oral, published and unpublished sources. A more
detailed compilation for the early 1930's may be found in C. A. Dawson's "Group Settlement,"
p. 108. For accurate changes in the western boundaries of the West Reserve see below Chart VI.

a few German words while serving in the Austro-Hungarian imperial army. Thus the common East European background made adjustment relatively easy. As in Russia, the Mennonites readily hired Slavic farm hands, particularly as village herdsmen, because they were known as hard workers and modest in their demands. As a rule, the old pattern of dominance and subordination between the two groups was also preserved in Canada. The Ruthenians were inclined to consider every German as a born master because in the Old Country the Germans with whom they came in contact had been mostly omnipotent officials and army officers, or aristocratic landlords and managers of large estates. The Mennonites, on the other hand, looked down upon the Ruthenians as poor farmers and petty thieves. They called them dirty and unprogressive, and criticized them because their women had to carry heavy loads while the men walked ahead empty-handed.

Like the German Lutherans, some of the Ukrainian farm hands wanted to settle in the Mennonite colonies. But by then no more land was available in or near the West Reserve which they could afford to buy. Thus they turned to township 5-6 East in the Municipality of Hanover. In the early days part of it had been occupied by Mennonite homesteaders. Since then, however, the whole area with its inferior, swampy soil and remoteness from all means of communication had been all but abandoned. It was here that between 1900 and 1914 the Ruthenians created a settlement which became known as the Sarto district.

Daughter Colonies

The preceding section has shown that even before the ban was definitely lifted on the lands reserved to the Mennonites, considerable portions of the reservations had already fallen into the hands of outsiders. Most of this land was held for resale to Mennonite farmers. Still other areas were voluntarily yielded to non-Mennonites, some of them Anglo-Saxons, but most of them members of two other immigrant groups, the German Lutherans and the Ruthenians, who were thus enabled to establish compact settlements of their own. The territories given up in this way were of a poorer quality, at least at that time, and were located along the fringes of the Reserves. Simultaneously, however, the Mennonites expanded their own land holdings in other directions, partly beyond the limits of the three municipalities which included the core of their settlements, partly by the foundation of daughter colonies outside Manitoba.

As early as 1889, reports reached the Canadian Government that the Manitoba Mennonites were in search of more land and that there was danger of their emigrating to the United States. A Government agent was despatched to investigate the matter on the spot. His report reflects the situation very well:

I met [wrote the officer with regard to the East Reserve] with some grumblers who appeared to be inclined to leave their lands and go over to the United States where they have friends and relatives . . . the greatest grievance, however, about which the Mennonites in this country complain, is that they have not land enough for their fast-increasing families in their Reserves here, and that even some of the land which they possess, is in many places too stony and sandy for proper and advantageous cultivation . . . [The children who, at the time of their immigration, had been small] have grown into men and women now, have married, and have got issue of their own. The old homestead is not now sufficient to support the whole family. Where the father has had means he has bought land, either adjoining or at some distance, for some son or son-in-law as the case might be. He is, however, unable thus to provide for three or four boys, or as many girls, and hence a keen desire on the part of the younger people for pastures new. This is perhaps the principal reason why we have heard of dissatisfaction and emigration schemes amongst the Mennonites. . . . The old people would willingly remain where they are; but if the younger people go it may not be so easy to keep the former back, as these people dread and are adverse to separation from their kindred.

Concerning the West Reserve, the agent reported that there

the trouble is greater, notwithstanding that they have had better crops there than in the East Reserve. The Western Reserve is much larger, contains a great many young men, who are also more enlightened, numbers of them knowing the English language thoroughly. These wish to spread out, and unless good inducements are held out to retain them on this side of the boundary line, they may do a good deal of harm.[7]

What strikes one most forcibly here is the fact that it has not always been religious issues which caused the Mennonite migrations. These periodic eruptions and strong urges for migratory moves were motivated by socio-economic factors to a greater extent than commonly thought. The Mennonite institutions were particularly adjusted to the ethos of typical colonizers; while blocking the pulverization of farm holdings and maintaining a rather comfortable level of living for all, they required at the same time continuous additions of new land,

---

[7] Report on Mennonite Colonies by Henry C. Jacobson, Dominion Government Intelligence Officer, to the Minister of Agriculture, Ottawa, of September 9, 1889 (*Sessional Papers*, 1890, vol. 5 no. 6, pp. 146ff.).

primarily unimproved and thus inexpensive land, either through contiguous expansion of the original colonies or through the foundation of daughter colonies. In a way, the tendency to migrate is characteristic of all peasant societies with their usually high fertility rates. Yet in the case of the Mennonites many of the alternatives with which other peasant societies have solved the ever present land problem, were excluded by the way of life sanctioned by their religion. As a perpetual minority they were unwilling to see their young people go into industries or urban trades, thus risking their loss through assimilation. At the same time, the standard-size family farm on reasonably fertile land appeared to them the safest bulwark in their struggle for self-preservation as a group. As long as opportunities of establishing their surplus population after the traditional pattern still existed, they also rejected any measure adversely affecting their customary standard of living. On the other hand, their long history of periodic migrations made the Mennonites less attached to home and soil than most other peasant groups. Like the Jews they were not "at home" in any definite geographical space, but wherever they went they recreated their "home" by recreating their institutions and pattern of life. Their talk of migrating to the United States en bloc was perhaps not meant seriously, but was mainly used to exert pressure upon the Canadian Government. Still, the mere toying with a thought usually so abhorrent to peasant farmers indicates that they put greater weight on social than on local stability.

The cry for more land, that is, for more land suitable to their type of farm economy and social organization, came at the opportune moment when the Dominion Government began to open up the North-West Territories for large-scale immigration and colonization. It was then a relatively simple matter for any individual to obtain assistance for transportation, housing and supplies from one of the many land agencies set up to promote settlement, or to acquire a homestead on the easy terms of the Dominion Lands Act. Like other Manitoba farmers, many of the Manitoba Mennonites were thus going west after 1890. They were joined by other Mennonites from Ontario, Kansas, Nebraska, Minnesota, North Dakota, and even Prussia and Russia. The Mennonite immigration from the United States in particular was actively supported by the Dominion Government which, in and after 1891, sent Hespeler and Manitoba Mennonites repeatedly across the border to advertise the new settlement scheme. According to official documents 300 new Mennonite immigrants arrived in Western

Canada in 1891, 600 more in the following year.[8] Some of these apparently went to Didsbury and Carstairs in Alberta, where they were joined by Ontario Mennonites from Waterloo County in 1893.[9] The largest settlement of Mennonites outside of Manitoba, however, grew up along the new branch line of the Canadian Pacific Railway leading from Regina to Saskatoon. In November 1893 the immigration agent of Prince Albert reported to Ottawa: "The only colony we have in this district is that of the Mennonites. They are steadily coming, some from Manitoba, others directly from Russia. They occupy a stretch of country south of Duck Lake . . . in the townships 40-44, ranges 2-5 West of the Third Meridian."[10] This is the first official mentioning of the later so-called Rosthern district. In the following year, 200 more settlers arrived, and in 1894 twice as many. For 1895, 250 arrivals were reported, and by 1896, Rosthern and Hague were described as prospering Mennonite villages.[11]

At first, the movement of Manitoba Mennonites to Saskatchewan was unorganized and haphazard, and thus against the intentions of responsible leaders. It seems that the Fürstenland group took the initiative in creating a new Reserve in the Rosthern-Hague district. An Order-in-Council, of January 23, 1895, refers to a petition of Manitoba Mennonites stating

that their two reserves in that province are now overcrowded owing partly to the influx of their fellow-countrymen from the United States and Europe, and partly to the natural increase which has taken place since their first settlement in Manitoba; and that, in order to meet the growing needs of their families, and to encourage the settlement of their fellow-countrymen in Canada, it became necessary for them to ask the Government to establish a Reservation for them from lands in the Prince Albert district.

The document adds that the odd-numbered sections were to be bought from railroad companies, and that it was the intention of the Mennonites to assist new settlers from abroad with their own means. Finally, the assurance was given to the petitioners "that they will be enabled to carry out the principles of their social system and to settle together in hamlets by obtaining entries for contiguous land." Thereupon, the

---

[8] Cf. *Sessional Papers*, 1892, no. 7, app. 12; 1892, no. 37; and 1893, no. 13.

[9] For a very short time there also existed a small settlement of Ontario Mennonites at St. Elizabeth in Manitoba. Cf. L. J. Burkholder, *A Brief History of the Mennonites in Ontario* (Markham, 1935), p. 135.

[10] *Sessional Papers*, 1894, no. 13, p. 146.

[11] These and other details are given in *Sessional Papers*, 1896, no. 13, p. 8; and 1897, no. 13, pp. 14 and 125; see also Lehmann, *Deutschtum*, p. 165ff.

migration of members of the Fürstenland group in Manitoba to the area was officially encouraged and several open-field villages were organized by them around Hague and Warman. By 1897 the Mennonite colony in northern Saskatchewan extended over townships 40-44, ranges 3-6 West of the Third Principal Meridian. For that year the total number of families living there was given as 250, equal to approximately 1,200 to 1,400 souls.

It does not appear that any great financial efforts were made by the Manitoba Mennonites to attract immigrants from Russia and Prussia, while those from the United States were able to look after themselves. To settlers coming from the Manitoba colonies, however, loans were extended either by private individuals or the Fürstenland *Waisenamt,* which in this case required mortgages contrary to its established practice. Moreover, the *Oberschulze* levied a special tax of $10 per quarter-section, and of $2.50 from each landless family, to provide indigent families with the necessary means for moving to Saskatchewan. But only 18 to 20 families are said to have been supported in this way. More often, well-to-do Mennonite farmers seem to have privately contributed to the migration by buying up run-down farms in the Manitoba Reserves, thus enabling their former owners to leave.

Although no further grant of land was ever made collectively to Mennonites in Canada, other smaller colonies made their appearance elsewhere in the West. In 1901 nineteen families and five single persons from Plum Coulee joined their brethren from Ontario and the United States in Alberta, where several Mennonite settlements were founded before World War I: the first was Didsbury, followed by Drake (1904), Lost River (1911) and Carnduff (1915). In 1907 a colony was established at Renata in British Columbia. After 1903 the town of Herbert in Saskatchewan became a Mennonite center; by 1905 one hundred families, mostly new-comers from Russia, were living in the district. The colony around Swift Current was started in 1904 by members of the Sommerfeld church in the West Reserve, who like the Fürstenland people managed to revive village habitat in Saskatchewan.

Growth of the Manitoba Colonies

In addition to the founding of daughter colonies, which brought some relief from population pressure, the Manitoba Mennonites began to extend their land holdings also beyond the original boundaries of the Reserves. This movement was in part assisted by the progress of Provincial drainage projects by which more and more stretches of superior land were made available for settlement. In the East Reserve, the Greenland colony, first founded by Holdemann people on the village territory of Blumenort, was gradually expanded into the neighbouring French Municipality of St. Anne. The general area adjoining the East Reserve to the north was known among the Mennonites as *Brettensteppe* (meaning half-breed steppes), because it had been originally set aside for the French half-breeds, who had made little use of it. Although marshy and not very inviting, land could be bought cheaply here from the Hudson's Bay store at St. Anne, or from any number of speculators and owners of half-breed scrips. During World War I, the Holdemann people pushed their colony into the parish of St. Anne itself. By 1925 there were 15 Mennonite families in the parish, 10 of whom were new immigrants from Russia. All but 7, however, left again, because they did not wish to send their children to a French-Catholic school.

During World War I, the Kleine Gemeinde people established a new settlement in township 8-5 East, which includes the districts of Landmark and Prairie Rose. Eventually the compact Mennonite settlement was extended in the north of the Municipality of Hanover from Ile-des-Chênes, the Oak Island Settlement and the edge of the Parish of Lorette far into the hay marsh formed by the waters of the Seine River between Lorette and St. Anne. Towards the east, the Mennonites first acquired the school sections in township 7-7 East and farms given up by the Clearspring Anglo-Saxons, but eventually penetrated into the Municipality of La Broquerie within a short distance of Giroux and the tracks of the Canadian National Railway. (See Chart IV.)

The Bergthal group in the East Reserve at first showed much less expansionist tendencies than the Kleine Gemeinde group and its offshoot, the Holdemann group, mainly because the West Reserve offered them better opportunities for resettlement. In fact, they not only retreated along the southeastern border of their original territory to make room for German Lutherans and Ukrainians, but also permitted land in township 7-4 East to fall into the hands of outsiders. According to a survey undertaken in 1917, fully 35 per cent of the township was owned by non-Mennonite absentee landlords, mostly banks and speculators. Only 45.5 per cent of the area was occupied by

Mennonite farm owners or tenants, another 8.6 per cent by Anglo-Saxon farmers, and 9.3 per cent by German Lutheran farmers. In addition, one half-section was owned by a Polish farmer, and not quite one section by two aristocrats from Germany. In the beginning the whole township had been without proper drainage and adequate roads. By the time these drawbacks were removed, much of the land had fallen into the hands of speculators, blocking further agricultural development until the 1920's, when the new Mennonite immigrants from Russia seized available land wherever it could be found. Before that time only one new settlement was founded by the Bergthal group in this Reserve, namely Neubarkfeld, which was colonized from the nearby village of (Alt-)Barkfeld.[12] The Russländer immigration following World War I, not only rapidly filled the empty spaces left by the emigrants to Latin America, but was also responsible for the expansion of compact Mennonite settlement into townships west of the Municipality of Hanover, which, up to then, had been solidly French. In more recent years, a new settlement was founded to the south in the so-called Chaco by Mennonites who had returned from the Gran Chaco in Paraguay.

The Mennonite colony in the West Reserve showed quite similar fluctuations, although the pressure for expansion was greater here due to the better quality of land. Contiguous settlement at first did not penetrate beyond the railroad line connecting Rosenfeld with Winkler because of unsatisfactory drainage. Yet two isolated Mennonite villages, Kronsweide and Grossweide, were founded as early as 1887-1888 in the Municipality of Morris by members of the Bergthal group. At about the same time American companies started commercial wheat mines at Lowe Farm and Rose Farm[13] but failed when their heavy steam plows bogged down in the Red River "gumbo." These commercial farms were soon abandoned as were several homesteads taken up by Anglo-Canadians in about 1882 and later by American farmers from Illinois. After 1897 Mennonites began to move into this area, which was greatly improved by the drainage project organized in 1904 under Provincial auspices.

Another water-logged ridge, between Burwalde and the railroad station of Kronsgart, had been left uncultivated by the Anglo-Saxon

---

12 Both Barkfelds were abandoned when their whole population moved to Paraguay in the 1920's.

13 The original place names were actually Lowe's Farm and Rowe's Farm. Hope Farm, south of St. Jean Baptist, is of a similar origin.

CHART VI—WESTERN BOUNDARY OF WEST RESERVE,
1906-1943†

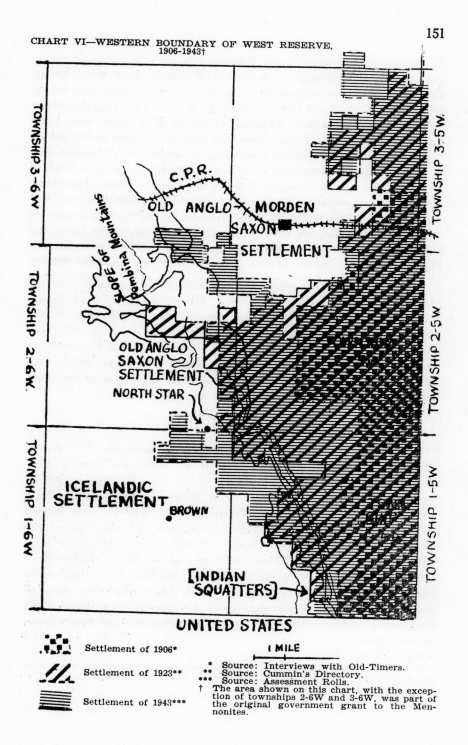

TOWNSHIP 3-6W

TOWNSHIP 2-6W.

TOWNSHIP 1-6W

C.P.R.

OLD ANGLO → MORDEN
SAXON
SETTLEMENT

SLOPE OF Pembina Mountains

OLD ANGLO
SAXON
SETTLEMENT

NORTH STAR

ICELANDIC
SETTLEMENT • BROWN

[INDIAN
SQUATTERS] →

UNITED STATES

TOWNSHIP 3-5W.

TOWNSHIP 2-5W.

TOWNSHIP 1-5W

Settlement of 1906*

Settlement of 1923**

Settlement of 1943***

1 MILE

* Source: Interviews with Old-Timers.
** Source: Cummin's Directory.
*** Source: Assessment Rolls.
† The area shown on this chart, with the exception of townships 2-6W and 3-6W, was part of the original government grant to the Mennonites.

farmers in the Municipality of Roland; this gave the Mennonites an opportunity of acquiring a tract of land which, after the drainage project got under way, turned out to be one of the very best in the whole region. Between 1905 and 1908, the remaining gap between the railroad tracks, Plum Coulee, Rosenfeld, Rose Farm and Lowe Farm was quickly filled by Mennonite settlers. A map published by C. A. Dawson and reflecting conditions in about 1923,[14] reveals that by then the solid Mennonite settlement completely covered a block of 15 townships, and portions of 9 more townships. These boundaries, however, were outdated at the time when the present survey was undertaken. Within 20 years Mennonite land holdings had connected the original West Reserve with the once completely separated Scratching River colony and the new Bathwell-Sperling colony of the Russländer immigrants, at a distance of over 30 miles from the American border.

While the greatest advancement was made to the north into the Municipalities of Morris and Roland, other inroads affected former Anglo-Saxon areas in the west, and French areas in the east. In the west the settlement frontier along the foot of the Pembina hills was as a whole stationary up to 1906 except near the Morden Experimental Farm where one Mennonite village (Schöndorf) was abandoned. Only at one point did the Mennonites invade the slopes of the First Lake Escarpment. As the saying was at the time:

> Wer seine Schulden nicht bezahlen kann,
> Siedelt bei 1-6 sich an.

(Those who can't pay their debts settle in township 1-6 West.) Later the same township was invaded by Icelanders coming from North Dakota, who proved more successful than the Mennonites in the rolling bush land. In recent years, however, the Icelanders have been partly replaced by Russländer immigrants, who by 1946 formed about 25 per cent of the township population. In other places the settlement frontier has been steadily, though slowly, advancing since 1906, particularly in townships 3-6 West and 3-5 West. Today Mennonites are found even on top of the hills but they have consistently avoided slopes. All these advances have been made not through pioneering on new land, as had been the case in many parts along the northern settlement frontier, but at the expense of old Anglo-Saxon settler families.

---

[14] *Group Settlement*, p. 108. Dawson's map is obviously based on *Cummin's Directory* for the year 1923.

The Rise of Towns

As the Manitoba Mennonites steadily increased their farm property, either by accretion along the original settlement frontiers in Manitoba or by creating daughter colonies in Saskatchewan and Alberta, they also invaded the railroad towns founded by non-Mennonites within their colonies. At the same time they expanded some of their farm-operator villages into rural trade centers. In the earlier days Mennonite churches and leaders insisted upon farming as the only acceptable occupation for members of the group. Nearby non-Mennonite towns served as trade and service centers, although small village stores run by some farmer in his front room soon came into existence in several places. How simple it was at the time to go into business is revealed by the following account given by a son of Klaas Reimer, of Steinbach, who was to become the leading storekeeper in the East Reserve:

> [My father] had driven to Winnipeg with [farm] products and dropped in at R. Y. Whitla's drygood store. The man asked my father whether he would like to take some merchandise along to sell among our people. Father said, he hadn't any money and couldn't do it. Thereupon the man had merchandise for about $300 wrapped up for him. He said, father didn't need to give him any money. If he could pay for it later on, that would be fine, if not, that would be alright too. The box in which the goods had been shipped became the counter and did not leave our house until the store was built which can still be seen on Main Street [in Steinbach] and which is called Central Store.[15]

Jewish merchants in Winnipeg, particularly, seem to have encouraged the establishment of small stores in the Mennonite villages. Later on these store owners frequently became prosperous businessmen, like Erdmann Penner who opened his first business in Tannau, at a strategic point along the trail leading from the East Reserve to Winnipeg. Afterward he moved to Niverville on the railroad, then to Neuanlage in the West Reserve, and finally to the new railroad town of Gretna, where he became the leading merchant. Another famous trading post in the East Reserve was Gröning's store in Schönthal. Although most of these village stores were rather short-lived they provided a fair income while they lasted. Much of the local trade was carried on by barter but certain provisions had to be bought either from one of the small Mennonite storekeepers in the villages or from non-Mennonite merchants in the larger trade centers.

---

[15] Cf. *Das sechzigjährige Jubiläum*, p. 28.

The advent of the railroad changed the commercial structure of the colonies, particularly of the more prosperous West Reserve. In 1892 the Canadian Pacific Railway reached the junction near the old Mennonite village of Rosenfeld. In the following year the town of Gretna was laid out on the land of three Mennonite farmers who moved to Eigenhof. In 1885, 48 of the town lots were owned by the railroad company, 24 by Hespeler, and the remaining 31 lots by different individuals, only two of whom were Mennonites. For many years Gretna remained an Anglo-Saxon enclave serving a solidly Mennonite hinterland, but later it was invaded by German Catholics and Lutherans. The Anglo-Saxon businessmen, many of whom became wealthy in the thriving border town, were always treated as strangers and gradually replaced by Mennonites. Gretna's stagnation and eventual decline after 1900 may be largely due to the stiff competition put up by other trade centers in which the Mennonite element was more dominant. Even many of the German families moved away in later years. The railroad town of Rosenfeld was founded at about the same time as Gretna by Anglo-Saxon businessmen. In 1897 it consisted of 3 stores and 1 hotel. By 1919 the German Lutherans, who had their settlement in this area, succeeded the Anglo-Saxons, but were never able to compete successfully with nearby Altona.

The town of Plum Coulee was founded in 1884.[16] Nine years later it included 4 stores with 3 Mennonite, 1 German and 2 Anglo-Saxon partners as owners, in addition to 2 lumber yards, one of which was owned by a Mennonite. By 1897 Plum Coulee had become the largest center for grain shipments from the Reserve with 2 flour mills and 7 elevators. That this town fared better than Gretna and Rosenfeld may be due to the fact that relatively more Mennonites settled here at a rather early time. It also gained some importance as a junction between the Pembina Mountain branch of the Canadian Pacific Railway and a line built in 1907 by the Great Northern Railroad between Gretna and Portage La Prairie, although the portion of the tracks between Plum Coulee and Gretna was torn up in 1926. At the turn of the century there were as many as 37 Jews in Plum Coulee. Generally speaking, Jewish immigrants were frequently drawn to the Mennonite towns in the same way and for much the same reasons as the German and Ruthenian immigrants were drawn to rural

---

[16] Originally, the town was situated one mile east of its present site in a coulee where railway surveyors had picked plums, but later floods suggested the move to a new location. Cf. *Altona Echo*, June 28, 1944.

CHART VII—ETHNIC COMPOSITION, FIVE TOWNS IN WEST RESERVE, 1901-1941

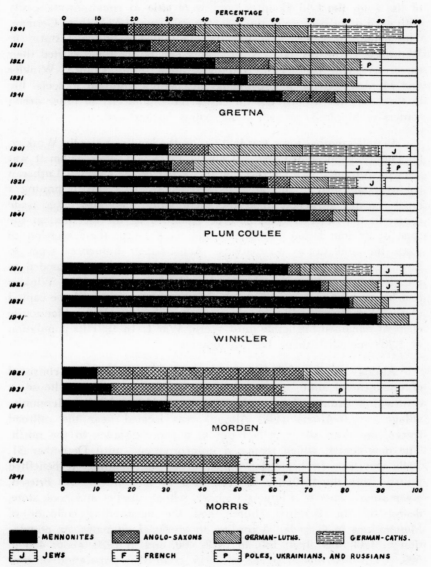

PERCENTAGE

GRETNA

PLUM COULEE

WINKLER

MORDEN

MORRIS

- ■ MENNONITES
- ANGLO-SAXONS
- GERMAN-LUTHS.
- GERMAN-CATHS.
- J JEWS
- F FRENCH
- P POLES, UKRAINIANS, AND RUSSIANS
- OTHERS

Mennonite areas. Both groups were familiar with each other's ways of life from the Old Country, and were able to communicate easily with each other because of the great resemblance of Yiddish to German. The parents of many Jews who later attained high social status in Winnipeg as consuls, lawyers, professors and businessmen started their career as small peddlers in Gretna, Altona, Plum Coulee, Winkler and Morden. As the Jewish immigrants became adjusted to social life in Canada, they usually left for either the capital city or other urban centers in Manitoba as well as for points farther west.

In 1892 another town was laid out on the land of Valentin Winkler, an Ontario pioneer of German Catholic extraction, after whom it was named. Although Winkler became the center of the German Lutheran colony established in this area, it exercised from its very beginning a much greater attraction upon the Mennonites than any other trade center in the Reserve. This may be explained by the fact that at the time of its foundation the Mennonites were losing their aversion to town life and urban occupations. Anglo-Saxon influences seem to have also been less pronounced here while the Mennonites tended to mingle more readily with the German Lutherans. By 1921 Winkler had become the largest town in the Mennonite colonies and the capital of the West Reserve. In Morden, on the other hand, the Mennonite element remained negligible until World War I. In 1921 its population of 1,268 included about 130 Mennonites.

Altona was founded as late as 1895, when its business consisted of one general store, a butcher shop, a hotel, a boarding house, a contracting firm, and a machine agency. Although the Mennonite village of Alt-Altona (Old Altona) was located near the railroad tracks, the town site was laid out at a short distance to the north. The new center, which remained unincorporated until December 31, 1945, was from its beginning predominantly Mennonite. It benefited greatly from the initiative of such men as the late D. W. Friesen, postmaster, owner of a large stationary, school supplies and book store, deacon of the Bergthal church and the outstanding collector of Mennonitica in Canada. According to unofficial estimates, its population in 1900 was about 150, in 1912, 400, and in 1920, about 450 to 500. (The first official census of 1946, counted a population of over 1,000, while the 1951 census recorded its population as 1,438.) At the time of Altona's founding, a grain elevator was built to be followed by 3 more, one of which has in the meantime been destroyed by fire. Although Altona's growth was slow, it became the seat of the rural municipality and an important center of Mennonite business and cultural activities.

Smaller rural trade centers were Haskett and Horndean. The former was located near a railroad built in 1906 from the United States border to Morden which, however, was broken up 20 years later. Yet Haskett has survived on a small scale as a border town. The area around Horndean had been uninhabitable before the drainage system was organized, and was without any source of fresh water. The first settlers had to dig up sod walls around their farms as a protection against north winds and floods. By 1911 a local farmer succeeded in having a flag station set up in front of his cow barn, which afterwards was used as the first store and post office of Horndean. Other businesses were added gradually, namely, a grain elevator in 1914, a garage in 1919, a lumber yard in 1917, a coöperative store in 1936, a second and third garage in 1938 and 1940, and a cafe in 1945, when the population of the town and its immediate hinterland was about 200.

The only railroad town in the East Reserve, Niverville, never attained the same significance as a trade center as did the West Reserve railroad towns. It was overshadowed by several other centers which developed out of old Mennonite villages, or sprang up on crossroads far away from any railroad connection. As late as 1946, Niverville's population did not exceed 260 souls. When the new town was started, the Reserve was on the decline due to the migration to the West Reserve. The rather primitive subsistence economy which prevailed for many years afterwards left little scope for a major railroad and trade center, while the few needs that did exist were easily satisfied by small village stores located more strategically in the colony. On the other hand, whosoever had more important business transactions to attend to apparently preferred combining this with a trip to Winnipeg instead of travelling to Niverville, an unattractive place with limited facilities. The grain elevator built in Niverville as early as 1877 by Hespeler was of little importance to a region producing hardly any grain for sale. When the demand for a major regional trade center finally made itself felt because of an increasing population and greater economic prosperity, Steinbach had already established itself as the unchallenged commercial capital not only for the whole municipality but for a rather extensive hinterland south and east of it.

Although Steinbach continued under the traditional organization of a Mennonite open-field village until 1912, its larger than usual population even at an early date indicates that it was more than just another farm-operator village. While its original plan provided for no more than 22 homesteaders, as many as 49 families lived here in 1898. Its population has been estimated as follows: 1874, 100; 1889, 256; 1905, 450; 1910, 500; 1944, 1,800. The official census figure for 1951 was 2,155. Until World War I, it was a very homogeneous and tightly knit community of Kleine Gemeinde and Holdemann people, where not even members of the Bergthal church were welcome. Although local businesses, such as the mill or the store, played some role in the village economy, Steinbach refused to accept a proposal by the Grand Trunk Railroad Company to run through it its line to southeastern Manitoba. As a result the tracks were laid out eight miles east of the town with a stop called Steinbach Station from 1899 to 1902, but its name was later changed to Giroux. In the beginning both Giroux and La Broquerie, being situated on the railroad, did draw some of the trade away from Steinbach; even some Mennonites opened stores there. But the trend was soon reversed once Steinbach abolished the open-field system, stressing business rather than agriculture. The movements of Jacob S. Friesen's printing press (now Derksen Printers Limited) are in a way typical. Between 1901 and 1912 it was located in Kleefeld, at that time a crossroad center; the two following years in Giroux, and finally, in 1913 it was moved to Steinbach.

The striking development of Steinbach after 1912, the only major trade center in the whole province without a direct railroad connection, is not easily explained. But it seems due in part to the same reasons which made Altona and Winkler eventually outgrow Gretna and Rosenfeld. In all three towns it was Mennonite businessmen who took the lead. It is true that the Mennonites have always traded quite freely with non-Mennonites. The idea of buying only "from our own people" or of boycotting others, for instance, Jews or members of the dominant group, is quite alien to them, even though it is a rather common phenomenon in other areas of nationalistic and inter-group tensions. As a matter of fact, Mennonite businessmen often complain that non-Mennonites have a better chance among their brethren than they themselves. On the other hand, Mennonite customers do show a preference for a type of trading based on personal consideration, trust, honesty, and coöperativeness rather than high pressure salesmanship, efficiency and individualistic competition implied in the principle of *caveat emptor*.

Without making a conscious choice along ethnic lines, the Mennonites thus extended their patronage mainly to businesses run according to their own standards. While Anglo-Saxons, following the rather ruthless American business practices of the time, usually did not do so well, many non-Mennonites, particularly Germans with a similar East European background, found precisely the same response as did the Mennonite businessmen. But even without this background, everybody willing and able to adjust to Mennonite business ways could find a chance to establish himself in these areas. For instance, in the almost purely Mennonite town of Altona, the restaurant owned by a Chinese[17] or the pharmacy owned by a Catholic from North Germany were both well patronized in recent years, while the most successful local physician was a Catholic of Polish extraction.

Another factor contributing to the rise of Steinbach was the flour mill, operated since pioneer days without major interruption but recently destroyed by fire. Its main business up to World War II was custom milling, of particular importance in a region of subsistence farming in which most of the grain grown was consumed domestically. Thus practically every farmer in the district visited Steinbach a few times a year to have his grain ground for flour and for livestock feed. These trips also gave him an opportunity to sell his modest surplus of farm produce, and at the same time to make all the necessary purchases in the local stores. While the better situated Mennonites often travelled to Winnipeg to do their shopping, it was above all the non-Mennonite immigrants and the poorer farmers of a large under-developed hinterland in the southeast corner of the province who depended entirely on the services of the near-by Mennonite town. Consequently Steinbach's present economic dominance has been achieved precisely because of the general lack of good communications in that part of Manitoba. Its strategic position at the edge of a largely unorganized and depressed hinterland which was inhabited by ethnic groups ill-adjusted to Anglo-Saxon ways of doing business, and the special services it provided for a region in which mixed and subsistence farming prevailed, have contributed substantially to the town's growth.

The preceding discussion, concentrating on the economic development of the Manitoba Mennonites until World War I, has revealed the

---

[17] The position of this Chinaman in the Mennonite community is quite unique. Although not accepted in the same way as for instance the German pharmacist or Polish doctor, who have become local leaders, he was nevertheless highly praised for his paternalistic efforts to keep young people in check, preventing them from excessive spending in his cafe, and was regarded a mainstay of the community.

160

rapid growth of their colonies, a steady increase of their land holdings, and a marked expansion and diversification of their business enterprises. They were able to build two little Mennonite empires based on the Municipalities of Hanover and Douglas-Rhineland, and on even wider trading areas which included also non-Mennonite colonies and economic dependencies. This rather complex Mennonite-dominated commonwealth was to a considerable extent segregated from the large society, but sustained by the expanding economy of Canada.

Cairn on the Post Road, near Gretna, commemorating arrival of Mennonites in Manitoba. Unveiled in 1950 in presence of, left to right: David Schellenberg, pioneer settler who donated land for Cairn; Hon. R. F. McWilliams, Lieutenant-Governor of Manitoba; Mrs. M. McWilliams, late president of the Manitoba Historical Society; Hon. W. C. Miller, member of the Provincial Legislature from West Reserve; Diedrich Klassen, pioneer Mennonite settler.

AN OLD FARM HOUSE IN NEUHORST (WEST RESERVE)

ROOF-THATCHING IN A PIONEER VILLAGE. FIRST SCHOOL IN BLUMENORT
(WEST RESERVE)

'VORDERSTUBE' IN OLD MENNONITE HOUSE, WITH 'SCHLAFBANK' IN
BACKGROUND

INTERIOR OF AN OLD MENNONITE FARMHOUSE

TYPICAL MENNONITE FARM BARN AND HOUSE AS SEEN FROM THE
BARNYARD

FARM HOUSE SEEN FROM VILLAGE STREET

DRAW WELL IN FRONT OF OLD
MENNONITE FARM HOUSE

TRADITIONAL SMOKE HOUSE ON
A MENNONITE FARMYARD

A PIONEER MENNONITE FARM WOMAN AT WORK

HISTORIC ROSENORT MILL. BUILT IN STEINBACH IN 1877, DISMANTLED
AND MOVED TO ROSENORT, (NORTHWEST OF MORRIS,) IN 1879. TORN
DOWN FOR ITS TIMBERS IN 1920. ORIGINAL BUILDER, J. H. FRIESEN.

C. F. KLASSEN
(1894-1954)
PROMINENT IN COLONIZATION
AND RELIEF WORK

HENRY H. EWERT
(1855-1934)
A LEADING EDUCATIONALIST
AMONG THE MENNONITES IN
MANITOBA

DAVID W. FRIESEN
(1879-1951)
A MENNONITE BUSINESSMAN IN
ALTONA

JOHANN FUNK
(1836-1917)
BISHOP BERGTHALER CHURCH
AROUND 1900

SOMMERFELDER MENNONITE CHURCH AT RUDNERWEIDE ON WEST
RESERVE

INTERIOR OF AN OLD COLONY CHURCH. NOTE HAT RACKS OVER PEWS,
AND SIMPLICITY OF INTERIOR

A MODERN MENNONITE CHURCH—MENNONITE BRETHREN CHURCH, WINKLER

INTERIOR OF A MODERN CHURCH. FIRST MENNONITE CHURCH (SCHOEN-WIESER), WINNIPEG. BISHOP J. H. ENNS PERFORMING A WEDDING CEREMONY

GRETNA—ABOUT 1930, ONE OF THE FIRST TOWNS AMONG MENNONITES ON WEST RESERVE

A MODERN STREET SCENE IN MENNONITE TOWN OF STEINBACH

GNADENTHAL—A MENNONITE VILLAGE ON THE WEST RESERVE

NEUBLUMENORT—A RECENT VILLAGE SETTLEMENT IN EAST RESERVE

BETHEL HOSPITAL SOCIETY—A MENNONITE HOSPITAL IN WINKLER

BETHANIA OLD FOLKS HOME NORTH OF WINNIPEG

A MORE MODERN MENNONITE HOME. CA. 1945

A MODERN SCHOOL IN MENNONITE TOWN OF WINKLER

A MENNONITE CITY INDUSTRY—MONARCH MACHINERY CO. LTD., WINNI-
PEG. J. J. KLASSEN, PRESIDENT AND FOUNDER

RURAL INDUSTRY—CO-OP. VEGETABLE OILS LTD., ALTONA

A MENNONITE INDUSTRY IN STEINBACH. C. T. LOEWEN'S WOODWORKING
FACTORY, SPECIALIZING IN SASH AND DOORS AND CHURCH PEWS

A MENNONITE INDUSTRY—WINKLER CO-OP. CREAMERY LTD., WINKLER

AFTER SUNDAY SERVICE. A RURAL MENNONITE CHURCH ON THE EAST
RESERVE

A HOLDEMANN MENNONITE (LEFT) AND AN OLD-TIMER (G. G. KORNEL-
SON) IN FRONT OF FORMER POST OFFICE IN HOCHSTADT (EAST
RESERVE)

CHAPTER VII

The Stumbling Block[1]

The Mennonite Private Schools

BETWEEN 1874 and 1883 the Manitoba Mennonites enjoyed complete school autonomy, as promised in the agreement reached by their delegates with the Dominion authorities as a condition of their immigration. This concession, included in clause 10 of Mr. Lowe's letter of July 25, 1873, was based above all on Section 93 of the British North America Act, Canada's Constitution, which reads, in part, as follows:

> In and for each Province the Legislature may exclusively make laws in relation to education, subject and according to the following provisions: 1) Nothing in any such law shall prejudicially affect any Right or Privilege with respect to Denominational Schools which any class of persons have by law in the Province at the time of the Union. 2) Where in any Province a system of Separate or Dissentient Schools exists by law at the Union, or is thereafter established by the Legislature of the Province, an appeal shall lie to the Governor-General-in-Council from any Act or decision of any Provincial authority affecting any Right or Privilege of the Protestant or Roman Catholic Minority of the Queen's subjects in Relations to Education.

Actually, this law had in no way been intended to regulate the school affairs of immigrant groups such as the Mennonites, but was exclusively meant to satisfy the claims of the two major culture groups united in the Dominion, the French Canadians who were concentrated

---

[1] A fuller version of this chapter together with pertinent documents will be found on pp. 204-237 of the *Mennonite Quarterly Review* (vol. 27) of July, 1953, under the title "The Mennonite School Problem in Manitoba, 1874-1919" and "Miscellaneous Documents Concerning School and Military Service."

in the Province of Quebec, and the Anglo-Canadians in the other original provinces. By leaving educational legislation to the Provinces a guarantee was given primarily to the French that they would be able by democratic procedure to protect their cultural interests in Quebec without interference by the Dominion Parliament, where they might have been in danger of being outvoted by an Anglo-Saxon majority. Yet, not all the French lived in the Province of Quebec, which itself included an Anglo-Saxon minority. In order to extend cultural autonomy to these minorities also, the jurisdiction of the Provinces over the school was limited by further constitutional provisions. As revealed in the quotation from the British North America Act, the legal provisions referred to the religious rather than the ethnic side of school administration, and carefully avoided mentioning the French and the Anglo-Saxons as distinct national groups possessing corporate rights. This was suggested by the fact that at that time public as well as private schools were "sectarian." The "dissentient or separate schools" referred to in the Constitution were essentially private parochial schools, while the "denominational schools" were actually public schools organized along religious lines which coincided largely with the major ethnic division between French Catholics and Anglo-Saxon Protestants.

Although the Province of Manitoba did not yet exist at the time of the Confederation, it adopted, following the example of Quebec, denominational schools as the sole official system of public education in 1871. The Provincial school board consisted of a Protestant (Anglo-Saxon) and Roman Catholic (French) section, each of which was empowered to set the standards for all schools under its jurisdiction, to prescribe text books and curricula for the teaching not only of religion but of all subjects, and accordingly to determine the language of instruction. While schools were built and maintained by local boards of trustees, they were subsidized out of the so-called Legislative Grant, a Provincial school fund, which was divided in proportion to the number of Protestant and Catholic school children, and allocated by the section of the Provincial school board having jurisdiction in each particular case. There was nothing, however, by which any religious minority could be prevented from establishing and maintaining private schools out of their own means without submitting them to the supervisory power of a Provincial school board.

This was the legal frame work of Provincial school administration, firmly secured not only in a Provincial statute but in section 22 of the Manitoba Act (a Dominion statute) and the British North America Act (a law passed by the English Parliament), which prompted John Lowe to assure the Mennonites that they would enjoy complete freedom in "the education of their children in schools." Accordingly, upon their arrival the Mennonites set up their own school system after the pattern which had existed in their Russian colonies. Among them the school was essentially a responsibility of the church which laid down general rules, appointed teachers and exercised a strict supervision over all matters concerning education. The maintenance of local schools was delegated to the village commune which also collected the school tax prescribed by the church, which was computed in proportion to property owned in the village territory and took care of the school building. Out of this general property levy also the teacher was housed and provided with fuel, grain, hay, and other contributions which represented one part of his income. On the other hand, the teacher's salary and current school expenses (chalk, books, etc.) were covered by the tuition fee which was computed according to the number of children of school age but collected just like any other tax.

Although there were several Mennonite school systems in early Manitoba, one for each church, they were very much alike. The *Allgemeine Schulverordnung* (general school regulations) of the Chortitz church refers in a preamble to the intention of the Canadian Government, "having granted us the education of our children in the schools by law," that the children should be instructed "according to the principles of our creed." The school was described as a "nursery of Christianity" in which a knowledge of the Bible can be acquired. Accordingly, its main objective was religious instruction and moral education in addition to the teaching of the three R's. School attendance was made compulsory for eight months of each year and for children of school age, that is, from 6 to 12 years for boys and from 6 to 14 years for girls.

Teachers, who were always men and usually married, were appointed once a year, on April 1, by the executive council of the church which also supervised final examinations. These were held publicly in one place for all the schools in a colony, were non-competitive and consisted of songs, recitations from primer and Bible, and exhibitions of work done by pupils during the year. In 1879 an

examination of school teachers took place in Chortitz (East Reserve).
In the presence of elders and preachers of both the Bergthal congregation and the Kleine Gemeinde, 36 teachers were at the time examined
by William Hespeler and two Mennonites (apparently men who had
been certified school teachers in Russia). All teachers were obliged
to attend three or four teachers' conventions a year, at which sample
lessons were given to school classes. The first of these meetings seems
to have taken place as early as the winter of 1876-77. Considering
the time and circumstances, the Mennonite educational system seems
to have been fair enough. It was an essential part of their Protestant
culture and democratic institutions, which required literacy and a
rather high educational standard from every member of church and
secular community. As soon as the most pressing needs were taken
care of, school facilities were provided for and attendance was enforced,
which really was more than could be said of many other pioneer
settlements in Manitoba.

The real weakness of the Mennonite private school should not
be sought in its limited curriculum and conservative teaching methods,
or in its autonomous church-controlled administration. Generally speaking, school and education do not thrive in a vacuum but require the
intellectual stimulus which only interaction with a rather large area
of high civilization can provide. Manitoba's English school could easily
have met with the same fate as the Mennonite German school had
it not remained in constant living contact with the old civilization of
Great Britain and the new civilization which was arising, on a broad
foundation, in the United States. Even in Russia, Mennonite intellectual
life and culture had been somewhat isolated; in Canada they were completely cut off from intercourse with any congenial area of high
civilization. The Mennonite private school also suffered from a lack of
trained teachers, partly because villages, and therefore schools, were
more numerous in Manitoba than in Russia, and partly because some
of the more liberal-minded teachers did not emigrate. Thus, almost
any male who had some schooling in the Old Country and was not fit
for homesteading, was called upon to serve as a school master. The
conditions under which these men had to work were by no means
attractive. In the earlier years one teacher, for instance, received an
annual salary of $40, free lodging and board, whereby the parents of
the children took turns in feeding him at their table. But even as late
as 1890, his salary was no more than $120. In addition he was entitled
to a residence and garden (valued at $20), free pasture for 10 cows

and 2 oxen (valued at $15), fuel ($15), and free tuition for his four children ($20). Moreover, his field of 20 acres was plowed at the expense of the commune (valued at $30) so that his total salary was equivalent of $220. For keeping summer school in July he was paid a dollar a day just like any working man. When he was attending a teacher's convention, he received a daily allowance of $1.25. Finally, he could pick up a few extra dollars by serving as herdsman, janitor, or sexton.

At first the Protestant section of the Provincial School Board seems to have taken no exception to the way in which the Mennonite schools were being conducted or to the use of the German language and foreign texts. At that time its members were more concerned with the power struggle raging between the Anglo-Saxon Protestants and the French Catholics than with the assimilation of a fraternal religious community. Indeed, they offered subsidies out of the Legislative Grant, which in many cases were accepted. By registering with the Board, a Mennonite parochial school, however, would automatically become part of the public school system. Although state supervision over public denominational schools was largely nominal, many Mennonites feared that by the acceptance of a Provincial grant they would eventually deliver their schools to the worldly state.

In 1877 Shantz felt confident in testifying before a Parliamentary committee that the Manitoba Mennonites, despite the privilege granted them, did not want separate schools. His opinion is in part borne out by the census of Protestant (public) schools in Manitoba for 1878 which listed ten Mennonite school districts with 750 pupils (414 boys and 336 girls) while there were 56 English school districts with 3,733 pupils.[2] Only about one-third of all the Mennonite schools, those of the Fürstenland people, were not registered with the Board and thus remained officially "separate" or private schools. But in 1880 the Protestant school census mentioned only six Mennonite public schools with 115 pupils, while the English school districts had increased to 101 with 4,378 pupils.[3] By then the Bergthal and Kleine Gemeinde people in the East Reserve had followed the example of the Fürstenland group and had withdrawn their schools from the public school system. Although they lost thereby the benefits of the Legislative Grant, they "thought better not to act in these matters differently than our brethren

---

[2] Weekly *Manitoba Free Press*, December 21, 1878.

[3] *Free Press*, October 11, 1881.

in the western reserve who had never yet accepted the grant, and we wish to be uniform in our doings." In this way they cut themselves off from all financial subsidies.

Intra-Group Conflict

While other schools in the Province soon began to outgrow the shortcomings of the pioneer period with the help of men and ideas brought in from the older parts of Canada and from Great Britain, the Mennonite schools stagnated and eventually deteriorated as the fund of their educational heritage was gradually exhausted with the passing years. Some of the Mennonites saw the danger of isolation and sought closer coöperation with the Provincial school authorities. The replacement of Mennonite institutions of self-government with the municipal system of local administration gave them the opportunity to organize public school districts within their settlements, and thus to benefit from the educational improvements inaugurated by the Provincial authorities.

At first, however, the movement for district schools was primarily motivated by financial considerations. The Mennonite system bore heavily upon the poorer and larger families, since a greater part of the school tax was assessed according to the number of children of school age. Thus the organization of municipalities was welcomed by many, mainly because under it all the money necessary for school purposes was to be levied on property. In several places, particularly in the Municipality of Douglas, existing private schools were converted into public schools, in others they were retained. Serious troubles arose, however, in those localities of the West Reserve where Bergthal people demanded that a school district be organized while the Fürstenland people opposed such a move. The latter group bluntly refused not only to coöperate with the new municipal administration but also to give up their parochial schools. They considered the organization of district schools under the auspices of municipal councils, even though the administration was in the hands of Bergthal Mennonites, as a direct violation of the Mennonite principle of church control over schools and of the privileges granted to them by the Dominion authorities.

A letter dated September 9, 1885, signed by D. H. Wilson, Provincial Secretary, and addressed to Isaak Müller, of Blumenort, then

Oberschulze of the Fürstenland colony, is very revealing.[4] After referring to a personal interview with Müller, Wilson informed him that he had conferred with the Deputy Minister of Justice at Ottawa as to the application of the Manitoba School Act to the Mennonites in the province. The Minister had agreed with the writer's viewpoint that—

no condition laid down in Mr. Lowe's letter of July 23, 1873, addressed to the delegates from Southern Russia, contradicts the jurisdiction of the local [i.e., Manitoba] legislature with regard to educational affairs. After having carefully examined the said letter, I may further say that I am not of the opinion that the same is acceptable to the consideration which you are inclined to lend it. It is by no means the wish of the Government vis-a-vis your people to pursue an arbitrary policy in these matters, but it is our desire to deal with you in such a generous spirit as your own good and the wish of the majority will permit. In consideration of the above, where a sufficient number desire the education of their children in accordance with the School Act, the Act empowers these to levy from the taxpayers an amount necessary for the efficient operation.

Accordingly, whenever in some locality a Bergthal majority petitioned for a district school, even though the Fürstenland people continued to send their children to their own parochial schools which had to be supported privately, the right of the Municipality to collect the school tax from the Fürstenland people was clearly established. Economic considerations were not the only factor in the drive of the West Reserve Bergthal people to replace the Mennonite parochial school with public district schools. As indicated in an earlier chapter, this group was generally more inclined to adjust themselves to the customs of their Anglo-Saxon neighbours. They were quite receptive to the argument put before them by members of the Provincial School Board, in particular by its chairman, Dr. George Bryce, that they should improve the schooling of their children in order to give them a better chance in the competitive society in which they would have to make a living. In the second place, increasing urbanization among this group underscored the need for a more adequate education and particularly for instruction in the English language. It is significant that many of the leaders in the school reform movement were businessmen from Gretna, Winkler and Altona, all towns within the domain of the Bergthal church.

As a whole, the Mennonites were not opposed on principle to learning English. But they feared, with some justification, that English

---

[4] A copy of this letter is included in the unpublished Elias diary. The original was obviously written in German.

instruction in the school would inevitably lead to a decline in the knowledge of the German church language among the younger generation. It should be realized that for a Mennonite, whose mother tongue is a distinctive Low German dialect, the learning of literary or High German is tantamount to learning a new language, so that the addition of English implied not only bi-lingualism but actually tri-lingualism. Moreover, there were simply not enough Mennonite teachers who were able to teach the English language. To the con-servative church leaders, finally, who insisted upon withdrawal from the world, the language of the outgroup meant dangerous avenues and channels through which strange and undesirable ideas would find entrance into the religious and social life of their flock. This concern was often expressed by saying that young people who knew English "could not be kept at home," and by quoting the old saying: "*Je gelehrter, desto verkehrter*" (the more learned, the more confused). A Fürstenland elder once said "that a knowledge of the English language would make it all the easier for [the children] to lapse into the great world of sin outside of the Mennonite communities."[5] The desire for knowledge beyond that needed for participation in religious functions, local community life, and the occupation of a simple farmer was considered a worldly pretense. If it was not outright evil in itself, it certainly was an occasion for sin.

The struggle for better education among the Mennonites lasted for many decades. By the end of the 1880's, the number of public schools in the Mennonite colonies was once more declining, and the quality of the private schools, too, was decidedly on the downgrade. In view of this situation, a group of members of the Bergthal church in the West Reserve, including Elder Johann Funk and four preachers, went to the root of the evil and stressed better teacher-training as the first step toward better schools. They formed an association which, with the help of private contributions, opened a Mennonite normal school in Gretna in the fall of 1889. But the man hired as teacher was incapable of handling the motley crowd of almost 60 pupils, ranging from candidates for the teaching profession to first-graders. When he resigned at the end of the session, Dr. Bryce and the Menno-nite school association combined their efforts to secure the services

---

[5] A. Willows, A History of the Mennonites, Particularly in Manitoba (M.A. thesis, University of Manitoba, 1924).

of Heinrich H. Ewert, then principal of the Mennonite normal school at Newton, Kansas.

Heinrich Ewert was the son of Wilhelm Ewert, one of the 12 Mennonite delegates of 1873.[6] He spent the formative years of his life in Thorn (West Prussia), where he went to the Bürgerschule (junior high school). It was only after his immigration to Kansas in 1874, that he came in contact with the brethren from Russia. He attended an English grade school, the State Normal School at Emporia, Kansas, the Des Moines Institute (Iowa), and finally the Theological Seminary of the Evangelical Synod at Marthasville, Missouri. Accordingly, his background differed greatly from that of the Russian Mennonites, among whom he was to work as a school teacher and minister of the gospel. In more than one respect Ewert was the type of man who could act as bridge-builder between two cultures and as a leader of his people in their adjustment to modern American and Canadian culture. But he was also in a way a marginal man and shared the fate of the marginal man. While he was working for a compromise, he was blamed by his own people for betraying their best interest and by the Anglo-Saxons for not achieving enough.

Ewert's appointment to the position in Manitoba coincided with the enactment of a new law, which brought about fundamental changes in the system of denominational public school. The Provincial School Board with its sectarian divisions was replaced by a department of education. The modern principle of state-controlled, secular, and tax-supported schools with one official language of instruction was adopted, but certain concessions were made in order to satisfy the claims of the French Catholics and to bring the strictly English public school system into agreement with the Constitution and section 22 of the Manitoba Act. This was done through the Manitoba Public Schools Act of 1890, causing a crisis in the relations between the French and the Anglo-Saxon element in Canada which shook the political and social foundations of the country.

After a long drawn-out struggle in courts and legislatures, the famous Laurier-Greenway Compromise was reached. Amendments to the Manitoba School Act, passed in 1897, permitted not only the teaching of religion in public schools, but also made possible a bilingual system of instruction in schools attended by at least ten pupils whose

---

[6] Cf. Paul J. Schäfer, *Heinrich H. Ewert, Lehrer, Erzieher und Prediger* (Altona, 1954).

mothertongue was not English. Moreover, rural school boards were obliged to employ one qualified Roman Catholic teacher (or one non-Roman Catholic teacher, as the case might be) if petitioned by a sufficient number of rate payers in a school district.[7] Although still phrased primarily in religious terms, the compromise obviously implied a limited school autonomy for ethnic minorities on a local level. In principle, English was made the official language and Anglo-Saxon culture the basis of the public school system; yet other culture groups, insofar as they constituted a majority in a given school district, could require that their children be brought up in the spirit of their own culture by teachers of their own nationality and religious persuasion. While these changes in the Manitoba school system resulted primarily from the struggle for political and cultural dominance by the Protestant Anglo-Saxon majority over the French Catholics, they had their repercussions upon other ethnic and religious groups, above all the Mennonites, who at the time were the most important minority in Manitoba, second only to the French.

If the Provincial authorities showed concern over the problem of public education in the Mennonite settlements, they were guided not so much by the conscious desire of using the school as a means for the effective assimilation of the Mennonites, as by the realization that the Mennonite private schools left a considerable portion of the population without adequate schooling — that is, inadequate according to the educational standards widely accepted in the Anglo-Saxon world. Since the Department of Education had no jurisdiction over private schools, the only hope of doing something about Mennonite education lay in the increase of the number of district schools and in their improvement. With this in mind, the authorities were very much interested in the Gretna normal school project. Although a private institution, it was recognized as a training center for Mennonite teachers; at the same time its new principal, Heinrich Ewert, was appointed official school inspector for all district (that is, public) schools in the Mennonite colonies.

The new school act, however, caused a considerable stir among conservative Mennonites, in particular the Fürstenland group. They were determined to make full use of the loophole left in the law by its failure to make attendance compulsory either at public or at recognized and supervised private schools. Accordingly, they violently

---

[7] Cf. George M. Weir, *The Separate School Question in Canada* (Toronto, 1934), p. 47.

opposed the efforts of the West Reserve Bergthal group under the leadership of their elder, Johann Funk, to develop the district school, coöperate with the Provincial department and make the Gretna institute a center of the school reform movement. They looked with particular suspicion upon Ewert in his double capacity of principal of a private normal school and inspector of public grade schools. As P. J. Schäfer aptly remarks, "they considered it an accomplished fact that the strange man, who was to come here, stood in the service of evil and would only create evil."[8]

However, not only the Fürstenland group took this attitude but also the majority of Elder Funk's own congregation. At the height of the controversy, no less than 415 of a total of 476 families belonging to the Bergthal church in the West Reserve broke away to found the Sommerfeld church with Abraham Dörksen as elder. From then on the partisans for or against the public school were divided, at least in the West Reserve, strictly along religious lines, with the Fürstenland and Sommerfeld churches opposing the reform movement which was under the auspices of the Bergthal church. In the East Reserve, the struggle was much less intense as all three churches more or less agreed upon a conservative school policy. In fact, here the Bergthal church changed its name to Chortitz church in order to demonstrate its disapproval of the West Reserve Bergthal church, from which it had been technically separated since 1885.

Heinrich Ewert reopened the Gretna school in the fall of 1891 with eight students. Although registration eventually rose to 40, actual attendance never exceeded 28 at any one time. In the face of the opposition against the school reform by all except the members of the Bergthal church, he and other leaders of the movement did not hesitate to invoke the state law in order to organize district schools wherever possible. If they could persuade a majority of rate payers in any one locality to petition for a public school, the Municipality would provide the necessary facilities out of taxes to be paid by all residents, regardless of whether they made use of the public school or continued to send their children to the Mennonite private school.

In places where the Bergthal group was unchallenged the old private school was simply converted into a public school; but in others the conservative minority preferred to pay twice, that is, for

---

[8] *Heinrich Ewert*, p. 50.

their own private school and for the public school, rather than permit their children to attend a district school. What made the strife between the enemies and friends of the public school so bitter was the realization that this double taxation was not imposed upon the conservative group by the Government, but was the result of deliberate action on the part of their own brethren. It was of little avail that the advocates of the public school were in a position to point at the rather liberal practice of the public school administration. In their compact settlements — and practically all Mennonites lived in such settlements — they were indeed able to control the teachers through the local school boards and to require instruction in their religion and in the German language, so that the public school was in reality a Mennonite school.

This was precisely Ewert's policy; throughout his life he considered the Mennonite public school not just an Anglo-Saxon school in which a few periods were set aside for religion and German. He was deeply convinced that Mennonite children should be educated in the spirit both of the Mennonite religious and the German national heritage. In fact, Ewert was more consciously German than most of the Russian Mennonites, but he realized also that Mennonite children had to be prepared for life in the Canadian environment and, to some extent, for participation in the large society and its cultural values. Ewert's conception of education and his cultural eclecticism were not easily understood, not even by the Mennonite teachers, upon whose coöperation, in the last analysis, the success of his work depended. The older school masters rarely measured up to the educational standards required for teaching in public schools. Modest as these requirements were in the beginning, they included at least some command of English and some knowledge of Anglo-Saxon institutions on the part of those who were to teach from Canadian text books and in the official language of the country. The authorities actually leaned over backwards and left everyone in his position "who understood school teaching only in some measure," as one old-timer reports. "I cannot remember," he adds, "one case that any one was deposed of his office."[9] Still, the Mennonite private school teachers usually qualified only for temporary teaching permits and had to work hard to keep up with ever stiffening Departmental requirements. They were forced to attend refresher courses provided for them at Gretna, and to pass examinations. Many became

---

[9] P. P. Epp, "Aus meinen Erinnerungen," *Mennonitische Rundschau*, July 4, 1934, p. 9.

discouraged and gave up, others strengthened the ranks of those fighting against the abolition of the private school.

Ewert considered the training of more and better Mennonite teachers as his primary task, more urgent even than the rapid conversion of Mennonite private schools into public schools. Neither he nor apparently the Provincial authorities ever contemplated the employment of girls or of teachers who did not have a Mennonite, or at least German, background, well knowing that this would have been entirely unacceptable to Mennonite parents. In a report of 1889, Ewert wrote:

The problem of furnishing the Mennonite schools with properly qualified teachers will probably remain difficult for some time to come; not so much because of the aversion of the Mennonites against higher education or of their prejudice against the English language, but mainly because the young people are not inclined to enter a profession which brings so much less than farming. . . . With the rich farm incomes in the North West it is difficult to induce young people from a farming community like that of the Mennonites to devote themselves to the teaching profession.[10]

Still he was able to register a gradual increase in the number of district schools under his jurisdiction. By 1902-03, the number had increased to 41, most of them one-room schools. These were staffed with Mennonite teachers, some of whom were from Minnesota and Kansas rather than Manitoba.

Political gerrymandering finally stopped the marked progress made in the field of education under Ewert's stewardship. In the election campaign of 1903, Conservative candidates played up to the conservative Mennonites (who usually did not vote at all) by supporting the enemies of the public school. They succeeded in engineering the abrupt dismissal of Ewert as inspector of public schools in the hope that, once his salary was suspended, he would not be able to continue as principal of the Gretna institute. But Ewert's friends privately collected a fund of $25,000 to assure the continued operation of the school. In 1905 a split occurred within the School Association when the original Gretna institute was removed bodily to Altona, the rising center of the Bergthal church. As a result, two Mennonite private high schools, with almost identical aims and supported by the same group of progressives, were in existence between 1908 and 1926: the Mennonite Collegiate Institute in Gretna under the direction of Ewert, and the Mennonite Educational Institute in Altona under the direction of another Mennonite from the United States, J. J. Balzer.

[10] Schäfer, *Heinrich Ewert*, pp. 63f.

Inter-Group Conflict

Thus far the school conflict was largely confined to the Mennonites themselves. It was brought about not by the direct interference of the state authorities but rather by their permissive attitude. Insofar as they failed to support the group mores, but suggested and rewarded alternatives, they weakened social controls, and fostered petty personal rivalries, such as are bound to arise in any community unless checked by political power.

A more direct, if feeble, attempt to bring about a reorientation of group values through the medium of the school was made in 1907. The Provincial Government decreed that the Union Jack, the symbol of the British Empire, be flown over every public school building. The measure was intended to "inculcate feelings of patriotism and materially assist in blending together the various nationalities in the Province into one common citizenship irrespective of race and creed."[11] Rodmond P. Roblin, Manitoba's premier from 1900 to 1915, declared in the Legislature: "While we welcome all, our duty to British subjects is to see that the children are taught the principles of the British Constitution. . . . What we need is to get the youth filled with the traditions of the British flag and then, when they are men . . . they will be able to defend it . . ."[12] As Roblin's biographer put it, his was a piece of "applied psychology." The symbolism of the flag "ever reminding them of what it represented in terms of robust citizenship," was used as part of a broader program designed to turn the immigrants "into intelligent citizens, schooled in Canadian tradition and British ideals of government."[13]

This kind of patriotism was ill-received by the Mennonites. Their religious doctrine forbade direct participation in affairs of state. The secular ritual of showing and saluting the flag was remindful of rendering an act of worship to Caesar's image; if they refused to do so, the Mennonites followed the example of the first Christian martyrs. Moreover, "they regarded the flag as a military emblem and believed that this was the thin edge of the wedge which, if consented to, would finally mean the loss of their military exemption."[14] True

---

[11] Quoted from Roblin's election manifesto of 1907.

[12] Quoted by Hugh Ross, *Thirty-Five Years in the Limelight: Sir Rodmond P. Roblin and His Time* (Winnipeg, 1936), p. 105.

[13] Ross, *Thirty-Five Years in the Limelight*, p. 104.

[14] I. I. Friesen, The Mennonites of Western Canada, with Special Reference to Education (M.A. thesis, University of Saskatchewan, 1934), p. 108.

enough, they did not hesitate to show the colors of the Empire, for instance during Lord Dufferin's visit, but then it was a gesture of courtesy or a festive display, not a public ceremony with the flag as its center.

Still another factor seems to have influenced their attitude. The idea of loyalty to the country in which they lived, and to its government, was by no means alien to the Mennonites. Many instances in their Russian history show a deep sense of reverence for the emperor, his family and his lieutenants. When they came to Canada this naïve trust in the ruler and even their love for him was transferred to the Queen of England and her Governor. But their allegiance was personalized; it also was qualified by the maxim of the Bible: render to Caesar what is Caesar's. It would seem that, in the thinking of peasants, such abstract notions as nation, citizenship or constitution were difficult to grasp. Their relationship to authority was conceived primarily after the model of the family. The Mennonites felt that, like children to their parents, they were subject to the "anointed" monarch and his officers, as long as the latter's commands did not contradict those of God, the father of all men. But they recognized no moral obligation to adopt the institutions of a politically dominant majority, or to merge into their culture. To them loyalty was primarily an act of personal obedience, while patriotism meant the undue attachment to this world which was forbidden by their religion.

Roblin's flag-flying policy elicited a response typical of the Mennonites: withdrawal. Since the Department of Education did not have jurisdiction over private schools, it was a simple matter to evade the obligation of flying the flag over school houses. Consequently, several public school districts were dissolved, particularly among the Kleine Gemeinde and Holdemann people who welcomed an opportunity to revert to their old policy, and also among the Sommerfeld group who, in this way, were able to strike out against Ewert and their former Bergthal brethren.[15]

In 1909-10 the Roblin administration was forced to engage an outsider, a German from Ontario, in order to rebuild the public school

[15] At the time, the Liberal *Winnipeg Free Press*, later a staunch advocate of a "strong" policy, warned that the aroused Mennonites might leave the country. It was suggested that a penalty of twice the cost of maintaining the flag should be imposed for non-observance of the regulation, thereby making it possible for those who were really acting from conscientious scruples, to retain the public school system.

system in the Mennonite Reserves. During the six years of his tenure, Inspector A. Weidenhammer (his name was changed to Willows) was able to increase the number of Mennonite pupils enrolled in public schools from 1,124 to 2,593, and the number of qualified teachers in the schools under his jurisdiction from 40 to 80. While the Mennonite public schools gave no cause for complaint, the situation in the remaining schools was quite unsatisfactory. In some of them English was taught part of the day, in others, particularly in those of the Fürstenland group, there was no English instruction whatever. "Some of them," wrote Willows after his retirement, "were doing fairly good work in German but in all of them the curriculum was very limited . . ."[16] He objected mainly to the short duration of the school year, and the neglect of Canadian history. With regard to the teachers, he remarked: "Many faithful and conscientious men were found by the writer among the teachers, men, who with better academic knowledge and some professional training would have become very successful teachers."[17]

Most of the new district schools organized during Willow's tenure were located in railroad towns or on the outskirts of the Fürstenland settlement, where members of the Bergthal and Mennonite Brethren congregations had become influential. While the Kleine Gemeinde and Holdemann people were wavering in their school policy, the Sommerfeld and Chortitz churches, though officially committed to the private school, were apparently unable or unwilling to enforce the principle among all of the members. These differences between the various Mennonite factions poisoned social life in the Reserves and had serious repercussions upon the cohesion of the Mennonite social system as a whole. Friends and enemies of the public school barely spoke to each other, and each accused the other either of heresy and treason, or of indolence and ignorance; the one group sought ever closer coöperation with the large society while the other retired ever further into stubborn isolation. Thus the Mennonite group was split wide open here as elsewhere over the school question precisely at a time when the outbreak of World War I and a rising tide of nationalism turned public opinion against them.

---

[16] A History of the Mennonites, p. 90.
[17] Ibidem, p. 92.

The Impact of Nationalism

At first nationalism did not affect the relationship between the Mennonites and the large society, although new ideas typical of National Liberalism had in part been responsible for changes in their legal status leading to social unrest. In Canada, too, nationalistic policies and attitudes did not play any significant role during the quarter century following their immigration. For the present purpose nationalism may be defined simply as that social and political ideology which postulates that the population of a state be identical with a distinctive ethnic system, having one common language and culture. This ideology also tends to emphasize loyalty to the legitimate government, a sentimental attachment to important national institutions, and the acceptance of a hierarchy of values in which the integrity and grandeur of the nation as such occupies an exalted, if not supreme, position. Wherever in a given state or society this unity of purpose and this cultural uniformity is not realized, it is considered as the right and duty of the nation and its govenment to bring about the ideal conditions not only by appropriate legislation but also by indoctrination.

Even where nationalism is mitigated by the notion of individual rights and by tolerance, particularly in matters of religion, there is, as a rule, no recognition of the corporate rights of ethnic minorities which by the historical accident of dynastic succession, treaties, conquest, or sometimes group migration are included in the socio-political system of the nation, that is, the "majority." Other types of political order, in particular the empire-state, have extended special privileges to religious, ethnic and similar groups in order to protect their heritage and native institutions, and to permit their continued functioning as separate social systems and sub-systems; the specific formulation of the right of minorities to a measure of political and especially cultural autonomy represents a rather recent modification of the concept of the nation-state. Such corporate rights have to be distinguished from individual rights of members of minority groups to be treated as the equals of any other member of the national society without any discrimination because of colour, creed, culture, origin, and so on. They rather take cognizance of the desire of every functioning social group to perpetuate itself and to resist assimilation, and to enable the minority, with the active support of the central government, to develop group institutions which compel members to conform to the values of their own group in spite of the direct and indirect pressures exercised by the dominant majority.

Before World War I the principle of corporate minority rights had been recognized only in a few states oriented to the ideology of modern nationalism, mainly in those countries comprising two or more ethnic systems of considerable size and political power. In Canada such recognition was implicit (but not explicit) only with regard to the French Canadians. Even today "minorities formed by persons having a common origin, language, religion, culture, etc., who have migrated or who have been imported into a country and have become citizens of the State; or by their descendants" are usually considered entitled to individual but not to corporate rights. Nevertheless, a recent statement on the subject acknowledges that "those who have entered the country under certain specified conditions (such as contract workers), or those who have been forcibly imported into the country (such as slaves), or elements brought by a State into its territory in pursuance of a plan of internal colonization, may have a valid moral claim to special measures of protection."[18]

Such ideas were alien to Canadian political thinking, for they represent a later development in political philosophy and international law; therefore they are inapplicable to an appraisal of political action affecting the Manitoba Mennonites at the time under consideration. Still the preceding discussion demonstrates the historical relativity of the attitude taken by the Canadian public as well as the Government when they finally adopted the current ideology of nationalism in their approach to the Mennonite group as an ethnic minority. By accepting the "melting pot" theory, which in fact is but the application of the idea of the nation-state to the peculiar conditions of the New World, they failed to realize that even an immigrant group may have the moral right to be recognized as a corporate entity due to the particular conditions under which it had immigrated. On the other hand, the tradition of the Mennonites was influenced by their earlier contact with an empire-type of political and social order. Nationalistic concepts and sentiments were quite alien to them, not only because of their religious convictions, but because they were a peasant group without an intelligentsia or an élite aspiring to political power. They lacked precisely

---

[18] United Nations — Commission on Human Rights — Sub-Commission on Prevention of Discrimination and Protection of Minorities, *Definition and Classification of Minorities: Memorandum submitted by the Secretary-General*, (Lake Success, 1950), Sections 75 and 79.

those social forces which are primarily responsible for the emergence of nationalism and modern nations. Accordingly, they defined the social situation in a completely different manner than the Anglo-Saxon majority, believing that they had indeed, if not a legal, certainly a valid moral claim to corporate rights and privileges.

The patriotism of Premier Roblin and his Conservatives had not yet constituted full-fledged nationalism. It was tied in with the imperial principles of British colonial administration rather than with the ideology of an independent Canadian nation. It is not accidental that the Liberal party was the first power group in the Province which adopted a platform directly aiming at the assimilation of minority groups. In their party convention of March 26, 1914, they demanded national schools, obligatory teaching of English in all public schools and compulsory school attendance. Years later, in an editorial of May 18, 1920, the *Winnipeg Free Press* with great clarity and succinctness brought to the fore the reasoning behind this step. The writer, perhaps John Dafoe himself, declared that state schools were the symbols of a new freedom; for the clerical leaders were fighting against it with the weapons of the sixteenth century. The modern democratic state, he insisted,

cannot agree that the parents have the sole right of determining what kind of education their children shall receive . . . a doctrine which in its practical working means every time absolute clerical control of education. The children are the children of the state of which they are destined to be citizens; and it is the duty of the state that they are properly educated.

If every group were allowed to ask for school autonomy, he continued, all the tongues and dialects of Europe would be perpetuated, and "our national school system, which is gradually turning this province into a real community, will be blown to pieces."

The outbreak of World War I was in part responsible for the upsurge of national sentiment and the acceptance of nationalistic ideologies among the general public which, in 1916, swept the Liberal party into power. The war and its aftermath also put the Mennonites at a disadvantage, both as a German-speaking minority and as conscientious objectors. As Professor C. B. Sissons, of Toronto, put it,

when the use of the German language was an offence added to conscientious objection to war, the Mennonites, who had remained true to their faith, found themselves in a very uncomfortable position. Especially was this the case in Manitoba, where the deplorable educational conditions discovered in many of the non-English-speaking districts under the Roblin regime had led to a demand for drastic reform.[19]

The movement against bilingual schools antedated the war, having its roots in marked changes in the ethnic composition of the province since the turn of the century. The Laurier-Greenway compromise did not explicitly grant school autonomy to national minorities. Still, in its application school districts were deliberately organized so as to include an ethnically homogeneous population, while the local boards were enabled to appoint teachers from among their own group and to insist upon instruction in their own language. Although English and other cultural subjects like history had to be taught in conformity with the Provincial regulations, in actual practice they took second place in bilingual schools, which were conducted in the spirit of the cultural traditions of the minority rather than of the Anglo-Saxon majority. This arrangement did not create any particular administrative difficulties as long as it concerned but few minority groups confined to ethnically homogeneous settlements. As a matter of fact, in the beginning it really affected only the French and the Mennonites, since the third major minority group in the province, namely, the Icelanders did not object to full participation in the life and culture of the large society.

This situation changed radically when, at the turn of the century, other groups of East European immigrants began to reach the province in large numbers. Unlike the Mennonites and Icelanders, most of these did not migrate and settle in compact units, although several group settlements were organized locally, either by design or as an effect of unplanned ecological processes. Generally speaking, Canadian immigration policy favored the deliberate dispersal of immigrants in order to prevent the formation and consolidation of large segregated ethnic communities. Yet the resulting settlement pattern, combined with a relatively high degree of mobility not only among the urban but also the rural populations, made the application of the principles of local school autonomy according to the original scheme increasingly difficult.

Moreover, mass immigration from the Continent threatened the absolute majority of the dominant group when, by 1916, no more

---

[19] "Trek of Mennonites has its Tragic Aspects," *Free Press Prairie Farmer*, November 16, 1921; see also his article "The Mennonites of Western Canada," *The New Outlook*, March 7, 1928, where he says: "When the war spirit got hold of the West, and to poor equipment were added the dual sins of pacifism and German speech, the patience of public and officials could no longer stand the strain. Recourse was had to compulsion."

than 58 per cent of Manitoba's population were of British origin.[20] Government and public became seriously alarmed at the prospect of Manitoba being turned into a multi-national country. As the leading Winnipeg newspaper expressed it in later years: "This is a land of freedom. . . . But we do not want a perverted sense of that principle to lead to isolated sections and divisions of the population. We want to be one people with a sense of national unity and with each section of the country interested in the progress and welfare of the rest of the country."[21] The answer was a policy of assimilation, with Anglo-Saxon ways of life setting the pattern for all—a policy in which the public school occupied a crucial position.

The bilingual schools actually prevented assimilation, and created administrative complications and, in some places, outright confusion. This was brought to the fore in private and official surveys which produced the following over-all picture.[22] Apart from the French, the Mennonites, and the German Lutherans, it was above all the Roman Catholic Poles and the Greek Catholic Ruthenians who, under the leadership of a nationally self-conscious clergy, took full advantage of the legal provisions.[23] Where they had the power to do so, they organized public schools which for all practical purposes were national minority schools and in which English was usually taught quite inadequately by teachers who themselves did not have sufficient command of the language, and who, in some cases, were openly hostile to Anglo-Saxon traditions and culture. Local school boards exercised almost complete control not only over teachers but indirectly also over the method and content of instruction. Teachers who refused to teach the language (and *in* the language) of the local majority were often threatened with dismissal. School administration was made extremely complicated and unwieldy as the different types of schools required adjustments in teachers' training, supervision, curricula and textbooks.

[20] Cf. *Bilingual Schools*, Address in the Legislature, on January 12, 1916, by Hon. R. S. Thorton, Minister of Education, Department of Education, Winnipeg, February 1, 1916.

[21] *Manitoba Free Press*, editorial of August 3, 1920.

[22] In addition to sixty-five articles published by the *Winnipeg Free Press*, a *Special Report on Bi-Lingual Schools in Manitoba* was issued by the Department of Education on February 1, 1916. It was based on findings of school inspectors which were summarized by Chas. K. Newcombe, Superintendent of Education. See also Thornton's address, and the full treatment of the problem, from different standpoints, by C. B. Sissons, *Bi-Lingual Schools in Canada* (London, 1917) and G. M. Weir, *The Separate School Question in Canada* (Toronto, 1934).

[23] Before 1916, there existed 126 French, 61 German, and 111 Ruthenian and Polish bi-lingual public schools in Manitoba.

Serious conflicts arose in ethnically mixed school districts, particularly in view of the fact that their ethnic composition changed frequently. As R. S. Thornton pointed out, "each district becomes in succession a storm center, and peace returns because one or the other section is driven out of the settlement. In most cases the English people are driven out of the settlement and those who cannot afford to move have to stay and endure conditions." But the bilingual school spelled conflict also among the various minority groups. It was, for instance, found that in five school districts separate minority schools could have been requested by no less than three different minority groups, had they chosen to do so. In 110 school districts, one or more local ethnic minorities had to send their children to schools which were taught in the language of another minority, for instance, Polish children were forced to attend Ruthenian schools, Finnish children Polish schools, and so on. In such districts the arrival or departure of a single family could alter the situation at any time and deprive the majority of its precarious privilege.

In several school districts with a non-Anglo-Saxon population, the English-language school was accepted. In these, the Departmental Report explained, "it was plainly evident that a condition of unstable equilibrium existed and English was the language of compromise." In many other districts, particularly in the towns and cities, ethnic minorities were required by law to send their children to a purely English school unless they maintained private schools of their own. In all these cases good educational results were said to have been obtained with children of foreign origin.[24]

In view of this situation, which had arisen since the introduction of bilingual public schools, the Provincial authorities came to the conclusion that

there should be some common school, teaching the things which are common to all, and leaving to individual effort those matters which are of private concern. There should be one standard of teachers eligible to teach in all schools of the province. There should be a Normal training to which all teachers should measure up. There should be a school inspector eligible to inspect every school under the Government. . . . We come from many lands and cast in our lot, and from these various factors there must evolve a new nationality which shall be simply Canadian and British.[25]

---

[24] C. B. Sissons, *Bi-Lingual Schools in Canada* (London, 1917), pp. 144 ff.

[25] R. S. Thornton, *Bi-Lingual Schools*.

The new school policy was adopted with the School Attendance Act of March 10, 1916. By the repeal of clause 285 of the Public Schools Act of 1890, English was made the sole language of instruction in all public schools of the Province. In addition, all children between the ages of 7 and 14 were compelled to attend public schools unless private education was provided for them in a manner acceptable to the school authorities.

These measures were not primarily directed against the bilingual schools in Mennonite school districts. In fact, the same reports which initiated the campaign against the bilingual school, contained the admission that, as Professor Sissons put it, "among the progressive Germans of Southern Manitoba . . . were found real bilingual schools, that is, schools in which the pupils learned to read, write and speak two languages. The method to achieve this end was scientific."[26] The Departmental Report of 1916 indicated that "the pupils speak English fairly well. This seems particularly true in the towns. English is the language of instruction though the mother tongue is frequently used with beginners. On an average one hour a day is given to the teaching of German."[27] Yet, less than three-fourths of the Mennonite children were in public schools, while at least 1,000 attended inadequate private schools, of which there were more than 20 in the Fürstenland settlement alone.[28]

For some time after the enactment of the new school law the Administration under Premier T. C. Norris and the Minister of Education R. S. Thornton considered the Mennonite schools a rather minor problem. Their policy of "wait and see" gave the Mennonites a chance to avail themselves of the legal loopholes that had been included in the Public School Attendance Act, primarily made in order to honour the school rights guaranteed to the Roman Catholic (that is, French) minority in section 22 of the Manitoba Act of 1870. While school attendance had become compulsory, minority schools were permitted to operate privately under section 4, chapter 97 of the School Attendance Act which reads as follows:

The Department of Education may, at least once in each year, upon the request of the board of trustees or the authorities in control of any private school, enquire into the qualifications of the teachers and the

[26] Sissons, *Bi-Lingual Schools*, p. 133.

[27] Sissons, *Bi-Lingual Schools*, p. 143; see also *Winnipeg Free Press*, January 21, 1916.

[28] Cf. Willows, History of the Mennonites, p. 96; Friesen, Mennonites of Western Canada, p. 132.

standard of education of such school, and as often as such enquiry shall be made the Department of Education shall furnish the said board of trustees or other authorities a written report of the result of such enquiry and transmit a copy of such report of the school inspector and the school attendance officer of the school district in which such private school is situated.

Thus, to escape the obligation of sending their children to the culturally uniform public school, the Mennonites had nothing else to do but to declare their schools once more as private.

As reported by Willows, then still inspector in charge of the Mennonite public schools, a meeting was arranged by the Mennonite Advisory Committee between church leaders and the Minister of Agriculture, who represented many potential Mennonite voters in the Provincial Legislature:

The school situation was fully discussed, and the advice that was given on the occasion is largely responsible for having created the . . . Mennonite school problem. As a direct result of the advice received, a large number of existing public schools were again operated as private schools.[29]

The inevitable result was a further deterioration of educational facilities in Mennonite settlements. The men who, like Ewert and Willows, had worked for a steady improvement of the school in coöperation with the Department of Education were disowned by the authorities themselves, while those who had advocated the private schools all along seemed to be vindicated by the events.

The abolition of the bilingual public school had been justified on account of its inefficiency and the frictions it caused. The immediate effect was a much greater inadequacy of the school in Mennonite districts and increasing frictions between the minority and the majority; this, in turn, was used as a convenient rationalization to demand complete suppression of all Mennonite private schools. Behind this demand, of course, lay ulterior motives, primarily national sentiment and resentment in and after World War I, and the determination of the Anglo-Saxon majority to forge Canada's population, outside Quebec, into one nation with one uniform language and culture.

The law had given the school administration full power to suppress any private minority school by the very simple device of finding fault with it. Wherever a local private school was condemned because of an inadequate building, poor equipment, ill-trained teachers, low standards,

---

[29] **History** of the Mennonites, pp. 96f.

etc., children attending it did not fulfill the requirements of the Act of 1916, and could be forced to go to a public school. If there was none, the Municipality had to provide for one by organizing a school district. If this was rejected, the Department of Education was by an earlier statute entitled to appoint, at its own discretion, an official school trustee who would see to it that a public school was established and conducted according to the regulations of the Department.

In the fall of 1918 the authorities began to bring all the power at their disposal to bear upon the Mennonite group. Not only were all Mennonite schools condemned as inadequate (with the exception of the few which by then were still operated as public schools) but Mr. J. F. Greenway was appointed official school trustee for all districts lacking the required school facilities. School buildings which had been erected by the Mennonites privately were requisitioned to serve as public schools. Moreover, parents who failed to send their children to a recognized school, as well as ministers of the church who counselled them against doing so, were hailed before the magistrates, fined and in several instances even jailed. The Fürstenland people, particularly, who never permitted public schools to operate in their settlement and who now adopted a policy of passive resistance, were severely hit by this Government action. On September 27, 1918, thirteen parents in the Wakeham school district (Haskett) were fined five dollars each for not sending their children to school. They paid the fine after having spent three days in the Morden jail. In the same year the elder of the Fürstenland church was fined twenty dollars for having advised parents in Schanzenfeld against sending their children to the public school at Winkler. The teacher of the Schanzenfeld private school was also fined, and it was remarked that he knew no English. On July 18, 1919, eleven persons were fined at Morden for the same offenses. As late as March, 1920, six farmers of Hamburg were fined twenty-five dollars and cost each for not having sent their children to the district school at Plum Coulee. This list is far from complete.

The Mennonites made great efforts to avert what they considered a disaster to themselves and a glaring injustice, in view of the promises made by the Dominion authorities in 1873. Two test cases were appealed, but they were decided against the Mennonites by the Manitoba Court of Appeal on August 12, 1919.[30] It is not the purpose

---

[30] It was not until July 30, 1930, that the Privy Council in London dismissed the application for leave to appeal from the adverse judgment of the Manitoba courts, finally closing the case as far as its legal side was concerned.

of the present study to discuss the legal merits of these decisions, even if the arguments adopted by the courts seem to be open to criticism.[31] At the same time, the Mennonites submitted several petitions to the Provincial Administration and Legislature. They emphasized that they were unable "to delegate to others the all important responsibility of educating their children, convinced as they are, that instruction in other than religious schools would result in the weakening and even loss of faith, and would be generally detrimental to the moral and spiritual welfare of the children."[32] But they declared their readiness to provide for adequate instruction in English; to strive toward "the highest standard of education which is possible to attain under our Mennonite teachers with their present qualifications"; to intensify the training of Mennonite teachers; to facilitate inspection by the Department of Education; in short, to "place our schools beyond just criticism."[33] Yet all their efforts to save their parochial schools were unsuccessful. For it was no more a question of educational standards which prompted the authorities to destroy the Mennonite private grade schools once and for all, and to replace them with English public schools. It was part of a consistent national policy aimed at the assimilation of ethnics to safeguard national unity and cultural uniformity. In this policy the school figured prominently as the most effective means to wean the children of immigrants away from the traditions of their group and to indoctrinate them with the ideals and values of the dominant majority.

---

[31] The text is reproduced in W. J. Tremeear (ed.), *Canadian Criminal Cases* . . . Volume XXXI (Toronto, 1920).

[32] Petition of October 14, 1921, as quoted by I. H. Dörksen, *Geschichte und wichtige Dokumente der Mennoniten von Russland, Canada, Paraguay und Mexiko* (not dated).

[33] Quoted by Friesen, Mennonites of Western Canada, appendix, letter No. 17, p. 3.

CHAPTER VIII

Regroupment

The Exodus

BETWEEN 1921 and 1930 approximately 6,000, or one-third, of the Mennonite group in Manitoba left for Latin American countries, while about 8,000 Mennonite refugees from Communist Russia arrived in the province. Although this was purely coincidental, the two events did have a strikingly complementary effect upon the structure of the group. In the following discussion we have to deal with three distinct divisions of Mennonites; in order to keep them apart we shall give each a proper name, the one under which they were popularly known among themselves. Those who left Canada after World War I shall be called the *Auswanderer* group, those who stayed behind, the *Kanädier* group, and those who immigrated from Russia in that period, the *Russländer* group. There were significant differences in the character of these groups. Of course, all three of them had been one people with substantially the same culture until 1874, when the more conservatives of them migrated to the New World. In the intervening 50 years the Mennonites in Russia had become more rapidly modernized than their brethren in Canada, perhaps precisely because they had been relieved of the more traditionalistic elements as a result of the first migration. In addition, however, the emigration from Russia in the 1920's was quite selective so that the Russländer group did not represent a true cross-section of the Mennonite people in Russia at the time of the Revolution but was weighted in favor of certain better educated and more enterprising classes. Accordingly, the immigrants and their Canadian hosts were in many respects utter strangers, although they did share common memories and common traditions.

On the other hand, the exodus to Latin America also changed the complexion of the Kanädier group, which continued to form the core and backbone of Mennonite society in Manitoba. For the Auswanderer group was affiliated with the Fürstenland, Sommerfeld and Chortitz churches, and thus represented the most conservative, tradition-bound and unacculturated portion of Manitoba's original Mennonite population. Much more than either the Kanädier or the Russländer group, they stood for those cultural values which had characterized the Russian Mennonites before their separation in the 1870's. In point of fact, one discovers a striking parallel in both cause and effect of the two migrations, that from Russia to Canada in the nineteenth century, and that from Canada to Latin America after the first World War. In both cases it was ideological and political changes in the large society which strained internal group relations to the breaking point. In both cases the withdrawal of rights which were considered by the Mennonites as an essential requisite for a way of life in accordance with the principles of their religion, provided an issue around which diffuse unrest crystallized into a social movement. In both cases the Mennonite commonwealth itself was split wide open over the question of what practical steps were to be taken to meet the new situation. This led to feuds between the advocates of emigration, and those who worked for a compromise and who finally adjusted themselves to given conditions. Eventually the separation followed the dividing lines within the group which had existed before the issue arose. Each time it was individual branches of the Mennonite church which organized the emigration, negotiated with foreign governments, provided for the necessary financial arrangements and used their spiritual power to force their members to fall in line. The subgroups participating in the migration were each time those who clung more tenaciously to tradition, who had preserved a greater social coherence, and among whom the church authorities exercised stricter social control. In both cases the issue itself also symbolized a much more general and diffuse conflict situation which had arisen earlier between the Mennonite group and the large society. With this in mind, we now turn to a more detailed analysis of developments in the Manitoba colonies during and after World War I.

The war not only intensified already existing tensions over the school question, but led to further frictions over Mennonite participation in the war effort. As the thunder clouds gathered, representatives of the Mennonites hastened to submit a petition for clarification of their status to the Dominion Government. Unlike school autonomy, the legal basis of which was at least open to doubt, military exemption for conscientious objectors, and specifically for Mennonites, was firmly anchored in the Constitution as well as in several Dominion statutes and Orders-in-Council. Moreover, military conscription was a hot political issue in Canada over which Anglo-Saxon and French sentiments clashed. It required careful maneuvering on the part of the Conservative Dominion Government. Thus the right of the Mennonites to complete exemption from military service or any other kind of conscription was never seriously challenged in Ottawa. Locally, however, emphatic protests were launched, both during and after the war, by such patriotic organizations as the Great War Veterans, Sons of England, Orangemen and British Citizens League. The extent of this movement against Mennonite privileges can be judged from the voluminous files deposited in the archives of the *Winnipeg Free Press*, the intellectual center for the propagation of National Liberalism in the West. While this agitation never went beyond the stage of resolutions and petitions, it may have indirectly influenced Dominion legislation by which the Mennonites were disfranchised and further Mennonite immigration was prohibited.

While the Mennonites were assured of military exemption, they were expected to contribute financially to the national effort. But new difficulties arose when they objected to subscribing to Victory Bonds and Red Cross drives because this was considered a direct support of the war. Only after they had been assured that their money would be used for charitable purposes did they give generously. They bought almost $700,000 worth of Victory Bonds, and in 1918 alone they donated almost $100,000 to the Red Cross and other patriotic funds. Many of them refused to take interest on Victory Bonds or any money loaned to the Government for charitable purposes.

By the Dominion Elections Act all conscientious objectors and persons of German origin were disfranchised.[1] When on September 20, 1917, the War-Time Elections Act was passed (largely as a political maneuver to assure re-election of a government favoring overseas conscription) the Mennonites together with Hutterites and Doukhobors were named specifically in sub-section 154 as being excluded from voting. In the debates preceding the enactment of the law,[2] the Menno-

---

[1] *Revised Statutes of Canada,* 1916, Vol. 1, ch. 6, section 67.
[2] Cf. *Hansard,* 1917, vol. 6, pp. 5807ff.

nites were hardly mentioned at all. But the Liberals, who had supported the Union Government in matters of compulsory conscription, opposed the disqualification of whole groups of "foreigners," most of whom were their voters.[3] It does not seem that the Mennonites were greatly aroused at the slight; many of them were forbidden by their church to participate in elections, while the others probably considered disfranchisement a fair price for military exemption.

More serious were measures taken by the Dominion Government against the further immigration of Mennonites and Hutterites to Canada. There was much resentment against conscientious objectors who fled to Canada from persecution in the United States, and acquired land, claiming military exemption under laws which had never been meant to apply to cases such as theirs. In the spring of 1919 the Prime Minister took cognizance of this situation and explained that according to a recent Order-in-Council the privileges granted to the early Mennonite immigrants did not apply to those who entered the country afterwards.[4] Two months later another Order-in-Council prohibited the landing of "any immigrant of the Doukhobor, Hutterite and Mennonite class" on the following grounds:

Owing to conditions prevailing as the result of war, a wide-spread feeling exists throughout Canada, and more particularly in Western Canada, that steps should be taken to prohibit the landing in Canada of immigrants deemed undesirable owing to their peculiar customs, habits, modes of living and methods of holding property, and because of their probable inability to become readily assimilated or to assume the duties and responsibilities of Canadian citizenship within a reasonable time after their entry.[5]

These events were taken by many of the Manitoba Mennonites as serious danger signals indicating that their social and legal positions in Western Canada were no longer safe. Their correspondence with various governments indicates clearly the points on which they desired more definite guarantees. Negotiations were initiated with Argentina, Mexico, Paraguay, the United States (Attorney-General Palmer rejected the application as undesirable), and—oddly enough—the Province of Quebec. By and large, the petitions were drafted after the model of the charters and concessions which their ancestors had once obtained from the Governments of Russia and Canada. For instance, representatives

---

[3] Cf. *Winnipeg Telegram*, September 21, 1918.

[4] *Manitoba Free Press*, April 9, 1919; reproduced by E. K. Francis, "Miscellaneous Documents Concerning School and Military Service," *Mennonite Quarterly Review 27* (1953): 234f.

[5] Order-in-Council, P. O. 1204, *The Canada Gazette*, June 14, 1919.

of the Fürstenland church in the West Reserve asked Premier L. A. Taschereau, of Quebec, whether the following five privileges could be granted "by law forever": 1) entire exemption from any military service; 2) the privilege of affirming instead of making affidavits; 3) "the fullest privilege of exercising our religious principles and rule of our church without any kind of molestation or restriction whatever"; 4) "the privilege of our own private school buildings and maintaining them at our own expense, and to educate our children in the same, according to our own customary German language without any restrictions"; 5) the right "to administer and invest the estates and inherited property of our people, especially that of widows and orphans, in our own trust system, called the Waisenamt, according to our own rules and religion without any restrictions."[6]

In a petition of October 5, 1921, to the President, Government, and Congress of the United States of Mexico, by the elder and three preachers of the Sommerfeld church, the following additional demands were made: permission to organize a mutual fire insurance; duty-free import of machines, stock and seed grain for ten years; the right to leave Mexico if conditions should turn out to be unsatisfactory; and finally inclusion of all the privileges into the existing law and the constitution of the country. The required guarantees were given by the Governments of both Mexico and Paraguay, and preparations for emigration to Mexico were at once begun.[7] This came much as a surprise to the advocates of a "tough" school policy who, in their materialistic frame of mind, could not imagine that the threat of the wealthy Mennonites to emigrate was meant seriously.

This time economic motives do not seem to have played any role in the decision to emigrate. In fact, members of communities leaving Canada who did stay behind were usually forced to do so by their poverty. On the other hand, land prices in Canada after World War I were favorable to the seller, and large areas of land could be purchased in Mexico at a much lower price. In fact, the Mexican Government, engaged in a great agrarian reform, was anxious to have Mennonite

---

[6] The French Canadian newspaper *Le Matin* commented that the Mennonites saw in Quebec an atmosphere of tolerance, of justice, and of liberty, denied to them elsewhere in Canada, and expressed the hope that they would be received cordially. For, the paper continued, "they ask permission to live in their own way which is not incompatible with the normal administration of law; for liberty to instruct their children . . . a liberty which we ask for ourselves as French Canadians." (From an undated newspaper clipping.)

[7] Cf. *Free Press Evening Bulletin*, September 17, 1921.

192

model farmers take over some of the confiscated land, while private owners were eager to sell before their estates were liquidated. Close to half-a-million acres in two blocks, one situated in the State of Durango, the other in that of Chihuahua, were purchased by the Mennonites at a price of nearly four million dollars, most of which was paid in cash.

The Auswanderer group going to Mexico included 3,200 to 3,300, or about 75 per cent, of the Fürstenland people in Manitoba, 800 (18 per cent) Fürstenland people from the Hague-Rosthern colony (in Saskatchewan), 1,500 (55 per cent) Fürstenland people from the Swift Current colony (also in Saskatchewan), and approximately 1,000 members of the Sommerfeld church in Manitoba and Saskatchewan.[8] Many of the emigrants carefully avoided burning all bridges behind them. They made certain they had properly acquired Canadian citizenship, and left substantial deposits in Canadian banks. In later years some of them actually returned to Manitoba.

Compared with the migration to Paraguay, that to Mexico was a relatively simple matter. Special trains were chartered, which brought the Mennonites, with their household goods and livestock, from a railroad siding in Manitoba almost to the doorsteps of their new homes. The cost involved was reasonable and return was within easy reach. The trek into the Gran Chaco, the "Green Hell" of Paraguay, on the other hand, was a risky undertaking leading into fever-infested tropical forests in the interior of South America, which could only be reached by a long sea voyage and by river boats. It was the hunting ground of savage Indian tribes and the object of a bitter struggle between two countries, a conflict which eventually led to the war between Paraguay and Bolivia. To go there, frequently meant an irrevocable step, and a new beginning under unfamiliar conditions. The emigration to Paraguay was delayed because in 1922 the country suffered a serious economic depression. Altogether 1,765 members of the Sommerfeld and Chortitz churches left Canada for the Gran Chaco between 1926 and 1930,[9] of which as many as 355 had returned by 1936. According to incomplete private lists, 819 individuals and 13

According to I. I. Friesen, Mennonites in Western Canada, pp. 140f.

[9] Cf. W. Quiring, *Deutsche erschliessen den Chaco* (Karlsruhe, 1930). See also Joseph Winfield Fretz, *Pilgrims in Paraguay: The Story of Mennonite Colonization in South America* (Scottdale, Penna., 1953), pp. 11f.

families migrated from the East Reserve, and 341 persons from the West Reserve, while 246 came from Rosthern in Saskatchewan.

Both movements involved large-scale financial transactions, and the disposal of land in Canada. The Auswanderer group refused to sell to Mennonites who had decided to stay behind and who were regarded as renegades; thus their farms were put up for public sale. According to a blueprinted map circulated by Mr. J. H. Black, a lawyer at Morden, who was employed by the Fürstenland people, more than 60,000 acres were offered. These were described as "of the finest improved agricultural land ever put on the market," and the absence of crop failures for the past 45 years was stressed. Eventually two stock companies were formed, the Intercontinental Company at Winnipeg, and the Corporacion Paraguay at Asuncion. These agreed to buy all the Canadian property of the emigrants, including buildings and some of the livestock and machinery, altogether 44,000 acres at rates varying from $6.50 to $42.00 per acre, while the rest was credited to a fund in Paraguay with which nearly 138,000 acres of virgin forest were purchased from the Casados interests at a price of almost $700,000.

Most of the land sold in Manitoba by the Auswanderer group was eventually bought up by the Russländer immigrants, after all sorts of non-Mennonite middlemen had taken their cut. About 255 Mennonite farms of 80 to 200 acres each changed hands between 1926 and 1930 alone. Some Kanädier Mennonites increased their holdings. Particularly, members of the Fürstenland group in the West Reserve who stayed behind acquired land at a good price. Some of the wealthiest farmers to be found today in the West Reserve are those who used this opportunity to their advantage.

The exodus of the Auswanderer group momentarily caused a great deal of confusion and disorganization in the Manitoba colonies. Yet the shock was cushioned by the simultaneous arrival of the Russländer group who quickly filled the gaps left by the emigrants. Relations between the Kanädier and the Auswanderer groups were never completely broken off. Mennonite periodicals printed in Canada continued to carry news items from Mexico and Paraguay. They were supplemented by a lively correspondence and even occasional personal visits between friends and relatives living in three different countries. Newspapers like the *Steinbach Post* or the *Mennonitische Rundschau*, both printed in Manitoba, have many subscribers in Latin America. The attitude among the Kanädier group toward the Auswanderer group seems to have changed considerably. Old hositilies and tensions have lost their edge, and have been replaced by a keen interest in the welfare of the brethren in far-off lands.

The Background of the Russländer Group

In 1874 the Mennonite people living in Russia were a homogeneous, isolated peasant society. Social stratification, division of labor, schooling and diversification of cultural interests, as well as contact and inter-action with the larger Russian society, were limited. In the course of the following 50 years, the isolation of peasant communities and their economic self-sufficiency were rapidly breaking down all over Eastern Europe. Localistic social systems, such as the Mennonite colonies in Russia, became more and more integrated into the complex structure of a modern high civilization. While it is true that the Russian Empire had been rather late in taking its place in the concert of modern European nations, social and cultural life in European Russia was quite comparable with that of any other Western country by the outbreak of World War I. Thus the Mennonites in Russia had become an integrated part of a highly differentiated, heterogeneous, secularized, and to some extent, urbanized, industrialized, and capital-istic society with developed institutions of higher learning and a flourishing national literature, whose achievements in the sciences, fine arts, music, drama, ballet, and so on were considerable.

Russia's Mennonite population had grown from about 37,000 to 104,000 in 1915. They still were basically an agrarian community with land holdings of almost $2\frac{1}{2}$ million acres in 45 colonies distributed throughout the Russian Empire from the Crimea to the Caucasus, the Ural, and far into Siberia. In addition, there were several large Mennonite-owned estates comprising 750,000 acres. These Mennonites had prospered economically and had largely accepted the ways and values of a capitalistic society. Rural trade centers with medium-sized local industries and commercial establishments had sprung up in their colonies, giving rise to a new middle-class of Mennonite factory owners, managers, clerks and businessmen. Many Mennonites had moved to Russian cities where some of them acquired high social positions as members of parliament, mayors, industrialists, bankers and mill-owners. Nine factories in Southern Russia with nearly 2,000 laborers, whose output in agricultural machines amounted to as much as 7 per cent of Russia's total production, were owned and managed by Mennonites.

In the two principal colonies on the Chortitza and Molotschna Rivers about 100 stores, 180 flour mills, 26 factories and larger workshops, 38 brick yards, and 2 printing presses were counted by the end of World War I. In 1910, 71.2 per cent of Russia's Mennonite population were farmers, 0.7 per cent industrialists, 1.0 per cent merchants, and 2.2 per cent skilled craftsmen.[10]

Economic progress was paralleled by great achievements in the educational sphere. Illiteracy was practically unknown among the Mennonites, although it was high among the Russian peasants. At the outbreak of World War I, the Mennonite school system included 400 elementary schools, 1 theological seminary, 2 business colleges, 4 high schools for girls, 2 normal schools and 13 *Zentralschulen*, a school type roughly comparable with senior high schools.[11] The following figures for 1910 are available for the Chortitza colony: of those who had attended school, 84.5 per cent had only a grade school education, 11.6 per cent had attended a secondary school, 1.9 per cent a normal school, 1.8 per cent a junior college, and 0.2 per cent had undertaken graduate studies.[12]

In particular, the *Zentralschulen* were centers of Mennonite culture and intellectual life in Russia. Practically all the men teaching grade school in any one of their scores of colonies had been trained in these institutions, which were located in the major settlements in the Ukraine, and thus in the heart of Mennonite social life. Those who prepared for teaching in secondary schools had to attend advanced Russian academies of university rank in the larger cities. The Mennonite teachers constituted a well trained, responsible and active class of intellectual leaders. Some of them were also ordained ministers and took a lead in the spiritual life and charitable activities of their church. Their authority and social status made them the backbone and unifying element in the total structure of the Mennonite commonwealth in all of Russia.

Several factors seem to be responsible for the high regard paid to education and the teaching profession by the Mennonites in Russia,

[10] Cf. *Die Mennoniten-Gemeinden in Russland während der Kriegs- und Revolutionsjahre, 1914 bis 1920.* (Heilbronn, 1921), p. 31; Adolf Ehrt, *Das Mennonitentum in Russland von seiner Einwanderung bis zur Gegenwart* (Langensalza, 1932), pp. 85ff., 96; Heinrich H. Schröder, *Russlanddeutsche Friesen* (Döllstädt, 1936).

[11] Cf. *Mennoniten-Gemeinden in Russland*, p. 31.

[12] Ehrt, *Mennonitentum in Russland*, p. 100.

in contrast to the attitude taken by their Manitoba brethren. There is no doubt but that the emigration of the more conservative or "unmanageably pious" elements, as P. M. Friesen called them, had freed the Russian group of much dead weight and accelerated their adjustment to the general cultural trends after 1880. Moreover, the Mennonite society in Russia was dominated by prosperous middle-class farmers, teachers and, in part, businessmen, who had a common interest with the emerging Russian bourgeoisie. Education was a means of rising in the status scale of the large society and of competing successfully in the new capitalistic economy.

The conflict over the control of the school between the state on the one hand, and the ethnic church and community on the other, had been carefully avoided in Russia. In 1881 the supervision of the Mennonite schools had been transferred from the Department of Crownlands to that of Education, which was responsible for all schools in Russia. Yet the Mennonites continued to enjoy almost complete school autonomy. When in 1897 instruction in the Russian language was officially prescribed for all the parochial schools of foreign colonists, it was left to the discretion of the Minister of Education and of a well-trained, non-political bureaucracy to introduce the Russian language and other educational reforms gradually and with the necessary psychological tact. At the same time, instruction in the mother tongue and in the religion of the school children was explicitly retained, "with a number of periods necessary for the acquisition of these subjects."[13]

In this way, Russian ideas and culture were absorbed gradually by the younger generation of Mennonites without being resisted either by their teachers or by their religious leaders as an imposition on the part of the large society and an intrusion by the state. In later years many of the young Mennonites and future community leaders attended Russian universities, colleges and academies, above all, those in St. Petersburg, where they came in still more intimate contact with Russian civilization. After 25 years of exile, many of those who later came to Canada were still enamored with the social and cultural life of the middle classes in Tsarist Russia, and homesick for a world that had long since disappeared.

This, however, was not the only contact which the Mennonite social system had with an area of high civilization. Wealthy middle-

---

[13] Cf. J. J. Hildebrand, *Zeittafel*, p. 268.

class Mennonites sent their sons to the University at Dorpat, with its rare blend of Russian and German culture. Still more of them attended schools and universities in Germany, then at the apex of her power and prestige. Yet pan-Germanistic concepts were largely absent in the thinking of the Second Reich, which was oriented toward a *kleindeutsch* rather than a *grossdeutsch* political philosophy. Thus the young Mennonites from Russia were thought of, and felt themselves to be, representatives of the great Russian nation, despite their German speech and background. Still, common language, religious affiliations, and cultural and racial affinities helped Mennonite students, seminarians, teachers and other travellers to eagerly absorb German ideas, literature and technology which they transmitted to their colonies back home in Russia.

The Forest Service has to be mentioned as a last important factor that shaped the cultural profile of the Mennonite community in Russia prior to the Revolution. Where every able-bodied youth is being drafted for a considerable period of his life, the army functions as much as a socializing factor as the public school. Particularly in countries including large peasant populations, the army has tended to strengthen the effect of the state-controlled public school, mainly by multiplying and intensifying contacts between different elements of the population; by instilling loyalty to the symbols of the state; and by redefining social roles and the means of gaining prestige. The process of levelling ethnic and regional differences, and of breaking down the isolation of localistic systems, which was initiated by the national school, has often been consciously supported by the national army. Yet the Russian Mennonites were able to retain not only a measure of school autonomy but even an autonomous system of conscription. Young Mennonites, instead of being conscripted for the army, were drafted into the Forest Service, which was organized very much like a military unit. They wore uniforms, were under military discipline and stood under Russian command. But their units were limited to Mennonites recruited from all over Russia and they were supervised in their off-hours by their own officers. Each of the five *Forsteien* (forest camps) was managed by a Mennonite *Ökonom,* who also acted as chaplain and as teacher of the Russian language. The duties of the "commandos" (forest units) consisted in logging, reforestation, road construction and work in state-owned saw mills, and, during war time, in guarding the crown forests, armed with nothing else but sticks.

The Mennonite colonies were responsible for the upkeep of the camps and were taxed for it corporatively. In 1913 about 1,000 young Mennonites were enrolled in the Forest Service at an expense of 350,000 rubles to their communities. Thus, this peculiar institution not only fostered acculturation but strengthened the social bonds among the widely scattered Mennonite settlements. In 1910 the need for coöperation led to the organization of a commission for church affairs including representatives of all the different branches of the Mennonite church. The commission, though religious in its designation, was really a national executive committee of the whole Mennonite commonwealth in Russia and contributed much to its unity and inner coherence.

The outbreak of World War I found the Mennonites in the position of one of several national groups included in the Russian Empire. Their colonies were united into a firmly knit ethnic system which was supported by many common interests, the need for coöperation on vital issues and by common religious, educational and semi-military institutions. The Mennonites were well adjusted to social, economic, cultural and political conditions in Russia, and to the large society. They even had developed a distinctly Russian patriotism. Thus, when war broke out, many of them entered the voluntary medical service in the Semski Soius, a sort of Red Cross, although they were liable to being called up for the Forest Service only. In 1915, 1,331 of them served in the Forest Service, 261 at road work in the Crimea, 804 in administrative civil functions (e.g. as hospital managers), and 3,093 in the medical service. At its height the total number enlisted in all these services reached 14,000 men. About 125 lost their lives either as stretcher-bearers on the battlefields or from diseases contracted in hospitals. The costs for the medical services were borne by the Mennonite communities.

Because of war-time propaganda and the general fear of spies and fifth columnists, heavy restrictions were imposed upon all Germans living in Russia, regardless of whether they were citizens or not. The use of the German language and social gatherings, even in private homes, were forbidden, and several Mennonites, including an elder, were jailed and exiled for alleged subversive activities. More serious was the enactment of laws providing for the expropriation of "Russian subjects of enemy origin, that is, the emigrants of non-Slavic extraction from states presently at war with Russia, viz. Germany, Austria, Bulgaria and Turkey, and their successors."[14]

In order to avoid the loss of their land and farms, the Mennonite leaders used a subterfuge. They proved, not quite incorrectly, that their people were of Dutch, not German, origin, and that the country from which they had immigrated had, at the time, been a part of Poland, not of Germany. This argument was finally accepted by the Russian authorities in January 1917, but not before some of the larger Mennonite estates had already been "liquidated" or ruined by commissioners of enemy property. As a result of these experiences, their concepts and sentiments of loyalty and national allegiance became seriously confused. At first they had been taught in school that they were, above all, Russians. When the war broke out, they were persecuted as *Germantsy*. Finally, their own leaders stamped them as Hollanders.

The Mennonites set great hope upon the Kerenski regime, which suspended the expropriation laws and adopted the principle of national self-government. The General Mennonite Congress was organized as a kind of secular parliament supplementing the General Conference of Mennonite churches. It was planned that the Central Bureau for Community Affairs would finally take over the autonomous administration of all Mennonite schools, the Forest Service, the Medical Service, etc. The November Revolution of 1917, however, ended all prospects of establishing an autonomous Mennonite nation within a decentralized democratic Russian republic.

Local soviets, often led by vindictive former servants of Mennonite masters, set up their regime of terror but were soon expelled by the advancing Austrian and German armies of occupation. Although the occupation lasted no longer than half a year, it had a profound influence upon the sentiments of the Russian Mennonites towards those who were technically the enemies of the country of their adoption, but who actually came as their liberators. The forces of the Central Powers restored law and order, and returned the property confiscated during war and revolution. For the first time, the Mennonites in the Ukraine were confronted with authorities who spoke their own language, who favored them, who entrusted them with important offices, and in whom they had confidence. For the first time, too, a new feeling of "belongingness" to the great and powerful German nation arose among

---

[14] Cf. Hildebrand, *Zeittafel*, p. 285.

the Russian Mennonites. When the troops of the Central Powers retreated, they left in their wake a social vacuum and a state of general anarchy. For some time the Mennonite colonies tried to carry on independently, while they were waiting for the arrival of regular Red troops and agents of the central Government. But in the surrounding country all social and legal order was breaking down. Bands of gangsters made their appearance, robbing, pillaging, raping and murdering. The largest of these was led by a former criminal, known under the name of Machnov, and said to have once been a young herdsman on a Mennonite farm.

The raids of the Machnovtsi put the Mennonites in a dilemma. Throughout their history they had claimed that Christians should suffer rather than do violence. Now that they were no more protected by other Christians who did not hesitate to wield the sword, they had either to perish or to take up arms themselves. Many Mennonites joined the *Selbstschutz*, an irregular army organized by the Germans in Southern Russia for their self-protection. After a few months of skirmishes and minor battles, during which but few lives were lost, they had to lay down their arms in March of 1918, when the Machnovtsi were joined by Red Army regulars in their battle against the forces of "capitalism and the counter-Revolution." The Bolshevik Government, unable to restore the power of the central administration in the Ukraine, surrendered to Machnov the Province of Tavrida in which the Molotschna colony was situated. Bloody revenge was taken not only on former *Selbstschutz* members but on the whole Mennonite community.

Once more the tide of civil war was turning when, in the summer of 1919, the White armies of Denikin occupied Southern Russia with the backing of the Western Allies. In October of that year, Machnov's partisans broke through the defense lines and inflicted the fate of Lidice upon several Mennonite villages. When famine and disease were added to their terror, about ten per cent of the Mennonite population lost their lives. Three more times did the waves of civil war sweep across their colonies: the regular Red Army replaced Machnov in January 1920, General Wrangel's White Army was in power from June to November of the same year, until the Red Army finally returned to stay.

As soon as the war had come to an end, its dire aftermath evoked the traditional humanitarian spirit of the American and Canadian peoples. Among the various relief committees organized at the time, one was also set up by the Mennonites of Canada and the United States, which at first coöperated with the Society of Friends in France. It was in 1921, when Hoover's Relief Administration came to an agreement with the Soviet Government, that American and Dutch Mennonites were permitted to carry on relief work in the Ukraine. In this way contacts with the brethren in Russia were re-established. In 1920 a delegation of Russian Mennonites visited the United States. They were officially charged with the mission of mobilizing aid for Russia, but explored at the same time possibilities of escape from the Red Paradise. They found the situation in Canada particularly promising for a large-scale transfer. The reasons for their choice were revealed in a statement by the late Bishop Toews, of Rosthern:

Mexico in every respect, its laws and regulations, and the mode of living on the part of the lower classes, reminded too much of Russia. The United States were closed to immigration, especially if immigrants were to be brought over by organized efforts. . . . Canada especially was thought suitable as a country that might be recommended for settlement, although even here it was hardly possible to arrange compact settlements the same as our brethren had in Russia.[15]

The motives for the migration of several thousands of Russian Mennonites, between 1922 and 1930, partly to Canada, partly to South America, are obvious. They were not the only Russian citizens who tried to escape the Red Paradise, but few others had a comparable chance to do so. To put it briefly, they were, in the true sense of the word, refugees from political and religious oppression. Many had lost their property, and often their families, during the Revolution, and were too worn out to attempt a new start in Communist Russia. When, after 1926, a more radical policy was adopted by Stalin aiming at the Bolshevization of the peasantry, the liquidation of the kulaks,[16] and the extermination of the last remnants of a bourgeois élite and intelligentsia, when hundreds of thousands of them were sent to concentration camps to be starved and worked to death, emigration became for many the only hope of survival. When finally a crusade against God and religion was proclaimed and when their schools were converted into institutions of Communist indoctrination, even the most adaptable, who had been willing to compromise almost at any price, realized that they had lost

---

[15] *Report of the 24th Session of the General Conference of the Mennonite Church of North America* (1926), p. 292.

[16] Although the liquidation of the kulaks, that is, middle-class farmers, was officially decreed on February 1, 1930, their suppression was already part of the policies of the First Five Year Plan.

all roots in a Russia that had become the laboratory of World Revolution.

The Second Immigration to Canada

After World War I Canada entered upon a second phase of its immigration and colonization policy. It was then realized that other methods had to be used than those employed during the heyday of Continental immigration between 1890 and 1914, when the progress of colonization was blocked by the haphazard, and partly fraudulent, manner of land distribution in Canada's West. J. B. Hedges quotes the following appraisal of past mistakes:

Probably one-third of the men who made entry to the land never intended to become permanent agriculturists. They earned their 'patent,' as it was termed, with the least possible delay. As soon as they had title, they either sold or mortgaged it for what they could get, and a large portion of them left the country. Many are reported to have gone north to repeat the operation, others drifted to urban centers.

To this the author adds: "The unoccupied land was largely in the hands of mortgagees or was destined to soon be there. In most cases, the mortgages were held by large mortgage companies."[17]

Thus, action was taken by government agencies, municipalities, banks, boards of trade and railroad companies to remedy the situation. As an immediate result, a Department of Colonization and Development was created by the Canadian Pacific Railway Company, and put under the management of Colonel Y. S. Dennis, of Montreal. This agency became instrumental in bringing the majority of Russländer Mennonites to Canada. Its policy was aimed at the colonization of privately owned, but not actually farmed, land in the West. Its original interest was in winning settlers from the United States. The plan failed, however, because of the depression which settled upon American agriculture after 1921. At the same time, the Dominion Government, then still in the possession of much unclaimed land, concentrated its efforts on the rehabilitation of war veterans, and assisted immigration from the British Isles. These attempts, too, were not particularly successful in promoting agricultural colonization, for immigrants from the United Kingdom usually aspired to a higher social status, preferring urban occupations to pioneer farming.

---

[17] *Building the Canadian West: The Land and Colonization Policies of the Canadian Pacific Railway* (New York, 1939), p. 349.

It was at this stage that the Dominion Government was first petitioned by a delegation of the Mennonite Conference of Central Canada to admit the refugees from Soviet Russia. The moment chosen was not propitious because of pending elections. After the victory of the Liberal party, however, the new Prime Minister, Mackenzie King, proved favorably disposed to the plan. Not only did his party rely heavily on the vote of the multi-national population of Western Canada in addition to that of the French-Canadian block in the East, but the Prime Minister himself had lived in his younger days among the Ontario Mennonites and had sat, from 1908 to 1911, for Waterloo North in the House of Commons. Thus Bishop Toews was able to describe him explicitly as "our friend."[18]

Before the project could be realized, the ban against the entry of Mennonites had to be lifted. This was done by Order-in-Council of June 2, 1923, which, however, was never published in the *Canada Gazette* so as to escape the pressure of public opinion. The permission to immigrants was made dependent on the condition, agreed upon by the Mennonite Board of Colonization, (1) that the Mennonites admitted to Canada would find shelter and support among their brethren, (2) that they would be placed on land as farmers, and (3) that none of the immigrants would become a public charge. It was further understood that the privilege of complete military exemption granted to the earlier group in 1873 would not apply to them.[19]

Even before immigration was made possible legally, a member of the Cabinet brought the Mennonite petitioners in contact with Colonel Dennis, who, as a young surveyor, had met the first party of immigrants in 1874, while travelling down the Red River on the Hudson's Bay Company steamer "International." In 1914, when he heard of Russia's plans of expatriating the Mennonites because of their German origin, he "thought it of the utmost importance that every effort be made to move them since they were excellent farmers and would undoubtedly have sufficient capital to make an auspicious start in the West."[20] Before 1919 Dennis had also seen war service in Russia and had undoubtedly gathered some first-hand experience as to conditions

---

[18] Christian Neff (ed.) *Bericht über die Mennonitische Welthilfskonferenz . . . 1930, in Danzig* (Karlsruhe, 1931), p. 74.

[19] Cf. Toews' report of 1926, p. 292, as quoted by I. I. Friesen, Mennonites of Western Canada, p. 171.

[20] Hedges, *Building the Canadian West*, p. 289.

204

there. When Colonel Dennis was approached in March 1922, he agreed to coöperate with the Mennonites who intended to purchase land vacated by the Auswanderer group in Manitoba, at the price of $25 an acre and of $150,000 for a whole village. This land was to be mortgaged, and the mortgages were to be sold to Canadian and American Mennonites. For this purpose the Mennonite Board of Colonization was founded in Gretna in April 1922, but was soon transferred to Rosthern, Saskatchewan, with Bishop Toews as its manager. The original project of establishing a stock company with a capital of ten million dollars was widely resisted in Mennonite circles, mainly because of the harsh terms included in the proposed contract with the Canadian Pacific Railway.

The railroad company agreed to transport the immigrants from any Baltic or Black Sea port to Saskatoon at the reduced rates of $140 for adults and $90 for children. But many of them did not have any money, while the funds of their American and Canadian brethren were already strained to the limit because of the necessity of preparing for the reception and settlement of the refugees. Thus the company proposed to bring them on a credit basis, "under which a Mennonite organization in Canada was to assume responsibility for the liquidation of the debt by installments."[21] It soon became evident that the Rosthern board alone was unable to cope with the financial problems involved in the project.

In 1919 Colonel Dennis had inaugurated the Canadian Colonization Association, later an adjunct to the Department of Colonization and Development of the Canadian Pacific Railway Company, with the purpose of developing areas tributary to existing railway lines. The first major enterprise undertaken by this institution was the settlement of the Mennonite refugees in Western Canada. In this it was assisted by the Canadian Mennonite Board of Colonization, the Mennonite Land Settlement Board, the Mennonite Immigration Aid, and the Central Committee of Mennonite Immigrants. This somewhat complicated organization succeeded in placing the larger part of the 20,835 immigrants on farms in Western Canada between 1923 and 1930. About 800 more were placed in a similar manner by the Canadian National Railway Company, while others were settled under private arrange-

[21] Hedges, *Building the Canadian West*, p. 370.

ments.[22] The principal function of the Mennonite Land Settlement
Board was, according to Hedges,

to find owners of improved land who were disposed to sell their holdings,
to bring such owners together with Mennonite immigrants, to see that
contracts for sale of such lands were fair to all concerned, and to provide
after-care and supervision for the new settlers. . . . The aim and purpose
of the immigration promotion now was to build the settler into the
economic life of the country.[23]

Once again a Mennonite immigration set the pattern for a whole
period of land settlement in Canada's West. The methods evolved
with the active participation of Mennonites as organizers were to
benefit many other groups of immigrants in the years between the two
wars. During the Depression native farmers, too, were assisted in
the same way when they were in danger of losing their property to
commercial mortgage companies, banks and other finance interests.
By 1930 a total of 2,000 Mennonite families, about 30 per cent, settled
on land and in villages abandoned by the Auswanderer group in the
West Reserve, and another 10 per cent in the East Reserve. Perhaps
25 per cent were settled in about a dozen larger blocks near Arnaud
and St. Elizabeth, Culross, Boissevain, Manitou and the Turtle Mountains, Starbuck and Springstein, and near Oak Lake and La Salle.
Almost 20 per cent lived in Winnipeg. Upon their arrival in Canada,
the immigrants were taken into private homes either by Kanädier
Mennonites or by earlier Russländer immigrants. At the close of
1928, 3,000 families, or 10,000 persons, had been placed by the
Canadian Colonization Association alone on privately owned farms
comprising 700,000 acres at a contract price of almost thirty million
dollars.[24]

Much land was offered to Mennonite immigrants at favorable
prices by private owners who had bought it at inflated prices after the
war and who were unable to operate it economically after conditions
deteriorated and wages increased. Also, land which had been vacated
in the Reserves by the Auswanderer group, and which was now in
the hands of big finance interests or of private speculators, was
sometimes leased to the immigrants. More often, however, such land

---

[22] Under the auspices of the Canadian Pacfiic Railway Company alone, 2,759 immigrated in
1923, 5,048 in 1924, 3,772 in 1925, 5,940 in 1926, 847 in 1927, 511 in 1928, and about 200 between
1928 and 1930.

[23] *Building the Canadian West*, p. 371.

[24] *Building the Canadian West*, p. 374.

was sold through the services of the Mennonite Land Settlement Board. Frequently no down payment was required, but the so-called Mennonite contracts provided for up to 15 annual installments to be paid with half the crop of each year. In many cases the settlers were able to pay half the purchase price in five years, but in others considerable reductions had to be granted because of the Depression. As a rule, the policy of the Canadian Colonization Association was successful in keeping farms in the hands of their new owners and in persuading creditors and mortgagers to desist from foreclosures, which would only have multiplied their losses.

Three-Way Adjustment

The Russländer refugees had to make social adjustments in no less than three different directions: toward each other, toward the large society, and toward their Kanädier brethren. Unlike other Mennonite migrations (that of 1874-1878 or the one to Mexico), this one did not consist of the wholesale transfer of compact colonies, including most of their personnel and institutions, to an underpopulated area where outside influences and pressures were weak. This new class of immigrants came from many different settlements and walks of life. They were homogeneous only in so far as they had a distinctive common background and were united, though in a rather general way, by a strong ethnic we-feeling. But in a social system which comprised over 100,000 people living in widely scattered communities, there had been limited opportunities for face-to-face relations and specific common experiences. While most of the leaders may have known each other personally, many of those who were thrown together by the migration had actually been strangers in the Old Country. It was in fact the migration itself, the need for mutual assistance and coöperation, and impressive common experiences before, during and after the movement, which forged all these divergent elements into a specific social group. This adjustment between the refugees themselves was effected without serious frictions, mainly because they were forced to coöperate in order to survive.

Adjustment to the large society was complicated by the treatment which the immigrants experienced from Canadian officials and public. Not that their experience was exceptional or that they were subjected to a particularly vicious kind of discrimination. On the contrary, they were given special consideration by the immigration authorities. The psychological shock, implicit in every migration, was in their case cushioned by the fact that they were welcomed by native Mennonites, that they arrived in slow stages, and that they were, by and large, permitted to remain together. Still, precisely because they suffered and acted as a group, and remained in constant contact with each other, a kind of collective resentment developed among them against what they felt to be unwarranted hardships and injustices inflicted upon them collectively by Canada and her agents. It is also true that Canada's public opinion was not altogether favorable to the large influx of destitute foreigners of German descent, so that fewer concessions were made in the application of immigration laws than possibly could have been made in this particular case.

Canada's immigration regulations exclude from entry persons with certain contagious and mental diseases. Under normal conditions a preliminary medical examination by authorized physicians takes place before visas are granted. Yet the Soviet Government did not permit Canadian officials to operate within Russia. Thus hundreds of Mennonites left that country who were afterwards rejected at the port of embarkation. Many of them suffered from trachoma. Once they had left the Soviet Union, however, they were refused re-entry. Thus a concentration camp was established in Atlantic Park at Southampton, England, where they could wait until they were cured, while the Mennonite Relief Committee had to pay for their upkeep. In 1926 the camp had 400 inmates and cost ran as high as $160,000.

Another refugee camp was organized on the Lechfeld in Bavaria by the German Mennonites, with the active support of the German Government and President Hindenburg (who personally donated 200,000 marks). Between July and December 1923 alone, 658 refugees were admitted, and at one time as many as 750 lived in the camp. Hundreds of Mennonites often stayed for several years in Germany, both inside and outside of camps, awaiting admittance to Canada. They were well received as *Volksdeutsche* and exposed to the ideas of Pan-German nationalism. They came to consider the German Reich and her people as their rescuers and developed strong emotional ties. It would probably be safe to say that it was first their contact with the German occupation armies and then the temporary sojourn of many in Germany which engendered strong national attachments among the Russländer group.

Soon after the arrival of the immigrants to Western Canada, it was noticed that they were in many ways more akin to Canada's large society and its cultural level than to the Kanädier group. On January 1, 1925, the Saskatoon *Guardian* observed that "recent new-comers at once upon their arrival . . . proceeded to erect a school for their children," which the paper called "welcome news." It added: "Canada has no more industrious, honest and respected citizens than some of those who bear the name of Mennonites, and if these new-comers . . . are willing to abide by our laws and learn our language, they should be accorded a hearty welcome." In a similar vein, the *Grain Growers Guide* of January 11, 1927, described the Russländer immigrants as progressive and eager to have schools, while *The New Outlook* published a sympathetic article in which Professor Sissons wrote: "They are keen to pick up English, and their evident readiness to put off the old and put on the new does not serve to commend them to some of their Canadian brethren."

Yet toward the end of the 1920's public opinion was once more mobilized against Mennonite immigration from Russia. Colonization in the West had then reached a temporary saturation point. Years before the great depression agriculture began to feel the pinch of declining wheat prices and markets. It was feared that immigration would increase unemployment. Thus it was resented in the Prairie Provinces. When the Conservatives took over the Government of Saskatchewan in 1929, one of the first actions of the new Premier, Dr. I. T. M. Anderson, was a strong protest to Ottawa (given prominence by premature publicity) against the contemplated immigration of another batch of 5,000 Mennonites. Premier Brownlee of Alberta (United Farmers), too, declared that admission of foreigners to Canada had been altogether too indiscriminate.[25] And John Bracken, Premier of Manitoba, insisted that unemployment was greatly aggravated by the flow of new immigrants.[26] In addition to economic considerations, the old "foreigner scare," too, played a role in this movement. For instance, Premier Brownlee reported that his government had been literally deluged with demands that the flow of immigrants be stopped.[27] As a result no more than 958 persons were admitted to Canada between 1928 and 1930. Afterwards the new

[25] Cf. *The Canadian Annual Review*, 1929-1930 (Toronto, 1930), p. 497.

[26] *Canadian Annual Review*, 1929-1930, pp. 463f.

[27] *Canadian Annual Review*, 1928-1929, p. 490.

Conservative Dominion Government barred all people from overseas, except for a small trickle of selected classes. At the same time it became increasingly difficult to obtain the necessary documents from the Russian authorities who demanded prohibitive fees. But Canada insisted upon regular passports on the grounds that this alone would permit the deportation of undesirables, although only one Mennonite has ever been deported. By transferring their non-preferred quota to the Mennonites, the two Canadian railroad companies were able to bring over at least some of the refugees waiting in Germany. But the bulk of the Russländer migration was afterwards directed to Paraguay and Brazil, partly with the support of the German Government.[28]

The depression of the 1930's hit the Russländer immigrants in Canada badly: for they were burdened not only with personal debts contracted in better years but with the collective obligation of looking after their destitute members and of repaying nearly two million dollars, plus interest, to the Canadian Pacific Railway Company. They had to care for all psychiatric cases which had occurred before naturalization in order to prevent their deportation. For this purpose every member was taxed with five, and even ten, cents a month. Perhaps as many as half of the immigrant settlers lost their farms during the Depression. Some of them took over smaller holdings while others drifted to towns and cities. As Bishop Toews reported in 1936 to the Mennonite World Congress in Holland,

many of our immigrants detach themselves readily from the soil, when the undertaken obligations appear too oppressive. . . . In a free country like Canada, it is difficult to exercise any control. We have to confine ourselves to give advice where it is requested, and to give aid where it is necessary and possible.[29]

The main reason for urbanization among the Russländer group, however, must be sought in the middle-class origin of many of the refugees, who included a disproportionate number of former estate owners, teachers, physicians, nurses, business men, clerks, bankers, and so on. At first the provisions under which they were admitted

----

[28] The most authentic source concerning the Russländer migration are the reports of the late Bishop David Toews to various Mennonite congresses and conferences, particularly in Christian Neff (ed.), *Bericht über die Mennonitische Welthilfs Konferenz . . . 1930, in Danzig* (Karlsruhe, 1931), pp. 94ff., and *Der Allgemeine Kongress der Mennoniten . . . gehalten in Amsterdam, Elspeet, Witmarsum (Holland), 29. Juni bis 3. Juli, 1936* (Karlsruhe, n.d.), pp. 151ff.; see also the reports of the Canadian General Conference (published annually since 1903 under the title of *Konferenz-Berichte*, at first of the *Konferenz der Mennoniten im mittleren Kanada*, since 1932: of the *Allgemeine Konferenz der Mennoniten in Canada*, most recently as *Jahrbuch der Konferenz der Mennoniten in Canada*).

[29] Neff (ed.), *Der Allgemeine Kongress der Mennoniten . . . 1936*, pp. 152f.

to Canada compelled all of them to work in agriculture. Yet, in the face of great hardships and difficulties, a majority of these new farmers took up more familiar occupations when opportunities presented themselves after they had become naturalized. According to a list, published in 1944, of 78 former students of the *Zentralschule* at Chortitz then residing in Manitoba,[30] only 25 were farmers, 14 craftsmen (mostly carpenters and skilled laborers), 6 teachers, 5 businessmen, 5 housewives, 3 owners of industrial plants, 2 common laborers, 2 gardeners, one each was listed as chickenbreeder, beekeeper and author, physician, retired clergyman, president of a Mennonite hospital, sales clerk, postal clerk, bookkeeper, railway employee, author, and trucker, while 6 had no definite occupation.

The most burdensome task was the repayment of the debt to the Canadian Pacific Railway, which was the responsibility of the group as a whole. At the same time it provided a rallying point and a common interest which contributed much to intensive interaction and social cohesion among the Rußländer immigrants, and separated them to some extent from the Kanädier Mennonites. While nearly 7,000, or one-third, of this group had been able to pay their passage to Canada in full, 675 had paid only half of it, and the rest had been brought over entirely on credit. C. F. Klassen, one of the prominent organizers of the migration to Canada, characterized the situation as follows:[31] "What was business for the Canadian Pacific Railway, or was at least intended to be, was to us a great help in distress." He emphasized that the company was not a "mission society," although its president, Sir Edward Beatty, and Colonel Dennis "had been led by a certain idealism," while two other officials, J. N. K. MacAllister and T. O. Herzer, had shown "great understanding and ready consideration."

The original contract with the company contained provisions which could have never been fulfilled even under more favorable circumstances. They were apparently the best that the promoters of the scheme could hope the board and stockholders would accept. They probably expected, not incorrectly, that once the transaction was carried to the point where it could no longer be undone, necessary adjustments would be made. Still, "a businessman would hardly have

[30] *Die ehemaligen Schüler der Chortitzer Zentralschule in Canada* (Steinbach, 1944).

[31] "Auch eine mennonitische Angelegenheit," *Warte-Jahrbuch für die Mennonitische Gemeinschaft in Canada 2* (1944): 95-73.

signed," wrote Klassen in retrospection. It was the Mennonite board at Rosthern and Bishop Toews who took the responsibility, "trusting in God's help and in the honesty of the expected immigrants whom he did not know."

In the same article Klassen remarked: "Very many debtors have acted in integrity and honesty, and many of them have paid their debt for passages under great hardships. These have kept up the whole matter with God's help and saved it from failure." Others, however, did not honour their word even in times of prosperity, creating a situation under which many similar schemes would probably have collapsed. The way in which the Mennonite leaders handled this loan provides a striking parallel with the repayment of the Government Loan of 1875. They convinced their people that the good name of the Mennonites was at stake, that they had a moral obligation to implement the promise given on their behalf, and that it was a matter of Christian charity to assist their brethren. As Klassen put it in a conversation with the author: It was a duty to help those unable to pay so that they could meet their financial obligations and would not become "guilty in their own conscience." Those, however, who did not *want* to pay, were to be considered as morally sick, imposing upon their brethren the duty to cover up their sin. Even the younger Rußländer generation were impressed with the idea of collective responsibility.

In collecting the debt, a system was adopted which stimulated and utilized both coöperation and competition. All Rußländer Mennonites living in a certain locality, and all the local districts within a province, were made collectively responsible for the unpaid debts of any member residing within their jurisdiction. In this way tardy debtors were induced to do their utmost in order to avoid taking advantage of their neighbours and incurring public censure. Others made great sacrifices to help out those of their brethren who would or could not pay. Finally, in a spirit of keen competition, the individual districts and regions tried to outdo each other. All this was done at a time when the immigrants were starting from scratch, were helping their brethren in the Old Country, were contributing to funds for Mennonite collegiates, Bible schools, hospitals and other charities, and were building 115 new churches and places of worship. World War II, made it finally possible to repay the principal of $1,925,000 in full, after the railroad company had remitted all interest.

Despite common origin and religion, adjustment of the Russländer immigrants to the Kanädier group was in many ways as difficult as adjustment to the large society. The two Mennonite groups were divided by cultural and class differences. In the eyes of the native Mennonites the newcomers appeared worldly, overbearing and unwilling to do manual labor. The Russländer people, on the other hand, found their benefactors, on whose good will they were dependent, uncouth, backward, miserly and, above all, ignorant and uneducated. Particularly divergent attitudes toward the public school led to serious friction. The Russian group were very anxious to avail themselves of the best possible educational facilities, while the Kanädier group were still very touchy about the subject and resentful of any criticism of their education.

The many former teachers and intellectuals included in the immigrant group saw a welcome outlet for their frustrated energies in a crusade for the improvement of schooling among their brethren in Western Canada, particularly in Manitoba. Also in other fields, such as scientific farming and business, church organization and pastoral practices, charities and public welfare, the immigrants were more progressive and tended to take the lead, not always with the necessary tact and patience. Quite generally, European immigrants, especially those with better training, are, of course, often inclined to criticize and minimize the kind of culture with which they are confronted in the New World. While some submit to the painful and slow process of acculturation, many others never lose an attitude of superiority mixed with resentment at having lost their former—real or imaginary—social status. These live and pass away as strangers to both cultures, that of their native, and that of their adopted country— truly marginal men, uprooted, lonely and out of tune with their environment. Usually the isolated immigrant of this type has little chance of causing a great stir. In the present case, however, circumstances favored the combination of a solid group of Europeans, filled with a sense of mission, and a related indigenous group which, at the time, was in the throes of a crisis. The refugees, because they were essentially better adjusted to life in a high civilization, often took the initiative in preparing the ground for a reorganization of the whole group in Western Canada.

One portion of the immigrants settled within the compact Kanädier colonies. Many others were distributed in smaller groups throughout the province, forming isolated local communities of their own. Although the Reserves were the scene of early frictions, mixed habitat necessitated coöperation, and led to intensive interaction between members of both groups and eventually to amalgation. Adjustment was facilitated mainly by two factors. First, the arrival of the newcomers was spread over a period of seven years. Second, the coherence of the local Kanädier communities was in many places seriously disturbed by the emigration of the Auswanderer group, so that no organized resistance by cliques of natives developed.

Both groups coöperated at once not only in the economic but also in the religious sphere. Many immigrants became public school teachers and, because of their better education, attained other positions of responsibility and leadership in the Reserves. Of course, both groups considered each other as part of the same ethnic system; this notion was given considerable reality by the fact that they were indeed bound together by countless kinship ties, a factor of decisive importance in a largely familistic society. On the other hand, the outlying Mennonite settlements, mostly with a homogeneous Russländer population, were small and leaned heavily upon the old Reserves as a natural center of gravity. Still, under the influence of urban immigrants, Winnipeg gained some importance as a secondary Mennonite center, mainly for the Russländer group. While it is true that certain cleavages can still be found, the differences between the Russländer and the Kanädier are losing their sociological significance, and the two divisions must be considered as structural components of a comprehensive group, the Russian Mennonites of Western Canada and, more specifically, of Manitoba.

CHAPTER IX

Social Change

The Crisis

THE REGROUPMENT of the 1920's accentuated the state of flux in which the Manitoba Mennonites found themselves after the war. Like other ethnic groups in North America, they felt the effects of outside pressure, subtle but persistent, and at times not so subtle and quite insistent. Of greater importance was the psychological attraction which the amenities of a prospering society exerted upon the susceptible minds of the second generation ethnics. True enough, the steady disorganization which encroached upon other minorities on this continent was somewhat retarded among the Mennonites, for the sectarian character of their religion and, above all, compact group settlement tended to preserve isolation more effectively. But to a thoughtful observer of conditions in the Manitoba settlements the ultimate outcome seemed quite inescapable. Sooner or later the Mennonites, too, would be absorbed into the general stream of Canadian life; hallowed traditions and customs would die away with the immigrant generation; at least their grandchildren would easily overcome the cultural lag in their mores and would embrace more up-to-date ideas; even attitudes towards religion would become modernized and religious taboos less restrictive, thus permitting more intimate conversation with and even conversion to other Protestant churches; English would become the primary means of communication, leaving their folk dialect a relic to be occasionally paraded by some old-timer before curious visitors or wide-eyed youngsters.

There were many signs making such a course of events most probable when the sociologist of McGill University in Montreal, Professor C. A. Dawson, and his students undertook a survey of the West Reserve.[1] While this study was made shortly after the onset of the Depression, conditions still reflected, in many respects, the tail end of prosperity. Dawson reported that the Mennonites had given up their earlier type of subsistence farming and, like their Anglo-Saxon neighbours, had adopted a capitalistic system of agriculture, using the latest farm machinery, concentrating on cash crops, neglecting livestock and diversification, and at times overexpanding their holdings at inflated prices. They sought credit from commercial banks and finance institutions, patronized commercial insurance companies, and were doing a brisk business with commercial grain buyers and flour mills. Many Mennonites had left their picturesque villages with their ancient Frisian farmhouses, which included residence, stable and barn under one roof, and were now farming on scattered homesteads like other Canadians, from whom they had learned to build two-storey frame houses with detached barns, tool sheds and granaries. Yes, the Mennonites were "good farmers" even in the critical eyes of their Anglo-Saxon neighbours.

And what was even more important in the eyes of these very same neighbours, they were fast becoming more "normal" than they used to be, though they still were keeping pretty well to themselves. Old-world peasant clothes were going out of fashion. Power washing machines were coming into use. Canadian institutions and organizations were more and more accepted, first in the towns, then also in the open country. Among the latter, Dawson mentioned the Boy Scouts, Tuxies, Canadian Girls in Training, Women's Institute, Manitoba Teachers' Federation, Manitoba Consumers' Coöperative Association, Junior Red Cross, Seed Growers' Club and Agricultural Society. Various forms of commercial recreation such as dances and movie theatres were becoming popular, at least among the young people. Particularly while working out in non-Mennonite city homes, farms or industries, they became acquainted with Anglo-Saxon customs in food, clothing, language and amusement which, upon their return, they introduced into the Mennonite settlement. Political participation, once altogether forbidden by the conservative Mennonite churches, had increased to such an extent that a local Mennonite physician had been elected to the Provincial Legislature.

---

[1] C. A. Dawson, *Group Settlement: Ethnic Communities in Western Canada* (Toronto, 1936), pp. 95-171.

Dawson clearly recognized the role which the public school played in this change. "The school," he wrote, "has become the nucleus of Canadian agricultural, athletic and literary organizations where people participate in competitive games, debating, dramatics and other departures from Mennonite traditions."[2] With the school came agricultural clubs, and with them an alien spirit of competition. With the school also came school picnics, parent-teacher associations and various secular gatherings which broke the monopoly of family and church on the social life of the community. And above all, it was the school which forced the knowledge and use of the English language upon all Mennonite children. Even some of the churches were becoming modernized, particularly those dominated by the Russländer immigrants. In this respect the observer reported that contacts with other Christian denominations had resulted in an elaboration of ritual and church organization among the more liberal branches of the sect. He noticed many deviations from the traditional pattern, such as the introduction of Sunday schools, of youth organizations, of sewing circles, elaborate church choirs accompanied by organ music; also a beginning professionalization of the ministry in a few places, even English church services and a closer coöperation with Anglo-Saxon Protestant churches. Dawson also felt that what he called "the old sectarian spirit" was on the wane. Religion did not mean as much to some Mennonites, particularly the younger people and the town folk, as it did to their elders. While church attendance was still excellent, "in many cases," wrote Dawson, "it is submitted to as a formality without a great basis of conviction."[3] Rural ministers had been losing steadily in importance as community leaders and had in part been superseded by school teachers, municipal officers, and businessmen residing in the trade centers and the railroad towns.

Was it then surprising when Professor Dawson concluded his report with the following resumé:

The Mennonite group as a whole has ceased to struggle against the world, and has to a large extent even forgotten its own distinctive group character. . . . Through many channels, the world is insinuating itself into the community life and breaking down the distinguishing characteristics of a 'peculiar people.' Whether this assimilation will be complete fifty years hence, hundred years, or more, it is impossible at present to predict. . . .[4]

On the surface, Dawson's assessment of the situation in the early

---

[2] *Group Settlement*, p. 144.

[3] *Group Settlement*, p. 153.

[4] *Group Settlement*, p. 171.

1930's sounded convincing enough. What he observed, or believed to observe, in the Mennonite colonies were precisely those symptoms which elsewhere had heralded the breakup and disorganization of ethnic communities. There was no reason to assume that the Manitoba Mennonites would not go the same way as all others.

Dawson himself had noticed that "the process of absorption . . . is of the whole Mennonite community rather than of individual Mennonites;"[5] however, he had failed to see the significance of this difference, apparently believing that acculturation is always a sign of assimilation. In reality acculturation may frequently be but a device by which a minority adjusts itself to the large society as a group, so that both conflict and absorption are successfully avoided. In this case group members participate simultaneously in many activities of the large society—particularly in its economy—as well as in the ethnic community which continues to function as a distinctive locality group. Portions of the traditional culture and of the culture of the greater society form a workable combination which, however, remains unstable. When a crisis suggests a reëvaluation of the compromise, the process of acculturation may even be reversed and the ethnic group may seek a solution by reviving traditional behavior patterns. This is precisely what happened in the case of the Manitoba Mennonites.

The crisis came to them by way of the Depression. In this respect Dawson's study included a revealing item. He had compared farm budgets among different ethnic groups in Western Canada just four years after the onset of the Depression and had found that Mennonite farm incomes were considerably lower than those of non-Mennonites. At the same time, however, the Mennonites had been much more successful in balancing their budgets through reducing their inventory, farm expenses, and cash living costs. In Dawson's own words, they had met the economic landslide by reverting to an economy of self-sufficiency, and they had made the transition more quickly and more painlessly than others. "There is no doubt," he added, "that this adaptability is of great advantage to them in weathering periods of economic stress."[6]

Nevertheless the Mennonites did not escape the effects of the crisis. Many of them lost their life-long savings when the *Waisenamt* banks were forced into bankruptcy. While economic and financial

5 *Ibidem.*
6 *Group Settlement,* p. 130.

factors were the immediate cause of their downfall, more decisive was the fact that the old coöperative community banks had lost their meaning and were abandoned with little compunction. There also was the same mixture of human shortcoming and the pathetic inability to cope with modern conditions which has brought about the downfall of other church banks. They have usually worked well under a stable economy and in a homogeneous society with fixed standards and strict social controls, but almost everywhere they have shown a tendency to lose all sense of proportion when confronted with the fluctuations of business cycles and a new business ethics. The Mennonite *Waisenamt* banks are not alone in having confused the care of bank deposits and trusts with the care of souls, and in having failed to put a check on the manipulations of unscrupulous or inefficient functionaries for fear that this would hurt the cause of religion. In the era of Capitalism, the combination of business and religion, once perfectly legitimate and successful, has proved dangerous for both business and religion, and in the long run unworkable.

According to a survey made at the height of the Depression by the Agricultural Association of Southern Manitoba, about half of the 1,240 farmers in the strongly Mennonite Municipality of Rhineland alone had lost title to their farms through foreclosures or bank proceedings, while 455 farmers were so heavily in debt that they were paying a third of their crop to mortgage companies or other mortgage holders. Only 159 farmers, that is, 26 per cent of the farm owners or 13 per cent of all farm operators, had been able to retain title to their land.[7]

The New Farm Economy

The lessons of the Depression were learned slowly but once learned they had a lasting and permanent effect. Census figures for the years 1936 and 1941 showed dramatic changes in Mennonite farm economy.[8] Taking first an area in the West Reserve, the same which had been studied by Dawson, there was a definite trend toward more intensive and more diversified farming. Wheat production was drastically reduced in favor of coarse grain, mixed grain and other

---

[7] A similar report has been published more recently in *The Community Builder*, (Altona Co-operative Council, 1951, p. 3). There are discrepancies between these figures and the census data for 1936, which however do not influence the total picture.

[8] Cf. E. K. Francis, "The Adjustment of a Peasant Group to a Capitalistic Economy: The Manitoba Mennonites," *Rural Sociology 17* (1952): 218-228.

TABLE 5—LAND UTILIZATION, HANOVER AND RHINELAND, 1921-1946

	Year	Number of Farm Units	Total Area in Acres appr.	Land Occupied			Improved Land			Land Under Field Crops*			Fallow		Cultivated Pasture		Unimproved Land		Natural Pasture and Prairie	
				Total Acres	Per Farm Unit Acres	% of Total Area	Total Acres	Per Farm Unit Acres	% of Occupied Land	Total Acres	Per Farm Unit Acres	% of Occupied Land	Acres	% of Occupied Land	Acres	% of Occupied Land	Acres	% of Occupied Land	Acres	% of Occupied Land
HANOVER	1921	629	185,000	147,436	234.4	79.7	54,977	87.4	37.3	40,244	64.0	27.3	10,178	6.9	1,665	1.1	92,459	62.7	47,751	32.4
	1931	688	185,000	152,690	221.9	82.5	57,297	83.3	37.5	42,730	62.1	28.0	9,283	6.8	3,242	2.1	95,393	62.5	49,686	32.5
	1936	883	185,000	158,174	179.1	85.5	63,429	71.8	40.1	49,245	55.8	31.1	10,827	6.8	2,628	1.7	94,745	59.9	58,480	37.0
	1941	1,088	185,000	166,614	153.1	90.1	74,358	68.3	44.6	59,170	54.4	35.5	10,008	6.0	2,242	1.3	92,256	55.4	70,271	42.2
	1946	1,113	185,000	171,360	154.0	92.6	74,924	67.3	43.7	52,331	47.02	30.54	14,943	8.72	1,213	.7	96,436	56.3	82,065	47.9
RHINELAND	1921	1,125	231,100	220,598	196.1	95.5	187,105	166.3	84.8	144,230	128.2	65.4	28,194	12.8	13,857	6.3	33,493	15.2	31,082	14.1
	1931	1,308	231,100	228,252	174.5	98.8	205,394	157.0	90.0	151,029	115.5	66.2	37,582	16.5	11,587	5.1	22,858	10.0	20,656	9.0
	1936	1,240	231,100	225,706	182.0	97.7	204,904	165.2	90.8	170,988	137.9	75.8	21,767	9.6	11,502	5.1	20,802	9.2	15,378	6.8
	1941	1,249	231,100	228,852	183.2	99.0	219,829	176.0	96.1	176,773	141.5	77.2	19,722	8.6	17,670	7.7	9,023	3.9	6,444	2.8
	1946	1,221	231,100	224,466	183.8	97.1	213,091	173.7	94.4	163,020	133.5	72.6	23,208	10.3	21,307	9.5	12,375	5.5	12,067	5.4

* Includes farm gardens and orchards.

TABLE 6—FIELD CROPS, HANOVER AND RHINELAND, 1936, 1941 and 1946

HANOVER

	1936		1941		1946	
	Acreage	%	Acreage	%	Acreage	%
All Field Crops	49,245	100.0	58,715	100.0	51,912	100.0
Wheat	6,248	12.7	7,045	12.0	5,313	10.2
Barley	16,642	33.8	18,334	31.2	16,274	31.3
Oats	13,095	26.6	13,018	22.2	17,063	32.9
Rye	945	1.9	1,824	3.1	110	0.2
Flax Seed	444	0.9	1,540	2.6	1,117	2.2
Mixed and Other Grains	1,339	2.7	1,870	3.2	3,023	5.8
Cultivated Hay	9,419	19.1	10,726	18.3	5,650	10.9
Other Fodder Crops	571	1.2	2,633	4.5	1,627	3.1

RHINELAND

	1936		1941		1946	
	Acreage	%	Acreage	%	Acreage	%
All Field Crops	170,988	100.0	176,648	100.0	162,495	100.0
Wheat	89,820	52.5	59,290	33.6	59,395	37.1
Barley	29,423	17.2	37,861	21.4	38,821	23.9
Oats	29,585	17.3	25,725	14.6	27,738	17.1
Rye	4,722	2.8	5,321	3.0	377	0.2
Flax Seed	1,626	0.9	5,838	3.3	10,162	6.2
Mixed and Other Grains		0.0	33,870	19.2	4,251	2.6
Cultivated Hay	8,935	5.2	4,440	2.5	1,306	0.8
Other Fodder Crops	4,884	2.9	2,499	1.4	4,707	2.9

fodder crops, while livestock gained in importance proportionally. In these five years alone, the wheat acreage of all land under field crops decreased from 53 per cent to 34 per cent, while the acreage of barley increased from 17 per cent to 21 per cent. In 1941 mixed grains, not cultivated at all in 1936, occupied 19 per cent of all land under field crops. At the same time the number of cattle per farm unit increased by 11 per cent, that of hens and chickens by as much as 62 per cent, and that of swine more than doubled. Up to 1936 most of the farm produce, particularly grain, raised in the municipality had been sold, but a few years later a major portion of cultivated crops was used for the feeding of livestock.

Farm incomes reflected the same trend. In 1936 the larger proportion of a farmer's cash income was derived from the sale of wheat, and this despite an all-time low in wheat prices and exports. But in 1942-3 barely 18 per cent of the farmer's income was drawn from wheat while other grains, particularly barley, took the lead among the field crops. Still more important, nearly 55 per cent of his total money income now came from sources other than the sale of grain, and this in an area which includes some of the best wheat land in Manitoba. Livestock and dairy products, for instance, provided then about as much money income as all grains taken together. Generally speaking, the farmer in this region had turned his back on a pure cash crop economy. His model had become the diversified farm providing not only subsistence for the farm family but also a form of intensive home industry by which labor and resources can be utilized most economically throughout the year. Combined with a limited sale of some unprocessed farm produce, it offers a variety of sources of income whereby the farmer becomes less susceptible to the hazards of crop failures and market prices. A study of 1942-3 farm incomes in the West Reserve and in a comparable non-Mennonite area reveals significant differences. Income from wheat, for instance, played a much smaller role among the Mennonites, while that from animal products, particularly from poultry and eggs, was relatively more important. Income from livestock and animal products represented half

TABLE 7—FARM INCOME, HANOVER AND RHINELAND, 1931 AND 1941, AND OTHER MUNICIPALITIES, 1941.

Municipality	Year	Mennonites as a % of total population	Land Occupied (Acres)	Number of Farm Units	Total Rural Population	Farm Population	Total Income (Dollars)	Average Income		
								Per Farm Unit	Per Person On Farm	Per 100 Acres of Land Occupied
Hanover	1936	°	158,174	883	6,834	5,128	537,714	608.96	104.86	339.95
	1941	81	166,614	1,088	8,190	6,074	947,480	870.85	155.99	568.67
Rhineland	1936	°	225,706	1,240	8,537	6,738	925,731	746.56	137.39	410.15
	1941	94	228,852	1,249	8,936	6,874	1,958,640	1,568.17	284.93	855.85
Stanley	1941	78	204,689	896	6,204	4,809	1,337,094	1,492.29	278.04	653.23
Morris	1941	63	252,009	757	5,095	3,768	1,739,320	2,297.65	461.60	690.18
Macdonald and Port. la Prairie*	1941	9	657,822	1,967	11,306	8,458	4,529,537	2,302.76	535.53	688.57
St. Anne and Tache**	1941	25	193,270	1,084	7,109	5,626	1,366,745	1,260.83	242.93	707.11
Roland†	1941	28	114,927	362	2,150	1,514	874,160	2,414.81	577.38	760.62

° Not available.
* Fifty-three percent of the population was Anglo-Saxon.
** Forty-eight percent of the population was French.
† Sixty-four percent of the population was Anglo-Saxon.

CHART VIII—AVERAGE FARM INCOME IN PREDOMINANTLY MENNONITE AND NON-MENNONITE MUNICIPALITIES, BY SOURCES, 1941*

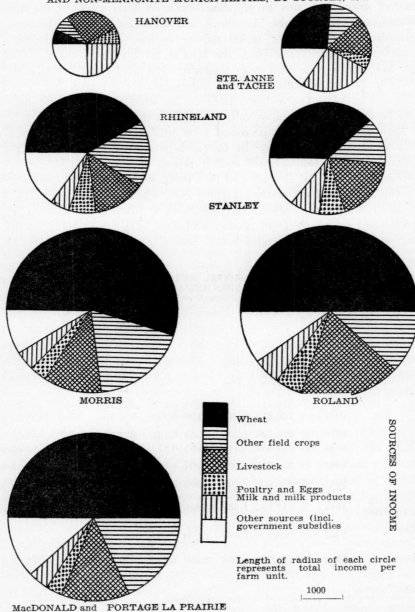

HANOVER

STE. ANNE and TACHE

RHINELAND

STANLEY

MORRIS

ROLAND

MacDONALD and PORTAGE LA PRAIRIE

SOURCES OF INCOME

Wheat

Other field crops

Livestock

Poultry and Eggs
Milk and milk products

Other sources (incl. government subsidies)

Length of radius of each circle represents total income per farm unit.

1000

* See also Table 5.

of the total Mennonite farm income, but only 35 per cent of the non-Mennonite farm income.

Census figures for 1946 indicate that the elasticity of Mennonite farm economy in Rhineland had been maintained, although hard grains had gained in importance over 1941, while the number of hogs had declined. On the other hand, a variety of row and vegetable crops had received increasing attention. Of the total acreage under field crops as much as 9.5 per cent was listed under such categories as "other field roots" and "other field crops." These figures require a word of explanation. According to a report received in 1947 from Mr. J. J. Siemens, of Altona, then vice-president of the Manitoba Sugar Beet Growers Association, the cultivation of this crop in Manitoba dates back to 1940, when a processing plant was constructed in Fort Garry near Winnipeg. Siemens indicated, however, that profits had been rather disappointing so that farmers in the Red River valley had turned to oil crops such as flaxseed and sunflowers. Moreover, vegetable crops such as peas were widely grown either for seed or canning. The local supply was largely absorbed by a small coöperative canning plant in Reinland, and a commercial canning factory in Winkler owned by Winnipeg packers. The diversification of Mennonite farm economy was also reflected in the steady increase of poultry, mainly hens and chickens. Many farmers with small capital and little land were making a good living in this way. Of the 80 hatcheries reported for the whole province in 1945, as many as 14 were located in areas of Mennonite concentration.

Developments in farm size tell a similar story. The standard size of 160 acres for a homestead had been set by the Dominion Lands Act. Yet the proportion of standard-size farms to all farm units has steadily decreased over the years. By 1936 only about two-fifths of all farms in both Mennonite Reserves were of standard size, while about three-tenths were above, and an equal proportion were below standard size. By 1941 about 40 per cent of all farms in the Municipality of Hanover were below standard size, 35 per cent of standard size, and 25 per cent above standard size, including only 9 farms (less than 1 per cent) measuring 640 acres or more. The corresponding figures for the Municipality of Rhineland were: about 31 per cent below standard size, including as many as 244 farms (20 per cent) measuring 50 acres or less, 35 per cent of standard size and 34 per cent above standard size, including 12 farms (1 per cent) measuring 640 acres or more. In a municipality adjacent to Rhineland, but with an ethnically mixed population, on the other hand, only 9 per cent of all farms were below standard size, 26 per cent approximately of standard size, but as many as 65 per cent above standard size, including 11 per cent in the largest size group alone.

Although the trend in the distribution of farms by size was similar in both the East and West Reserve, its causes differed. In the West Reserve lack of land and high land prices, together with the desire of Mennonites to see their children settle close to home, had led to a pulverization of farms. Everywhere in the wheat belt the shift to more intensive production methods had made the traditional quarter-section farm obsolete. But while elsewhere a remedy has been found in the expansion of farm size, the Mennonites were able to demonstrate that the forty-acre farm utilizing family labour to its full capacity and emphasizing specialized crops, poultry and the like, may guarantee a satisfactory living and good returns on relatively small capital investments. In the East Reserve, on the other hand, the larger-than-standard-size farm had been abandoned for other reasons. Since the Russländer immigration, and particularly since the Depression, many settlers with little or no capital had moved to this area. While much of the available land was marginal and undesirable, new farming methods offered adequate subsistence, even on smaller holdings, for Mennonite families with a relatively low level of living. Accordingly, the tendency here in recent years was not only toward creating many new below-standard-size farms on previously unoccupied land, but also to divide many of the already existing larger farms.

In the East Reserve mixed farming, rather than cash crop farming, had always been the rule. Consequently, the greater independence from capitalistic world markets guaranteed a greater resistance to the crisis. In point of fact, during the Depression many Mennonites from other parts of the province were attracted to the East Reserve because the chances of weathering the storm were better there than anywhere else. Thus population density rose between 1931 and 1941 from 16 to 23 persons per square mile, while the number of farm units increased by 16 per cent. Despite unfavorable soil conditions in the East Reserve the average cash income per farm unit in 1936 was almost as great as in the West Reserve, while gross cash profits were actually higher because of smaller expenditures, a lower level of living, and a greater reliance upon home-grown food. After 1936 the East Reserve enjoyed a period of prosperity such as it had never experienced before. This is reflected in the census figures for both farm income and farm value. In the five-year period from 1936 to 1941, the average value of the farm unit increased by 18 per cent in the East Reserve, by 10 per cent in the West Reserve, and the farm value per 100 acres of land increased by 38 per cent in the East Reserve, as against 2.5 per cent in the West Reserve. On the other hand, income per 100 acres of farm land increased by 65 per cent in the East Reserve, while in the more fertile West Reserve the farm income more than doubled with the upswing of the business cycle. In 1941 over one-fourth of the farm income in the East Reserve came from livestock, particularly hogs and animal products. In another year, 1942 to 1943, as much as 40 per cent of all farm income was derived from livestock alone, with another 17 per cent from poultry and eggs, and 32 per cent from milk and milk products. Income from wheat, however, was down to 1 per cent and that from other field crops to 6 per cent of the total farm income.

By the end of the second World War farm economy in the East Reserve rested on three types of farms. On the better lands in the northwest holdings were larger and conformed pretty much to the pattern observed in other grain-growing regions such as the West Reserve. The medium-sized mixed farm, however, was the most widespread type in the East Reserve, emphasizing dairy products and to a lesser degree poultry and eggs. The third type was the small farm specializing in one product such as poultry, potatoes or berries, which enabled many resourceful Mennonites to make a good living on notoriously poor soil by utilizing the supply of relatively cheap and efficient labour as well as the closeness to the Winnipeg market.

In both Reserves the Mennonites made better use of natural resources than the more commercially minded majority of Canadian farmers. While the average income per farm unit was as a rule lower among Mennonites because their farms were of relatively smaller size, in 1941 the average income per hundred acres of occupied land in the West Reserve, for instance, was 24 per cent higher than in a comparable non-Mennonite area. Still more striking were population densities in the two principal areas of Mennonite concentration. Optimum density in the farming districts of the West Reserve had been reached by 1901 with 22.5 persons per square mile, one of the highest in the province. In the following years new agricultural techniques did not greatly alter the upper limit, for the level of living rose correspondingly. The influx of Russländer immigrants into the Reserve who replaced the emigrants to Latin America did not change the pattern appreciably. In 1941 the population density in non-Mennonite townships adjoining the West Reserve, and comparable with it in economic conditions, was 12.1 persons per square mile or less than half of that in townships inhabited almost exclusively by Mennonites, which itself probably had no equal anywhere in purely agricultural districts of Western Canada. Nevertheless, even this figure was topped in 1946 by the population densities in the East Reserve, which includes much marginal and submarginal land such as is being rejected by others as almost worthless and condemned by economists as unfit for human settlement.[9]

Behind the cold figures one senses a profound reorientation of the Mennonite economy as a whole. It seems that the crisis had given them an opportunity to reassess their position. As long as the agrarian capitalism typical of Western Canada, and especially of its wheat growing regions, proved workable, they tended to follow the example of the host society. When its fallacies became apparent with the breakdown of world export, they readily reverted to older behavior patterns and, above all, to a modified form of subsistence farming. Once the myth of Anglo-Saxon superiority in the economic sphere was shattered, the Mennonites apparently gained a new pride and faith in their own group and its social heritage, and were inclined to approach more critically what the large society had to offer them as a substitute. They began to look down upon their neighbours, whom they considered (rightly or wrongly) as poor farmers, less able to resist the periodic crises of capitalistic economy. Of course, the economy of Canada's large society, too, had outgrown the "gilded age of agrarian capitalism." But it would appear that the Mennonites went very much their own way since the Depression.

Community reorganization among the Manitoba Mennonites, at least in the West Reserve, was signalized primarily by the spread of the

---

[9] See, e.g., the opinion voiced by W. L. Waines, an economist of the University of Manitoba, in the Report of the Sirois Commission on Dominion-Provincial Relations: "Prairie Population Possibilities." The noted adviser of the Canadian Government suggested that marginal areas of Canada's West be withdrawn from cultivation and their present owners resettled. The implication was that any further agricultural immigration was to be discouraged. Yet the present study indicates that the right type of farmers could make a satisfactory living in much of the as yet underpopulated areas of the Dominion, thus improving her strategic position, expanding inner markets and eliminating many of the social disadvantages which a population irregularly and thinly spread over her vast territory obviously entails.

coöperative movement. Of course, it did not originate here but first took hold among Canadian farmers at large as a measure of self-help and social reform during the Depression. But the innovation was so readily accepted by the Mennonites that the West Reserve soon became the main stronghold of the coöperative movement in the whole province. By 1946 the Federation of Southern Manitoba Coöperatives, with 26 affiliated organizations, covered territory which was almost exclusively Mennonite, with a total population of about 20,000. The coöperatives tended to replace the old church-connected institutions of mutual aid with institutions which were meant to be secular; this was interpreted by the Mennonite churches as a challenge to their position of dominance in the community. The struggle was fervent, but the secular trend was clearly winning out.

This is the story of the coöperatives in Southern Manitoba as told by its principal organizer and champion, J. J. Siemens, of Altona:

Rhineland Consumers Co-operative Ltd., Altona, was the first such coöperative to find its way into our area. Sixty-seven members and $670.00 represented its first beginning. The early years were difficult as the methods of open membership and neutrality in religion were not fully understood by the masses. However, it grew and proved its ability to effect real savings for the members, and as this became better known, membership increased, volume of goods handled increased, plant equipment and services rendered improved, and by 1937 the flood gates opened and the movement expanded into other lines such as stores, cheese and cream processing plants, hatcheries, machine shops, egg-grading stations, credit unions, burial aid societies, until 85 per cent of the people in the area belonged to either one or another of such economic units. Total membership by 1946 reached an all time high of 10,000 members. Savings for all these coöperatives and volume handled also increased to an all time high.

The first coöperative was organized in 1931 to provide gasoline, oil, and service station facilities.[10] In 1937 the Altona Co-operative Service Ltd. came into being. By 1944 its assets had increased to over $67,000, and its membership from the original 10 to over 800; annual sales amounted to almost a quarter of a million dollars. Connected with it was an egg-grading station, handling up to 100 cases a day. A group of farmers started the Rhineland Co-operative Hatchery in 1940, which two years later had a capacity of 100,000 eggs. The Farmers' Co-operative Machine Shop was opened during World War II when

[10] Cf. J. Winfield Fretz, "The Renaissance of a Rural Community," *Mennonite Life, 1* (1946), pp. 14-17, 39.

new farm machinery was scarce, and the old equipment was in urgent need of repair. It enabled farmers to do their own welding, rebuilding, and repairing, aided by a number of expert mechanics.

By 1945 all stores included in the Federation of Southern Manitoba Co-operatives[11] had 3,494 members and 43 employees; the oil stations 1,426 members and 16 employees. Membership of the stores increased between 1942 and 1945 by 70 per cent, of the oil stations by 16 per cent, and of the producers coöperatives by 126 per cent. The total turnover of the credit unions, which had 9,887 members and 160 employees, was $4\frac{3}{4}$ million dollars in 4 years, and total net savings were almost $300,000.

In view of urgent war-time demands for lubricants and food stuffs, the Dominion Government invited farmers in the Mennonite districts of Manitoba and Saskatchewan to grow, on a commercial scale, sunflowers, soy beans, rape and flax. This was the green light for the West Reserve coöperatives, which for some time had been anxious to introduce new row crops, and to process them locally so that profits would not go to outside processing companies as had been the case with sugar beets. In 1944-45 the Co-operative Vegetable Oils Ltd. was organized by some 800 farmers and businessmen, and after some delay a plant was constructed in Altona with the most modern equipment. It opened in March of 1946, with J. J. Siemens as its first president and D. K. Friesen as treasurer. By early 1947 close to 11 million pounds of sunflower seed had been processed by the plant which operated on a 24-hour schedule. The enterprise had considerable influence upon Mennonite agricultural development in providing not only a source of profit for its producer-members, but also an opportunity for further diversification, more intensive and scientific farming, the employment of extra labour to hoe and harvest this crop, and better utilization of mechanized equipment acquired for other row crops such as corn and sugar beets.

Two factors seem to have been mainly responsible for the spread of the coöperative movement among the Manitoba Mennonites: (1) The breakdown of their traditional economic institutions had left a vacuum which was filled by the coöperatives. (2) Because the principles of the coöperative movement bear a certain resemblance to the

---

[11] Cf. Report of the Federation of Southern Manitoba Co-operatives on its Third Annual Convention, July 12, 1946.

solidaristic type of peasant economy, the coöperatives seemed to the Mennonites a revival of familiar forms of socio-economic organization.

Yet the coöperative movement took permanent root only in one of the Mennonite colonies. Although it entered the East Reserve at about the same time, it was soon abandoned there. Several of the coöperatives were transformed into private stock companies so that by 1945-46 only a few coöperative stores, credit unions and cheese factories were still in operation. As a matter of fact, people were openly boasting that they got along as well and better without such "economic crutches." They pointed out that during the Depression, when literally scores of unemployed were shipped from across the Red River to Hanover, the Municipality had refrained from dealing out "unearned money." Instead of the dole, all who were able to work were given an axe or a pick and told: Now earn your warm meal a day. In this way the Municipality had been able to carry out valuable public works at rates which, though not measuring up to trade union standards, were alone feasible under the conditions. The unemployed, on the other hand, were saved from much frustration and were less inclined to grumble, loaf and develop inferiority complexes. Thrown without much mercy upon their own resourcefulness, they discovered many opportunities for rehabilitation, either by developing mechanical hobbies into gainful occupations, some of which have in the meantime led to the establishment of prospering workshops and factories, or by cultivating small plots obtained on easy terms and netting satisfactory profits from small garden crops, such as berries and vegetables.

By the end of World War II, a decidedly competitive spirit characterized all trade in this Reserve. Businessmen explained with pride the efficiency of their aggressive salesmanship and the progressive services which their methods had been able to provide for the whole community. This situation demands some explanation. Differences in the type of leadership come to one's mind first. The native Steinbach group, descendants of the more progressive Molotschna colony, and the still more progressive Russländer immigrants had set the pattern for the East Reserve. In the West Reserve, on the other hand, J. J. Siemens, a Kanädier member of the liberal Bergthal church, together with a group of personal friends in and around Altona, had been playing a role in the reorganization of the Mennonite community somewhat similar to that of Cornies in the Molotschna colony a hundred years ago. But even leaders of this stature cannot succeed unless other, more impersonal, factors have already prepared the field. The East Reserve had suffered much less in the Depression and had recovered much more quickly. Furthermore, when the coöperatives were first introduced here, there were still some of the older institutions in existence. Thus, unlike in the West Reserve, the coöperatives did not fill a vacuum but tended to replace the traditional peasant institutions. Finally, economic conditions improved before the coöperatives had a chance of becoming firmly established and of proving their worth as a means of self-help in a crisis. They were quickly given up as soon as individual enterprise promised greater economic gain, a gain which seemed to contribute to the general prosperity of the colony. Nevertheless, even in the competitive East Reserve, capitalism was accepted with a strong mental reservation, and for the time being, as it were.

The economic structure of the two major areas of Mennonite concentration continued to support strongly its ethnic unity. Originally, each Reserve had been a self-sufficient entity with farming as its main source of livelihood, supplemented by small businesses which were centered in the farm-operator villages. It was only with the advent of the typical Western railroad town that most of the trade was drawn away from the villages and into the hands of non-Mennonite townsfolk. But this was soon changed when Mennonites themselves began to monopolize the urban trade. At the same time several of the old villages were able to retain or regain some of the local trade. The tradition of the village smithy was carried on by garages and repair shops for motor vehicles and farm machinery. Filling stations were usually connected with either stores or garages although some enterprising farmers, too, had put up pumps at a corner of their place hoping for a few extra dollars. General stores existed in many of the surviving villages, the bigger ones drawing their customers from within a radius of two or more miles. A more diversified type of services was offered by the towns but in none of them were all necessary services available. Thus farming and business throughout the whole Reserve were closely interwoven and interdependent, adding to the social coherence and ethnic homogeneity of its population. Moreover, the towns left still enough room for small local businesses outside of them. It would seem that greater population density and prevailing village habitat increased the opportunities for small businessmen and craftsmen such as carpenters, shoemakers, and mechanics, to establish themselves in strictly rural places; more jobs were created, customers had better access to services, and rural community life was better balanced.

The Municipality of Hanover appeared to be part of a much wider trade area, including not only most of the Mennonite East Reserve but nearly all of South-Eastern Manitoba. The heart and center of this sub-region was Steinbach. While to the north and northeast its trade area was limited by the retail area of Winnipeg, it reached far into the sparsely populated parts of the southeast and south. Its western boundaries were somewhat blurred by competing French trade centers, but the Mennonite settlements around St. Elizabeth, Arnaud and Dominion City, which themselves were local trade centers, were tributary partly to Steinbach, partly also to towns in the West Reserve. Niverville and Grünthal were the only other minor trade centers in the East Reserve but these were clearly subordinate to Steinbach.

Because village habitat had mostly disintegrated in the East Reserve, business units outside the aforementioned centers were scattered irregularly over a wide area, not only in or near hamlets but also along the main arteries of communication, particularly on crossroads. Among them were general stores, garages and repair shops, licensed transfer services, and an egg grading station. Gasoline pumps were usually attached to either stores or garages, and most postal stations were combined with stores. The telephone exchange in Chortitz was installed in the house of a farmer and operated by his family. Also small stores were sometimes operated by farmers. Of the 8 cheese factories in the Reserve 4 were located in the open countryside. Combined with or next to cheese factories there usually was a general store. All the neighbourhood stores carried a few lines of household supplies and groceries, including canned goods, some hardware and working clothes, but expensive goods were purchased either in Steinbach or in Winnipeg.

The oddest example of a rural business aggregate was without doubt Plettenville. It was a product of depression and rural electrification. It consisted of a cluster of small business units, partly commercial, partly industrial, all of which were owned by members of the same family. Two of the Plett brothers operated a lumber yard, three others managed a box factory, while the youngest brother ran the paternal farm. Other business units combined with this family enterprise were a mechanical workshop, a small saw mill turning out shingles, a feed crusher, and a little store. The parents and the brothers with their families each lived in their own house, forming a veritable village by themselves; for ten brothers and the old couple made quite a crowd, and there were lots of blond-haired, blue-eyed children around. Moreover, three or four of their working men had built cottages on the Plett farm, which had become a teeming industrial settlement with lowing cows and shrieking pigs as an appropriate backdrop.

In order to maintain the continuity of our account of economic developments since the Depression, we have anticipated a good deal of another crisis which the Mennonite group had undergone since then. We thus have to retrace our steps in an attempt to assess the social effects of the second World War.

The Second World War

The outbreak of the war found the Manitoba Mennonites well on the road to recovery. Economically, wartime prosperity helped them to their feet, just as it helped other Canadian farmers and businessmen. In other respects, however, it completed a process of reorientation and community reorganization whose early stages had been climaxed by the Russländer immigration and the Depression. Now, in the second World War, Dominion policy concerning conscientious objectors had similar effects upon the group and its relation to the large society, as had the Provincial policy concerning the public school during World War I. Both times a conflict arose over a fundamental tenet of Mennonite religion. Both times the conflict not only divided the group itself between the conservatives and progressives, but, once the fight was over and decided in favor of the progressives, it left the community better adjusted to life in a modern high civilization.

The situation in World War II was much more complex than during the years 1914-18. Then the Mennonites had enjoyed complete exemption from military service on grounds of their religious conviction and under the agreement of 1873. By 1939, however, the principles of total warfare, even though accepted with some reluctance in Canada, made direct or indirect participation in the war effort much more general, so that the granting of exemptions to any particular class of citizens appeared to most Canadians as obsolete. Moreover, the validity of the so-called Mennonite privileges had been successfully challenged once before, namely, during the school conflict. Finally, while in World War I the privileges of 1873 applied to the whole Mennonite population of Western Canada, now a good proportion of them had been admitted to the Dominion with the explicit under- standing that neither they nor their children would be exempted from any laws covering Canadian citizens in general.

But quite apart from legal considerations, the progressive seculariza- tion of the group had not escaped public attention and the suspicion was widespread that many of them used their religious convictions as a pretext to avoid active participation in the armed conflict while at the same time violating other precepts of their faith whenever it was convenient to do so. It was well known, for instance, that during the years of Hitler's ascendancy some Mennonites had been in sympathy with what was going on in Germany. It made, of course, little difference to the aroused political emotions of Anglo-Canadians that a much larger proportion of non-Mennonite and non-German fellow-citizens had nursed similar feelings when Nazism seemed at the height of its power and before the country was drawn into the life-and-death struggle against it.

The reader who has followed the account of Russländer immigra- tion will not fail to infer some of the factors which, prior to the war, had evoked pro-German sentiments among many Manitoba Mennonites. To these must be added the efforts made by Germany in the 1920's and 1930's to strengthen the ties between German-speaking minorities all over the world with the motherland. Now, with increasing secularization, many of the more liberal-minded Mennonites, par- ticularly among the Russländer group, became susceptible to modern ideologies. We have seen that Mennonite group loyalty was originally based exclusively on their consciousness of being a distinct and separate religious body. As religious convictions waned, people tended to accept nationalism, to wit, German nationalism, as a logical substitute upon which to anchor their natural desire of "belonging." This trend was, of course, strengthened by the behaviour of the large society which was conditioned precisely by the same national ideals. The Russländer group, in particular, had experienced a serious shock when they were excluded from Russian society which they had learned to consider as their national group. But also Canadian society had refused to accept either Russländer or Kanädier Mennonites without certain reservations, and had remained suspicious of their German speech and other cultural peculiarities. The German nation, on the other hand, apparently was only too anxious to claim them as their own. A few Mennonites were able to realize, however dimly, that the Mennonite community itself, even if partly divested of its unifying religious content, might constitute a distinctive "nationality" offering the desired opportunity for intimate social participation and expression of we-feeling in a world more and more compartmentalized into mutually exclusive "nations."

Under the circumstances it is not surprising to find that most Mennonites showed little enthusiasm for participation in a war which (despite all protestations to the contrary) was not exclusively a struggle against the Nazi regime but involved also the suffering of the whole German people. Those who had not been secularized were genuinely opposed to bloodshed on religious grounds, even in defense against a worldly power whose injustice and inhumanity they abhorred as strongly as the most vociferous Western Liberals. Others, who in their search for national "belonging" had been leaning toward Pan-Germanism in one form or another, found a convenient way out of the dilemma by retiring into a sort of mental neutrality. For both camps, however, total abstention from the war was the logical solution.

By and large, the ideological dividing line followed rather closely the natural division between the Kanädier and Russländer groups. This is illustrated by an incident which occurred shortly before the outbreak of hostilities when representatives of the various Mennonite churches in Canada gathered in Winkler, on May 15, 1939, to discuss the threat of war and of universal military service.[12] In this meeting the complaint was made that too much German propaganda literature was being distributed and that this was causing bad feelings among Anglo-Saxon neighbours. To this a Russländer elder answered that not everything German was bad, and that it was after all no crime to cultivate one's mother tongue. From the report it becomes apparent that the Kanädier Mennonites were more sensitive to public opinion and more emphatic about loyalty to one's country, that is, Canada, as required by their religion, while the Russländer people were more inclined to defend Germany against criticism in the Canadian and American press.

The difference in attitudes between the two groups showed up again when the question of a substitute service for conscientious

---

[12] For the following see David P. Reimer, *Erfahrungen der Mennoniten in Canada während des zweiten Weltkrieges*, 1939-1945 (Steinbach, n.d.); also J. W. Nickel, "The Canadian Conscientious Objector," *Mennonite Life 3* (1948): 24-28.

objectors was debated. Curiously enough, this time the Russländer representatives were at once in favor of some alternative war service, including even service in a medical corps attached to the armed forces, while the conservative churches, mostly composed of Kanädier Mennonites, at first rejected any kind of compulsory service in lieu of the military draft. An explanation can be found in the different experiences which the two groups had had in the First World War, when the Russian Mennonites in Canada were completely exempted in accordance with the agreement of 1873. Their brethren in Russia, on the other hand, had been serving either in forest camps or in semi-military medical outfits, and had found the arrangement as a whole satisfactory.

A compromise was finally reached unanimously rejecting any kind of service in uniform, under military command or in war industries, but accepting various forms of civilian alternative service not directly connected with the war effort. These primarily included work in conscientious objectors' camps which were located in National Parks, and in forest and lumber camps in British Columbia. Later on, conscientious objectors were assigned individually to coal mines, hospitals, mental institutions and to farmers under special contract, according to which they received a standard pay of $25 a month while the balance of their normal wage, originally fixed at $40, was to be remitted to the Red Cross. The rates were repeatedly modified in later years.

These arrangements were made under considerable public pressure and to a large extent under compulsion. As early as the spring of 1939, a local physician belonging to the Kanädier group, a former Member of the Provincial Legislature, had warned an assembly of responsible Mennonite leaders that their own actions had turned public opinion against them and their status as conscientious objectors. He is reported as saying that "in the last war our young people remained at home while we were filling our pockets with money thanks to good crops and high prices."[13]

More explicit is a letter addressed by another physician, an Anglo-Saxon of Morden, to the bishops and ministers of the Mennonite church in December, 1940.[14] The writer belonged to an older Anglo-

[13] *Erfahrungen*, p. 53.

[14] Part of the letter was reproduced in the *Free Press Prairie Farmer*, January 1, 1941.

Saxon generation who, living in close proximity to the West Reserve, had witnessed the steady retreat of their own kin in the face of Mennonite expansion. Despite the understandable bias of such a man and some incidental misrepresentations of fact, the doctor's appeal reflected faithfully the attitudes of many non-Mennonites during the early war years. He first mentioned that the majority of young Mennonites appearing before members of the National War Service Board at the court house in Morden, on December 9, 10 and 11 of that year, had affirmed that they believed it would be wrong for them to take 30 days of training in a military camp. On the other hand, the writer continued, none of the young Mennonites to whom he himself had spoken had given any indication that he believed *personally* that it would be wrong for him to take any military training. Others had even enlisted in the C.A.S.F., presumably voluntarily, and about 150 young Mennonites had signed a statement that they wished to join the Non-Permanent Militia.

From this the author of the letter concluded that the defendants in Morden had acted under pressure exercised by church authorities and older members of the community. He added:

In your zeal to promote the idea of non-participation in military service, you have attempted and fairly well succeeded in denying these young men the right to the free exercise of their own conscience, the foundation upon which the Mennonite church was built. You of course know that the Canadian Legion made representations to the Government at Ottawa regarding the exemption from military service enjoyed by your people. We have seen your ways of life changing. We have seen your people doing and enjoying many things forbidden to the Old Colony church[!]. As your ideas have changed, and ideas of the young Mennonites have changed in regard to so many questions, is it not natural to assume that there must be a considerable number of the young people who do not hold to the old view regarding military service?

Apart from the rational argument, the criticism of course boils down to a protest against the successful exercise of social controls by the Mennonite group in a matter which touched upon the religious basis of their culture.

Canadian authorities and those concerned with public affairs in the country, therefore, saw themselves confronted with a rather bewildering situation which only few took the pains to understand in all its ramifications. Eventually a compromise was adopted in the best British tradition. Although it shared the fate of most British compromises, namely of pleasing nobody, it actually averted the danger of an open clash. The measures taken were the following: First, the right to refuse military service was recognized for all those Mennonites who had immigrated under the agreement of 1873, and for their descendants. In their case, no further proof was required that their refusal was motivated exclusively by religious convictions. Second, the Russländer Mennonites and their descendants were excluded from these benefits, and enjoyed only those rights which statute law afforded to any other Canadian citizen; accordingly, the burden of proof was upon them that they were bona fide conscientious objectors.

Certain judges were prone to hold against defendants the fact that they had never formally joined any Mennonite church, or had liberally broken Mennonite taboos, such as the prohibition of drinking and smoking. Although the courts undoubtedly acted in accordance with the letter of the law, it apparently escaped their attention that these and similar injunctions were not basic or universally enforced principles of Mennonite religion, and that in the eyes of the Mennonites themselves the unbaptized son of Mennonite parents was still a non-resistant Mennonite. More serious, and perhaps more justified, was the supposition made by some tribunals that a good number of these defendants were actually motivated by ethnic, if not by political, sympathies with the enemy. Whenever this was proven, their plea for military exemption was summarily rejected despite all protests of Mennonite elders and preachers, who attempted to save as many of their flock as possible. These ministers, far from being disloyal to their country, were convinced that the use of arms was inherently evil; moreover, they saw an opportunity to lead stray sheep back to the fold by defending them, regardless of church membership and personal conduct.

The actual number of Manitoba Mennonites who were permanently refused conscientious objector status, and the volume of subsequent convictions for failure to report for induction into the armed services, remained low. It is not easy to offer any accurate figures. A report made to a Mennonite preachers' conference on January 9, 1945, however, indicates that at that time "only just a couple of youths were in jail," that their convictions were usually "for neglecting written orders," that the terms were mostly for two months, and that after their release they were, as a rule, sent to a conscientious objectors' camp.[15] Altogether about 50 Mennonite objectors were sentenced to jail in

---

[15] *Erfahrungen*, pp. 162f.

Manitoba during the whole war, usually for their failure to observe proper procedures due to misunderstanding or obstinacy. Nothing indicates that they were deliberately deprived of their Constitutional right to refuse military service on religious grounds. In fact the official Mennonite records underline the readiness of the responsible authorities to help those who had gotten into conflict with the law. Yet, the convictions were widely misinterpreted and caused much ill-feeling.

In addition, the alternative service imposed upon conscientious objectors led to many frictions. Those recruited into conscientious objectors' camps were not entitled to government issues of clothing or any other privileges granted to members of the armed forces. The actual work done in those camps, often under trying conditions, appeared to them as of doubtful economic value, and was felt more as a punishment than as a useful contribution to the common weal. When later on the young people were employed in the forest service and lumber camps, or released to work in hospitals and on individual farms, there were complaints of overwork and occasional maltreatment combined with low wages, although frequent adjustments were made, particularly after married men were called up. These were entitled to retain an additional $10 of their wages plus $5 for each child. The following wage scales were in force in 1945 for those working in hospitals and institutions: Brandon, $52.50; Portage la Prairie, $57; Selkirk, $49; in three hospitals in the Metropolitan area, $38.10, $43 and $55 respectively, with lower wages during the first 3 or 6 months.[16] The farm contracts for alternative service work made it possible for Mennonite farmers to petition for their own sons to be assigned to them for farm work under the usual conditions. Mennonite leaders had to warn repeatedly that this privilege should not be abused, while the farmers grumbled that they had to pay considerable sums to the Red Cross under the title of wages for the services of their own children.

Of about 3,200 conscientious objectors in Manitoba, as many as 2,453 were Mennonites. Yet, approximately another 2,000 young Mennonites had joined the armed forces, mostly voluntarily, and many of them had been serving with distinction; at least one was decorated with the Distinguished Service Cross. There were also about 194 post-

---

[16] *Erfahrungen*, pp. 152 and 171.

ponements granted to Mennonite draftees. In judging these figures, however, one must keep in mind that, at one time, almost 80 per cent of all Mennonites of draft age were ipso facto exempted from military service either as farmers or teachers.[17] On the other hand, the Mennonite leaders were informed in 1944 that, according to a general ruling, male persons of draft age were not permitted to attend normal school during the war, nor could they hold a teaching permit, but that qualified teachers recognized as conscientious objectors were allowed to continue teaching school.[18]

During this emergency all Mennonite congregations in Manitoba united, for the first time since World War I, in common action by organizing the Mennonite Peace Committee. Its activities included above all negotiations with the authorities, the defense of conscientious objectors before the various boards and tribunals, and the religious care of those committed to alternative service. Mennonite preachers were permitted to administer to the spiritual needs of camp inmates, and to visit others periodically at their widely scattered places of work. This was done by volunteers whose modest expenses were refunded by the committee. It is clear from the accounts that the committee operated with minimal finances. Its expenditures amounted to $6,781.98 in 1943, and to $5,692.13 in 1944. The sums were raised by a per capita levy on the various participating churches. Yet the committee was able to prevent many unnecessary hardships, and to overcome many inner difficulties with which the war confronted the whole Mennonite group. Thanks to its work and to the understanding it found among those in charge of the Canadian war effort, serious incidents were avoided and a tolerable modus vivendi was eventually reached. This was mainly due to the calm and almost sophisticated view which Canadians generally were taking of the issues at stake. Nevertheless, there was much friction among the Mennonites themselves, who at one time were threatened by an open split. A Mennonite Central Relief Committee, organized for Canada in 1939, did split a year later over the question of military service.[19] Moreover, feelings ran high at times between Mennonites and their fellow-citizens, who regarded them as shirkers and war-time profiteers. But, toward the end of the war, the honest work done by the alternative service men

---

[17] Cf. *Altona Echo*, February 17, 1944.

[18] *Erfahrungen*, p. 157.

[19] Cf. Report of the Mennonite Central Committee of Western Canada, January 16, 1941.

was widely recognized, and the indignation of those whose children had to bear the brunt of the emergency was somewhat abetted.

The Mennonites, on the other hand, realized that they were getting off lightly in the face of the universal calamity. Although their charitable contributions made during the war are difficult to assess for individual provinces, Canada's contributions to the relief work carried out by the Mennonite Central Committee of the General Conference in Akron, Pennsylvania, amounted to $24,761 in funds, and $16,634 in clothes between January 1 and September 30, 1943.[20] In 1944, a committee representing Mennonite congregations in Western Canada alone, collected over $10,000 for relief work. One report of January 1945 states that the value of the relief work of all Canadian Mennonites in England during a four-year period amounted to over $40,000; another unpublished estimate valued the total aid sent to air raid victims in England at $130,000. In December of the same year total voluntary donations through the Canadian Mennonite Relief Committee were reported as having reached $75,000, not to mention substantial but unrecorded Mennonite contributions to war loan and similar drives.[21]

Some Mennonites objected to participation in the Red Cross, the official relief agency for Canada. We gather from a private correspondence that it was considered by them as "part of the war machine." One clergyman wrote:

Whether the Red Cross in each case is really working for the sake of charity, I do not know, but I believe to have heard that the whole thing smacks too much of business. After all, we know that in many of these organizations rather high salaries are being paid. In any case, the Red Cross is part of the war machine, and the war machine is made to destroy life.

Similarly, at a meeting of the Mennonite Relief Committee at Kitchener, Ontario, on September 18, 1939, the suggestion was made that the groups in the West should carry on with their own work, "staying clear of other organizations which are connected with army organizations. Our efforts should be purely from the standpoint of our Christian profession, following the example of the teaching of Jesus Christ."

[20] John D. Unruh, *In the Name of Christ: A History of the Mennonite Central Committee and Its Service 1920-1951* (Scottdale, Penn., 1952).

[21] Cf. *Erfahrungen*, pp. 166 and 174.

It was only after the Constitutional freedoms were restored that open propaganda was made among certain more conservative groups for emigration to some country which, once more, would give them full assurance that their cultural and religious traditions would be safeguarded for all future.[22] The supporters of the movement maintained that Canada had broken her word by imposing secular public schools upon the Mennonites and by pressing their young people into military service. They were also convinced that both, school and army, had supported a trend toward secularism among the younger generation which was threatening to destroy the basic values of Mennonite religion. But the majority of Mennonites in Manitoba have reacted quite differently to recent experiences. While times of economic want and out-group pressure usually tend to strengthen group cohesion, prosperity seems to lead to greater readiness for accommodation to conditions as they are.

Some 2,000 conservative Kanädier Mennonites left Manitoba for Paraguay in June 1948. A private information, dated November 1, 1951, by Mr. B. B. Dubienski, at the time Honorary Consul of Paraguay at Winnipeg, who had provided for passports, visas, exchange of clearances, and transportation for these emigrants, indicates that

the decision had been made by the elders shortly after the end of World War II, when they realized that they were incapable of resisting the inroads made by the rapid rise of modern standards of living, i.e. radio, rubber-tired tractors, telephones, cinemas, hotel beer parlors, etc., all of which tended to detract the younger generation from the traditional 'Old Colony' way of life. It is significant that the rift between these Mennonites and the Russländer group is constantly widening and has been a factor in the emigration to Mexico as well as to Paraguay. The latter have not missed an occasion . . . to let Canada know that the move to Paraguay was unsound, unpatriotic and organized by a few ignorant, uncompromising, old-fashioned preachers who were losing hold of their diminishing communities.

According to the same information, about 720 of the emigrants had returned to Canada by the end of 1951, while the others were settling down to become pioneers in South America.[23]

Since 1946 a new batch of about 8,000 Russländer refugees has arrived in Canada with novel experiences in Soviet Russia, and in both

[22] The matter of emigration was broached officially before, but not acted upon, in a meeting of preachers in Lowe Farm, on May 4, 1942. (*Erfahrungen*, p. 121).

[23] See also J. W. Fretz, *Pilgrims in Paraguay* (Scottdale, Penna., 1953).

242

Nazi and post-Nazi Germany behind them. An article published in the *Mennonitische Welt,* of November 1951, reported the number of Mennonite immigrants to Canada at that time as 6,979, of whom 2,275 went to Manitoba.[24] We are not prepared to assess the influence of this major shift upon the ideological trends within the group as a whole. But a strengthening of pro-German sentiment would not be surprising under the circumstances. In a way, the attitude of the Russian Mennonites somewhat resembles that of the Alsatians, who for centuries have been unable to define clearly their collective membership either of the German or the French nation. If we do not misjudge the situation, however, there apparently is also a definite tendency among the group to adopt Canadian national ideals as their own, perhaps also to view the Mennonite group as a distinct and separate ethnic unit with limited reference to any specific religious content but with emphasis upon its cultural character.

---

[24] Eventually the total figure was probably closer to 8,000. See also J. J. Thiessen, "Present Mennonite Immigration to Canada," *Mennonite Life 4* (1949): 33-36, and *Jahrbuch der Konferenz der Mennoniten in Canada,* 1950, pp. 109ff.

Epilog

By the end of the second World War, the Mennonite group in Manitoba did not show any signs of serious or permanent disorganization. On the contrary, group coherence was still strong, and there was a newly gained pride in Mennonite traditions. The Mennonites had remained by far the least urbanized of all ethnic groups in Manitoba, and most of their "urban" population lived in small rural trade centers within their own colonies. In these towns they had largely displaced the original non-Mennonite majorities. Intermarriages were still very rare except with their German Lutheran neighbours, a group of similar cultural background. The younger Mennonite generation had been educated exclusively in public grade schools, and probably every single Mennonite in the province was now thoroughly familiar with English speech and values. Nevertheless, all Manitoba Mennonites understood and spoke their Low German dialect. Modern trends in American Protestantism have had a certain influence upon Mennonite religion. Yet conversions to non-Mennonite churches had remained the exception, and were confined largely to such religious groups as the Seventh-Day Adventists or the Pentecostals. Participation in church activities, which were social as much as religious affairs, did not appear to have suffered, while commercial amusements and non-religious associations had found entrance in only a few places. As of old, family and kinship group had remained the solid core of the whole social fabric. While the original institutional basis of community organization had become disorganized upon close contact with a modern capitalistic society, an apparently successful attempt had been made at social reconstruction with the help of more adequate institutions, particularly agricultural coöperatives. No doubt the Mennonite social system showed a greater diversification than 25 years earlier, and resembled more closely that of Anglo-Canadian society at large. But

TABLE 8—MENNONITE POPULATION OF MANITOBA, BY ZONES, 1881-1941

	1881 Mennonites No.	1886 Mennonites No.	1891 Mennonites No.	1901 Mennonites No.	1911 Mennonites No.	1921 Mennonites No.	1921 in census sub-districts	1931 Mennonites No.	1931 in census sub-districts	1941 Mennonites No.	1941 in census sub-districts	Total Population No.	All census sub-districts	Mennonite population as a per cent of total population
Manitoba East and West	7,776	9,112	(2)	15,246	15,600	20,595(3)	49	29,352(3)	113	37,336(3)	126	729,744	204	
Reserve	7,769	9,100	11,210	15,170	15,355	19,958	13	23,017	15	28,415				
Outside Reserves						637	36	6,335	98	8,921				
Hutter. (est.) (3)	7(1)	2	(2)	76	245	700		1,000		2,000				
ZONES (4):														
South-Central						16,301	14	19,539	27	22,288	27	76,080	34	29.3
West Reserve only						16,092	8	17,015	10	19,525				
Outside West Reserve						209	6	2,524	17	2,763				
South-Eastern						3,988	9	6,713	12	10,404	10	39,018	13	26.5
East Reserve						3,866	5	6,002	5	8,890				
Outside East Reserve						122	4	711	7	1,514				
Eastern						5	1	15	3	90	6	31,578	11	.3
Interlake						6	2	21	3	80	7	25,387	14	.3
Central (est.) (3)						30	6	768	16	893	19	59,815	21	1.5
Western						11	5	911	34	650	27	94,534	57	.7
Northern (incl. Dauphin)						129	7	204	6	547	14	101,308	38	.5
Metropolitan						125	5	1,181	12	2,384	16	302,024	16	.8

1 The difference of 7 between the total figure for Manitoba and that computed for the two Reserves is apparently identical with the number of "Tunkers" who then lived in the province as these were counted together with the Mennonites.

2 Not available.

3 The number of Hutterites living in the Central Zone was estimated and subtracted from the census figures for this zone. However, the small Hutterite settlement at Blumengart, which is situated in the West Reserve, was not taken into consideration. This explains the difference between our totals for 1921, 1931 and 1941, and those included in the official census publications as well as in other tables in this book where a similar correction did not appear necessary.

4 See Chart IX.

CHART IX—DISTRIBUTION OF MENNONITE POPULATION IN
MANITOBA, 1941

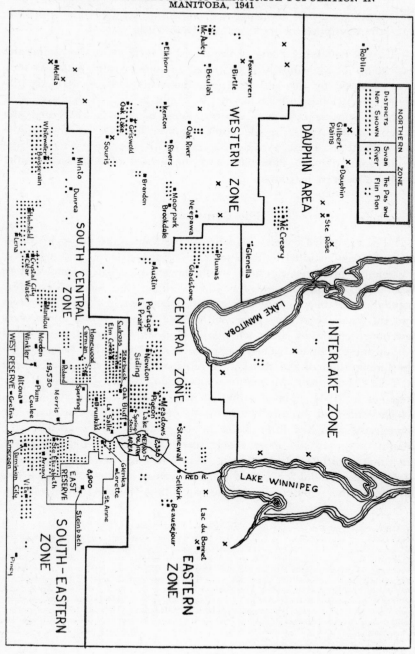

the Mennonite group also appeared more integrated than at any time since the disruption of its structure after World War I.

In the remaining pages of this book, conditions in the Mennonite settlements in Manitoba will be traced in some greater detail as they were observed by the author during the years 1945 to 1947, in the course of an extensive field survey. It should be noticed, however, that at the time some new factors, which once more were to change the pattern of the Manitoba Mennonite groups, had as yet not become fully effective. These include the return of the war veterans, the recent emigration to Paraguay, and the arrival of 8,000 Mennonite displaced persons in Canada.

The Community

The continued coherence of the whole Mennonite group in Manitoba was demonstrated by their tendency to live together and, wherever possible, to preserve or restore the homogeneity of their communities. Before the regroupment of the 1920's, almost the whole Mennonite population in the province had been concentrated in the two Reserves and the small Scratching River settlement. Except in the towns, very few non-Mennonites, and then mostly German Lutherans, were found within these colonies. Then came the exodus to Latin America and the immigration of the Russländer refugees. As a result, over 27 per cent of Manitoba's Mennonite population resided outside of the Reserves by 1931. The distribution was entirely due to the way in which land had been allotted by the colonization agencies to the immigrants who had little choice in the matter.[1] Ten years later the Mennonites were still more widely scattered throughout the province. As a matter of fact, 31 per cent of them were now found living outside of the Reserves, and few indeed were the census subdivisions which had no Mennonite population. At the same time, however, many of the

---

[1] In addition, some of the farm land in the Reserves, which had been sold by the emigrants, had been transferred into non-Mennonite hands, and more was lost during the Depression, although this did not alter the ethnic composition of the actual occupants. In the East Reserve, one trust company alone held title to a large number of farms in the 1930s. In the Municipality of Rhineland, on the other hand, 24 per cent of all rented land, that is, 8 per cent of all farm land, was owned by speculators and absentee landlords in 1936. The figure had decreased but slightly by 1941, when 3,340 acres were owned by a Gretna real estate man of German extraction, 4,681 by a few Jewish business men, 640 by an Anglo-Saxon outsider, 640 by various implement agents, 1,133 by commercial mortgage companies, 320 by one of the *Waisenamt* banks, 264 by the Municipality, and 2,999 by an array of small private investors such as a local physician, a local lawyer, a postmaster, a station agent, and similar people.

smaller Russländer settlements had declined or had been abandoned altogether, while the larger outlying centers of Mennonite concentration showed substantial gains. More significant still was the trend toward strengthening those settlements which, though not contingent upon one of the Reserves, were within easy reach of them. In the west and north of the West Reserve, up to a distance of about 90 miles from its outer limits, strings of well-established Mennonite settlements had made their appearance along the main arteries of transportation, in part extending into Saskatchewan. Simultaneously, the Russländer settlements located in the space between the two Reserves had greatly gained in strength, and the Mennonite population of the East Reserve had not only increased but, like that of the West Reserve, had overflown the boundaries of the original settlement in all directions. Thus, in the Red River Valley between the United States border and Winnipeg, and between the Pembina Mountains and the French settlements along the banks of the river, there existed a heavy concentration of Mennonites who, in many places, tended to displace the original owners of the land. Here a Mennonite domain was steadily building up which eventually might close the gap between the East and West Reserve, with the French wedged in along the river and scattered English-speaking farmers of various ethnic origins sandwiched between solid Mennonite colonies, while the towns along the fringes probably would remain predominantly non-Mennonite.

These developments were supported by a larger natural increase and a lesser degree of urbanization among the Mennonites. In the census for 1941, 9 out of every 10 Mennonites were listed as "rural," yet this figure includes some settlements which, though not incorporated at the time, must nevertheless be considered "urban." But even when this is taken into consideration, 83 per cent of the Manitoba Mennonites were residing outside of urban communities, and of these no less than 80 per cent were living on farms. As far as the urban Mennonite population is concerned, however, one has to distinguish between those living in the metropolitan area of Winnipeg and those living in rural trade centers within their own colonies, where they remained in intimate contact with a rural way of life, still felt to be the best safeguard against the intrusions of alien values. Critical remarks about city people and the iniquities of urban life were heard frequently among the Manitoba Mennonites. Even those who had become more sophisticated in matters of religion were convinced that the strength of the group lay in farming. It was widely realized that

TABLE 9—URBAN POPULATION OF MANITOBA, TOTAL AND MENNONITE, BY SIZE GROUPS, 1901-1941

Year		Urban and Rural	Urban No.	as a per cent of urban and rural population	Winnipeg No.	as a per cent of urban and rural population	as a per cent of urban population	Places with Populations between 1,000 and 29,999[1] No.	as a per cent of urban and rural population	as a per cent of urban population	Places with Populations under 1,000[1] No.	as a per cent of urban and rural population	as a per cent of urban population
1901	Total	255,211	70,436	27.6	42,340	16.6	60.1	21,317	8.4	30.3	6,779	2.7	9.5
	Mennonite	15,246	273	1.8	13	0.1	4.8	13	0.1	4.8	247	1.6	90.5
1911	Total	461,394	200,365	43.4	136,035	29.5	67.3	45,216	9.8	22.6	19,114	4.1	9.5
	Mennonite	15,600	609	3.9	43	0.3	7.1	30	0.2	4.9	536	3.4	88.1
1921	Total	610,118	261,616	42.9	179,087	29.4	68.5	60,134	9.9	22.9	22,395	3.7	8.6
	Mennonite	21,295	1,353	6.4	114	0.5	8.4	156	0.7	11.5	1,083	5.1	80.1
1931	Total	700,139	315,969	45.1	218,785	31.2	69.2	75,706	10.8	24.0	21,478	3.1	6.8
	Mennonite	30,352	2,820	9.3	909	3.0	32.2	1,219	4.0	43.2	692	2.3	24.6
1941	Total	729,744	321,873	44.1	221,960	30.4	69.0	77,356	10.6	24.0	22,557	3.1	7.0
	Mennonite	39,336	3,714	9.4	1,285	3.3	35.0	749	1.9	20.2	1,680	4.3	45.0

[1] Incorporated towns and villages.

Mennonite farmers were able to compete much more successfully with Anglo-Saxons than their brethren in urban walks of life, they also withstood such crises as a depression better than other classes. Even among urban Mennonites there was a latent readiness to return to the country and the farm, and those who actually had taken the step did not seem to feel the discomforts often connected with it as undue hardship. In fact, this ability to go back to the land apparently lent them a feeling of superiority over their neighbours whom they often ridiculed, rightly or wrongly, for preferring "softer jobs" in the city.

The inclination to move to the "big city" was much less pronounced among the Mennonites than among Manitoba's population at large. While in 1941 as many as 69 per cent of Manitoba's urban population lived in Winnipeg, only 35 per cent of the urban Mennonite population were found in the city, many of them but temporary residents such as young people, particularly girls, "working out" for a while before settling down in their own communities. The majority

TABLE 10—MENNONITE POPULATION OF MANITOBA, RURAL AND URBAN, BY SEX AND BIRTHPLACE, 1941*

Birth Place	Sex	Total No.	Total %	Rural No.	Rural %	Winnipeg No.	Winnipeg %	Other Urban No.	Other Urban %
All Birth Places	T	39,336	100	35,622	100	1,285	100	2,429	100
	M	19,943		18,178		591		1,174	
	F	19,393		17,444		694		1,255	
Man- itoba	T	30,390	77.3	28,134	79.0	534	41.6	1,722	70.9
	M	15,486	39.4	14,388	40.4	278	21.6	820	33.8
	F	14,904	37.9	13,746	38.6	256	19.9	902	37.1
Rest of Canada	T	1,018	2.6	847	2.4	67	5.2	104	4.3
	M	530	1.3	443	1.2	28	2.2	59	2.4
	F	488	1.2	404	1.1	39	3.0	45	1.9
Russia	T	6,834	17.4	5,631	15.8	641	49.9	562	23.1
	M	3,400	8.6	2,865	8.0	263	20.5	272	11.2
	F	3,434	8.7	2,766	7.8	378	29.4	290	12.0
Rest of Cont'al Europe	T	147	.4	108	.3	27	2.1	12	.5
	M	78	.2	57	.2	14	1.1	7	.3
	F	69	.2	51	.1	13	1.0	5	.2
United States	T	729	1.9	697	2.0	11	.9	21	.9
	M	350	.9	333	.9	6	.5	11	.5
	F	379	1.0	364	1.0	5	.4	10	.4
Other Coun tries	T	200	.5	195	.5	1	.1	4	.2
	M	90	.2	88	.2	—	—	2	.1
	F	110	.3	107	.3	1	.1	2	.1

* Unpublished data of the Canadian Bureau of Statistics.

of Winnipeg Mennonites were of the Russländer group, a considerable proportion of whom had belonged to the urban rather than rural classes in the Old Country. These, of course, had an understandable desire to remain in the city upon their arrival, despite all restrictions imposed on them by the immigration authorities, or to drift back to the metropolitan area as soon as these restrictions no longer applied to them. Nevertheless, even in the city the Mennonites showed a strong tendency to move into the same sections and neighbourhoods. They were concentrated mainly on Winnipeg's northside, the habitat of most minority groups of East European extraction, and in East Kildonan. The suburban settlement of East Kildonan is, according to one Mennonite sociologist, Professor J. W. Fretz, the only example of a true Mennonite colony found anywhere in a strictly urban community. It is described by him in these words: ". . . there is a solid settlement of Mennonites on three city streets, about half-a-mile in length. These people use the German language and have their own social and religious activities apart from the surrounding community."[2] At the time of our visit, it comprised over a hundred families, mostly labourers, clerks, and some businessmen. Many of them kept gardens and poultry on their small lots.

The Mennonites in the metropolitan area had an active social life, centered mainly around their churches and church institutions. In the summer of 1947 we counted more than 20 Mennonite-owned business units including 2 small factories, one producing bolts and hinges, the other wooden boxes. Still, the Winnipeg Mennonites had taken a leading role in only a few activities of the Mennonite group, mainly in the Bible school movement, the organization of charities, the administration of the Russländer debt to the Canadian Pacific Railway Company, and, to a lesser extent, in the publishing of Mennonite literature. As of old, the center of gravity for the ethnic group as a whole lay in the Reserves, not in the Provincial Capital.

With regard to the country towns located within the Mennonite Reserves, the most striking change that had occurred was the replacement of their original non-Mennonite majorities. Of course, Steinbach, unchallenged center of the East Reserve, had always been an almost exclusively Mennonite community. From a farming village of 47 families in 1889, it had gradually grown into a flourishing urban community of about 1800 at the time of its incorporation in 1948. The proportion of non-Mennonite residents was still very small, and included such people as the druggist, the bank manager, the physician, the Mounted Police constables and the town policemen. At the end of the war, Steinbach had the appearance of a boom town. Its Main Street was lined with substantial business buildings equipped with large show windows and neon signs. There was nothing provincial about the garages and stores, the beer parlors and at least one of the cafes. New shops and homes were continuously under construction. While most of the industrial establishments included plants for the processing of agricultural products and served local needs primarily, some of the factories had customers all over Western Canada and even in Ontario. Steinbach, too, was the only Mennonite town with a movie theatre whose patrons, however, consisted mostly of non-Mennonites living in its large trade area outside of the Reserve. Compared with Steinbach, the other towns in the East Reserve played

---

[2] "Factors Contributing to Success and Failure in Mennonite Colonization," *Mennonite Quarterly Review* 24 (1950): 130.

quite a subordinate role. Niverville, the only place located on a railroad, had remained stagnant. Grünthal, on the other hand, had become a little Steinbach, but on a much smaller scale. It drew its trade mainly from an underdeveloped, partly submarginal, hinterland extending as far as 15 miles to the south and southeast. The population of both, Niverville and Grünthal, was almost exclusively Mennonite.

The towns of the West Reserve had been founded by non-Mennonites, and, with the exception of Winkler, had long been dominated by them. Yet in 1941 the non-Mennonite majorities had become insignificant. In large part the growth of the Mennonite population in these communities since 1931 had been due to the influx of Russländer immigrants. However, the Kanädier Mennonites, too, had long lost their earlier aversion to urban living. Many retired farmers had moved into the nearby towns, while some of the young generation sought white collar jobs. With the expansion of Mennonite settlement a few towns at its fringes, which had long been solidly Anglo-Saxon, experienced a Mennonite invasion. In Morden, particularly, the Anglo-Saxon population decreased between 1931 and 1941 by 80 per cent, while the Mennonite population increased by 45 per cent. The situation in Morris was similar, although Mennonites did not gain the same ascendancy here because they had found strong competitors in the Slavic element. While Mennonite succession in two small railroad settlements, Lowe Farm and Kane, was practically complete, the little railroad hub of Rosenfeld was dominated by German Lutherans, who also had substantial minorities in other towns within the West Reserve, particularly in Winkler. Yet, Rosenfeld had gained far less than the neighbouring towns in either population or business volume, mainly because it was overshadowed by the prospering all-Mennonite town of Altona, just a short distance to the south. Gretna, too, once a strong Anglo-Saxon center but with German Lutherans and German Catholics together constituting a majority, had not been able to withstand the competition of Altona.

On the surface the Mennonite towns in the West Reserve compared with other railroad settlements throughout Manitoba in their economic or social structure. For instance, a survey of Winkler,[3] undertaken by the author in 1946, revealed a prevalence of retail trade and maintenance services. Next in importance were agencies for the processing

---

[3] To the population of Winkler, given by the 1941 census as 957, should be added the inhabitants of a large residential section, developed in recent years but not incorporated into the town.

and marketing of agricultural products. Then there were the usual educational, medical and recreational services and 6 churches, 4 Mennonite, 1 Lutheran, and 1 Adventist. Yet a comparison with conditions in neighbouring Morden did reveal several significant differences. Public offices, such as county court, Mounted Police post, land titles office, municipal office, experimental farm, customs office, in addition to the offices of several lawyers and the agricultural representative, were found in the older Anglo-Saxon rather than in the German and Mennonite town. Moreover, Morden, although not much greater in actual size than Winkler, had many more churches, namely, 2 Mennonite churches, and 1 building each for members of the United Church, Presbyterians, Anglicans, Roman Catholics, Lutherans and 3 smaller congregations. Winkler had very few recreational agencies, namely, a beer parlor and a few restaurants, while a dance hall, opened outside of the incorporated area in 1945, had folded up shortly afterwards. There was no picture theatre, and the few clubs were either defunct or led a precarious existence. Morden, on the other hand, had not only many more beer parlors, cafes and restaurants, it also had a dance hall, a movie theatre and no less than 7 active fraternal and sport organizations. Although some of these clubs had a few Mennonite members from Winkler and Plum Coulee, these were people who had drifted far along the road to complete assimilation. (See Chart VII.)

In addition to the towns, several villages survived in the Mennonite Reserves, most of them remnants of old open-field communities. Some had largely disintegrated, yet they still provided nuclei for open-country neighbourhoods. Table 11 summarizes the situation as we found it in 1947.

Neublumenort, unique in Manitoba and probably in all of Western Canada, deserves a few additional remarks. Here we have a genuine farm village which has been formed in recent years; it resembles one of the old peasant villages although there is no direct connection. While lying within the area of the former village of Blumenort, it is actually located some seven miles north of the old site which is almost completely deserted. The settlement had grown, without any deliberate design, around a cheese factory and store erected in the open country near a few odd farmsteads. In 1939 the Kleine Gemeinde church, as a matter of practical relief work for indigent members, had bought 20 acres nearby, offering 2½ acres to every family at the price of $30 per acre, which sum included fencing.

TABLE 11—MENNONITE PLACES IN MANITOBA[1]

Location	Foundation	Name	Settled By	Description

A) EAST RESERVE

Location	Foundation	Name	Settled By	Description
6-6 East[2]	o.f.[3]	Steinbach[5]	Kleine Gemeinde group	important town
7-4 East	1880	Niverville	non-Mennonites	small railroad town
5-5 East	o.f.	Grünthal	Bergthal group	farm-operator village and trade center
7-5 East	o.f.	Chortitz	Bergthal group	farm-operator village, small trade center
6-5 East	before 1890	Kleefeld	Kleine Gemeinde group	near abandoned site of Grünfeld (an open-field village and small trade center)
6-5 East	has grown gradually	Hochstadt	Bergthal group, further developed by Russländer immigrants	near abandoned site of Blumstein (an open-field village); farm-operator village, small trade center; actually forms one settlement with Kleefeld
5-5 East	o.f.	Schönsee	Bergthal group	rudimentary farm-operator village
7-6 East	since 1930	*Neublumenort[4]	Kleine Gemeinde group	farm-operator village and small trade center
7-6 East	since 1930	*Plettenville	family of Plett	small industrial village, family settlement

Other small trade centers, which cannot be called villages and were founded after 1918, are: New Bothwell (twp. 7-5 East), Prairie Rose (twp. 8-5 East), Landmark (twp. 8-5 East) and Greenland (twp. 8-6 East). These places have no connection with any former open-field villages.

B) WEST RESERVE

Location	Foundation	Name	Settled By	Description
3-4 West	after 1890	Winkler	non-Mennonites	important railroad town
2-1 West	after 1890	Altona	non-Mennonites	important railroad town
1-1 West	after 1890	Gretna	non-Mennonites	railroad town
3-3 West	after 1890	Plum Coulee	non-Mennonites	railroad town
3-1 West	after 1890	Rosenfeld	non-Mennonites	railroad town

TABLE 11—(Continued)

1-4 West	after 1890	Haskett	non-Mennonites	formerly on a railroad line, partly agricultural; near abandoned sites of Kronsfeld and Grünfeld (both open-field villages)
3-2 West	after 1890	Horndean	individual Mennonites	railroad settlement, partly agricultural
4-3 West	after 1890	Kronsgart	individual Mennonites	farm-operator village with railroad station, small trade center
4-1 West	after 1890	Lowe Farm	non-Mennonites	railroad town
4-2 West	after 1890	Kane	non-Mennonites	small railroad settlement
1-1 East	o.f.	Halbstadt	Bergthal group	farm-operator village, small trade center
1-1 East	o.f.	Sommerfeld	Bergthal group	well-preserved farm-operator village, small trade center
1-1 West	o.f.	Neubergthal	Bergthal group	well-preserved farm-operator village, small trade center
1-1 West	o.f.	Gnadenfeld	Bergthal group	rudimentary farm-operator village
1-1 West	o.f.	Silberfeld	Bergthal group	rudimentary farm-operator village
1-1 West	o.f.	Neuanlage	Bergthal group	rudimentary farm-operator village
2-1 West	o.f.	Alt-Altona	Bergthal group	farm-operator village, a sort of agricultural suburb of the town of Altona, half a mile north
2-2 West	o.f.	Altbergthal	Bergthal group	rudimentary farm-operator village
1-2 West	o.f.	Blumenort	Fürstenland group	farm-operator village
1-2 West	o.f.	Kronsthal	Fürstenland group	rudimentary farm-operator village
1-3 West	o.f.	Neuhorst	Fürstenland group	farm-operator village
1-3 West	o.f.	Rosenort	Fürstenland group	farm-operator village
1-3 West	o.f.	Schönwiese	Fürstenland group	farm-operator village
1-3 West	o.f.	Rosengart	Fürstenland group	well-preserved farm-operator village (with new additions)
2-3 West	o.f.	Gnadenthal	Fürstenland group	farm-operator village, small trade center

TABLE 11—(Continued)

2-3 West	o.f.	Blumengart	Fürstenland group	was bought by Hutterites after World War I who re-arranged building and made many new additions "Bruderhof"
1-4 West	o.f.	**Reinland**	Fürstenland group	well-preserved farm-operator village (with new additions), trade center
1-4 West	o.f.	Blumenfeld	Fürstenland group	farm-operator village
1-4 West	o.f.	Hochfeld	Fürstenland group	farm-operator village
2-4 West	o.f.	Neuenburg	Fürstenland group	rudimentary farm-operator village and small trade center
2-4 West	o.f.	Friedensruh	Fürstenland group	farm-operator village, small trade center
2-4 West	o.f.	Schanzenfeld	Fürstenland group	well-preserved farm-operator village, small trade center
2-4 West	o.f.	Chortitz	Fürstenland group	well-preserved farm-operator village, small trade center
2-5 West	o.f.	Osterwick	Fürstenland group	well-preserved farm-operator village, small trade center
3-4 West	o.f.	Reinfeld	Fürstenland group	well-preserved farm-operator village, small trade center
3-4 West	before 1890	*Hildebrandsdorf	family of Hildebrand	family settlement resembling an open-field village

C) SCRATCHING RIVER COLONY

6-1 West	o.f.	Rosenort	Kleine Gemeinde group	farm-operator village, small trade center
6-1 West	o.f.	Rosenhof	Kleine Gemeinde group	farm-operator village

---

[1] All those places have been included in this list whose population was more than half Mennonite.

[2] Locations are listed by township and range, east or west of the first principal meridian.

[3] o.f. — organized under the open-field system at time of immigration.

[4] * — unofficial place name.

[5] The names of railroad towns and locally important trade centers are in **boldface**.

By 1946 the community had grown to 26 households. Part of the buildings were arranged, though somewhat irregularly, along the east-west section line, while the others, including the school, formed a row along the north-south section line. The business units included a cheese factory, a store, a garage, a shoe-maker shop, and two gas filling stations. The people had managed to make a living with very little capital by concentrating on poultry and garden crops. One Mennonite was raising 17,000 chickens on a 500-acre farm, but most of the other holdings were much smaller. Community life was focussed on the Kleine Gemeinde church whose building stood south of the settlement along the highway.

The Church

At the end of World War II, there were no less than 24 different religious bodies of Mennonites in Manitoba listed by separate names. This seemingly extreme particularism, however, requires a few words of explanation. The traditional Mennonite term for their religious bodies is *Gemeinde,* which literally means "community" but is commonly translated as "church." The Mennonites themselves make the distinction between *kirchliche Gemeinden* and *Brüdergemeinden,* thereby indicating a highly significant difference between churches, properly speaking, and brotherhoods. Originally all religious communities of the Anabaptists conformed to the sociological type of a "sect," that is, a religious movement (or group) which stands in opposition to the institutionalized church; the latter, as a rule, is territorially defined. While the church is closely identified with the established social order, the sect remains critical of the "world," and prefers withdrawal to compromise. Because the word "sect" has an insiduous connotation it has been widely replaced by "brotherhood." Due to their typically loose and spontaneous organization, brotherhoods tend to be confined to rather small localized, at best regional, communities, which on occasion, however, enter into larger associations with like-minded groups. This is precisely the way in which the Mennonite church has grown and spread. Yet, when in the course of time members of the brotherhood formed segregated colonies, their religious organization assumed the role of a parish church. The established churches in the various colonies of Mennonites in Russia were characteristically named after the localities with which they were identified. For instance, the Bergthal church in Manitoba is directly derived

257

TABLE 12—MENNONITE POPULATION OF MANITOBA, BY CHURCH AFFILIATION, 1913, 1932 AND 1944*

	1913(2) Souls	1932(3) Souls	1944(4) Souls	Families	Members	Church Buildings	Bishops	Preachers
Total	14,325	20,699	34,420	(6)	17,471	(6)	19	216
Kirchliche Gemeinden (Churches)	14,153	16,799	28,920	5,960	14,971	65	19	155
Old Colony Church	3,946⎫	9,800	1,176	200	478	4	1	5
Sommerfeld Church	5,343⎬		7,650	1,800	4,000	12	1	13
Chortitz Church	2,110	2,450	3,223	600	1,448	4	1	11
Kleine Gemeinde, East Reserve	801	1,365⎫						
Kleine Gemeinde, Rosenort Colony	307	567⎬	2,955	500	1,430	5	1	16
Rudnerweide Church	—	—	3,130	600	1,442	10	1	21
Church of God in Christ (Holdemann)[1]	498	958	957	180	585	4	4	14
General Conference Churches	—	1,659	9,829	2,080	5,588	26	10	75
Bergthal Church, East Reserve	—		510	70	218	1	—	5
Bergthal Church, West Reserve	1,148		4,521	1,000	3,146	8	1	18
Blumenort Congregation	—		583	123	277	3	1	11
Lichtenau Congregation	—		300	66	123	1	—	5
Nordheim Congregation	—		177	36	86	—	—	2
Schönfeld Congregation	—	Not specified	232	40	109	1	1	4
Springstein Congregation	—		213	41	105	1	1	2
Steinbach Congregation	—		121	27	62	1	—	3
Elim Congregation (Grünthal, East Reserve)	—		470	90	194	1	1	2
Whitewater Congregation	—		889	180	340	2	1	9
Bethel Mission (Winnipeg)	—		300	100	70	1	1	1
Schönwiese Church (Winnipeg)	—		574	119	403	1	2	1
Schönwiese Church (scattered groups)	—		788	160	389	4	1	9
McCreary Congregation	—		101	13	41	1	—	1
Scattered Members	—		50	15	25	—	—	2
Brüder Gemeinden (Brethren)	172(5)	3,900	5,500	(6)	2,500	(6)	—	61
Mennonite Brethren	150(5)	3,500	5,000	(6)	2,300	(6)	—	60
Evangelical Mennonite Brethren	22(5)	400	500	(6)	200	2		1

* Many of the figures are not very accurate but frequently based on rough guesses.
1 Actually more of the "Brethren" than the "Church" type.
2 "Der Mitarbeiter, 1913."
3 I. I. Friesen, "The Mennonites in Western Canada" (1934).
4 Information Rev. Benjamin Ewert, Winnipeg, in: "Warte-Jahrbuch, 1944" and "Jahrbuch der Allgemeinen Konferenz, 1944."
5 In 1912.
6 Not available.

from the local church of the Bergthal colony in Russia, while the name of the Old Colony church of the Fürstenland people betrays the descent of this group from the so-called Old Colony on the Chortitza river. Thus one reason for the multiplicity of separate branches of the Mennonite church may be found in the many migrations of its faithful.

On the other hand, the religious organization of the Mennonites has also been subject to a variety of schisms in the different colonies. In a "free" church without a central authority other than the *Bruderschaft*, or assembly of its male members, and an elected elder or bishop, all that is necessary to accomplish separation is that the dissident group convene, elect their elder and have him ordained by the elder and preachers of some other branch of the Mennonite church favorably disposed toward them. Dissensions over matters of faith and doctrine rarely play a decisive role. More commonly such divisions are the expression of a protest by more zealous members against laxity in the observance of religious and moral principles, and in church discipline on the part of the majority. The differences are often formulated in terms of ritual concerning the form of baptism, the type of religious music, and the like. At times, however, these are but external symbols for more deep-seated antagonisms and personal rivalries which have arisen in some local community or colony. We have already met with one typical example of such a schism in discussing the separation of the Bergthal church in Manitoba from the Sommerfeld and Chortitz churches as a result of the school conflict in 1891.

The *Brüdergemeinden* or brotherhoods found among the Manitoba Mennonites are of a somewhat different origin. At the beginning of the nineteenth century a group of German Lutheran Pietists settled in the Molotschna colony where they made proselytes among their Mennonite neighbours. The movement grew in spiritual stature under the leadership of a certain Pastor Wüst, a dissident Lutheran clergyman from Württemberg.[4] Attracted by his sermons and revival meetings, many Mennonites refused to recognize the authority of the local parish churches and began to organize separate meetings. It is quite conceivable that the new movement would have joined some non-Mennonite religious body such as the Baptists, had not, under the Russian legal system, renunciation of the Mennonite faith also carried with itself loss of important rights and privileges, including military exemption and the holding of property in the Mennonite settlements. Ultimately, a modus vivendi was reached according to which the "Brethren" were recognized as a Mennonite denomination, thus re-

---

4 Cf. A. Kröker, *Pfarrer Eduard Wüst, der grosse Erweckungsprediger in den deutschen Kolonien Südrusslands*, (Leipzig und Hillsboro, Kans., 1903).

maining members of the Mennonite civil community without being members of its established church.[5]

As a common term for both types of Mennonite religious bodies, the churches and the brotherhoods, Mennonite historians and theologians in America have adopted the expression "branches of the Mennonite church." By the end of World War II, the following branches were found in Manitoba: First there were the old conservative churches which tried to preserve as much as possible of the historical traditions which had developed in Russia up to their emigration in 1874. They forbade the use of organs or pianos, part-singing, decorations, free sermon, free prayer, and the use of the English language in their church services. As far as personal conduct of their members was concerned they were opposed to fashionable dress, sports, radios, movies, sometimes even passenger cars and bicycles, but were more lenient with regard to dancing, alcohol and smoking. Most of them did not have Sunday schools, youth clubs, or evening services, while their Sunday morning service was regularly set at an earlier hour than among the more liberal churches. The most conservative of all was the Old Colony church of the Fürstenland people. When most of its members emigrated to Mexico in the 1920's, the few who remained behind either joined the Sommerfeld church or, as Dawson aptly wrote, "they stood aloof in austere isolation."[6] After about 80 families had returned to Manitoba, the church was revived in 1936; it flourished under the capable leadership of Elder Jacob J. Froese.

Two other churches in this group were direct off-shoots of the old church of the Bergthal immigrants. After its split in 1891, the East Reserve section was renamed the Chortitz church, while the conservative dissidents among the West Reserve Bergthal people reconstituted themselves as the Sommerfeld church, whose elder was ordained by the elder of the Chortitz church. Both groups coöperated in the emigrations to Paraguay, and maintained a basic unity in their religious practices and way of life.

Another Mennonite church of the old school, though more compromising, was the Kleine Gemeinde which had been founded in 1813 in the Molotschna colony as a reform movement.[7] Many of its members

[5] Cf. P. M. Friesen, *Konfession oder Sekte? Der gemeinsame Konvent am 7. März und die Kommission in Halbstadt am 11. und 12. April 1914* (undated pamphlet).

[6] C. A. Dawson, *Group Settlement: Ethnic Communities in Western Canada* (Toronto, 1936), pp. 150.

[7] Cf. *Eine einfache Erklärung und einige Glaubenssätze der sogenannten Kleinen Gemeinde* (Quakertown, Pa., 1901).

migrated in 1866 to the Borsenko colony and hence, in 1874, to Kansas, Nebraska and the Manitoba East Reserve. Some of the Nebraska group moved later to Meade County in Kansas, and some of the East Reserve group to the Scratching River settlement, some miles north of the West Reserve. In both Manitoba settlements, the Kleine Gemeinde functioned from the beginning as an established church in the same way as the Bergthal and Old Colony churches. An undisclosed number of the original Kleine Gemeinde congregation in Kansas were converted to the Mennonite Brethren and the Krimmer Brethren. In 1889, Isaac Peters, of Henderson, Nebraska, and Aaron Wall, of Mountain Lake, Minnesota, founded the brotherhood of Evangelical Mennonite Brethren, which was joined by some Kleine Gemeinde people in the East Reserve, Nebraska and Kansas.[8] Finally, many Kleine Gemeinde members in Manitoba separated to form the Canadian branch of the Church of God in Christ (Holdemann). All three original churches in Manitoba, the Bergthal, Old Colony and Kleine Gemeinde church, have constantly lost members, either to the various brotherhoods or to filial churches, without trying to balance the loss through missionary work.

The second group of Mennonite religious bodies in Manitoba could be described as reform churches. Reform may be in the direction of greater strictness, or of greater leniency. The first type, which stands half-way between the churches and the brotherhoods, included the Holdemann and the Rudnerweide church, although, according to more recent information, the latter seems to have moved since 1945 toward greater leniency and has become somewhat like the Bergthal church. Founded in 1859 by Johannes Holdemann in Ohio, the Church of God in Christ (Holdemann) had members in 11 of the United States, 2 Canadian provinces and in Mexico by 1945. Its Canadian converts came mainly from the Kleine Gemeinde but included also some non-Mennonite Germans as well as a few Anglo-Saxons in the Clearspring settlement near Steinbach. The practices of this branch of the Mennonite church were revivalist and evangelical. Like the Brethren, the Church of God in Christ had adjusted itself rather willingly to life in a secularized society, at the same time tightening its principles of moral conduct, and adopting the pastoral methods of American revival churches. The Holdemann people used the English

---

[8] Cf. *A Historical Sketch of the Churches of the Evangelical Mennonite Brethren, 1889-1939* (Rosthern, Sask., n.d.); also *Constitution of the Conference of the Evangelical Mennonite Brethren* (n.d.).

language freely, were aggressive in business, and interested in the affairs of the world and in new ideas. Yet as a church they were perhaps the most rigorous of all branches of Mennonites in Manitoba; for they retained not only the injunctions of the old conservative churches, but combined them with the stricter principles of the Brethren in regard to smoking or drinking. Unlike other Mennonite groups in Manitoba (not counting the Hutterites), they also insisted upon the external distinction of well-groomed beards and tieless shirts for the men.

The liberal type of Mennonite reform branches is exemplified in varying degrees by the churches united in the General Conference.[9] This organization was founded in 1860, but had been supported mainly by the immigrants who came from Russia in the 1870's and again in the 1920's, until it became the second-largest Mennonite group in the world. The first separate meeting of Conference churches in Western Canada took place in 1903. Thirty years later, the Canadian Conference was formed which, however, remained affiliated with the larger body, while most of the Canadian Conference churches were also members of the American Conference. In Manitoba the core of the General Conference, which may be best described as a union of liberal churches among the Russian Mennonites, was the Bergthal church, whose original membership of Kanädier Mennonites had been greatly strengthened when it was joined by many of the Russländer immigrants settling in the West Reserve. Other refugees, however, formed separate local churches in the new outlying settlements. In several instances members of some local church in Russia decided to continue their tradition and name when they were reunited in the New World, for instance, the relatively large Blumenort or Schönwiese churches. In addition, separate Russländer congregations were formed in the towns of the East Reserve. The immigrants who had belonged to the established churches in their various Russian settlements found the liberal spirit of the General Conference most congenial. After the emigration of the more conservative elements in the 1870's, these churches had adjusted themselves rather readily to the conditions of modern life. They had been subjected to similar social forces as had their more progressive Canadian brethren, they had been influenced by other Protestant churches and their theological literature, and they

---

[9] H. P. Krehbiel, *The History of the General Conference of Mennonites of North America*, 2 vols. (St. Louis, Mo., 1898 and Hesston, Kans., 1938).

followed their example in methods of pastorization as well as in ritual and ecclesiastical organization.

By the end of the second World War, the Conference functioned among the Mennonites in Manitoba very much like the United Church of Canada functioned among Anglo-Saxon Protestants, except that as a rule they still insisted strongly upon the use of High German in their church services. They permitted, and even favored, instruments, mixed church choirs, decorations, free sermons and prayers, Sunday schools, church services in the evening, youth clubs, women's auxiliaries, sewing circles, and so on, and they were less strict with regard to worldly pleasures, although even they forbade attendance at motion picture shows. They supported the Bethel Mission in one of the better residential districts of Winnipeg, which was served by a full-time elder. Its services were conducted in the English language in order to attract non-Mennonites as well as young Mennonites who worked or studied in the city. In addition, an itinerant preacher was stationed in Winnipeg, Elder Benjamin Ewert, a brother of Heinrich Ewert.

Finally, there were the brotherhoods which had abandoned the last vestiges of the old Mennonite ritual, used gospel songs instead of the traditional Reformation hymns, conducted their services in both the English and the German language, favored musical instruments and mixed choirs, cultivated free sermons and free prayers, and were not as much opposed to sports as most other branches of the Mennonite church. It is not positively known whether there existed a nucleus of Mennonite Brethren in Manitoba when, in 1880 or 1881, a certain Johann Funk, of Neuenburg, began preaching penance in their manner, causing considerable unrest in the Fürstenland portion of the West Reserve.[10] In any event, this dramatic outbreak of sectarianism and chiliasm was quickly suppressed. The brotherhood of Mennonite Brethren[11] was officially introduced to the province in 1884, when Elder Heinrich Vogt of Minnesota paid his first visit. He was followed by other missionaries from Kansas and Nebraska who made some converts among the Manitoba Mennonites. But the movement did not greatly progress until the arrival of the Russländer refugees. Some of the best educated and leading personalities among

---

[10] Unpublished diary of P. Elias.

[11] J. F. Harms, *Geschichte der Mennoniten Brüdergemeinde* (Hillsboro, Kans., n.d.); John H. Lohrenz, *The Mennonite Brethren Church* (Hillsboro, Kans., 1950); and Peter Regier, *Kurzgefasste Geschichte der Mennoniten Brüder-Gemeinde* (Berne, Ind., 1901).

the immigrants belonged to the brotherhood, which strengthened its position substantially. By 1945, about one-half of the Mennonite Brethren in Manitoba belonged to the Russländer group. Their main concern seemed to be with religion rather than folk traditions. They were more broad-minded than any other branch with regard to the use of English in church functions. At the same time, they were most insistent upon total abstinence from nicotine and alcohol, and emphasized high standards of personal moral conduct. Always stressing the need for religious education, they were responsible for the introduction of the Bible school idea to Manitoba. The Brethren also showed strong interest in missionary activities outside the ethnic group, fostered a certain evangelical emotionalism, and considered their ministers less as church functionaries and more as teachers and leaders, whose ordination did not even require the presence of an elder. All told, they were probably farthest removed from the historical type of the old Mennonite church.

The second brotherhood in Manitoba, that of the Evangelical Mennonite Brethren, was confined to Steinbach and a small mission chapel in the south end of Winnipeg. It had been imported by American immigrants shortly before the turn of the century. In its large church building at Steinbach services were conducted by 1946 in German and English on alternate Sundays. This, together with a fine choir and the ministrations of a full-time pastor (a former school teacher), had a strong appeal not only to the upper class in town, but also to its Anglo-Saxon population who were without a church of their own.

The School

One of the most striking changes in recent years has occurred in the field of education, mainly under the influence of the Russländer immigrants. At the end of the first World War, the schools in the Mennonite colonies had been "nationalized" with the avowed purpose of facilitating acculturation and, through it, the speedy absorption of the group into the national society. A quarter of a century later, a whole generation had grown up which had never attended a parochial Mennonite grade school. Day after day, year after year, the secular public school had taught young Mennonites the same language and the same culture it had been teaching to the youth of all Anglo-Saxon Canada. And it had been successful to the extent that the Mennonites had assimilated much of it as part of their own social heritage. What was even more significant, the school itself, the potent instrument of acculturation, had not only been accepted as a matter of fact by the old as well as the young, but the majority of Mennonites were taking a keen and active interest in educational affairs. School attendance in Mennonite school districts was excellent, and scholastic achievements were superior to the provincial average. There were less one-room and more two-room schools in rural areas with a Mennonite majority than anywhere else in the province. Because Mennonites continued to live in compact settlements, the public school which they attended was felt to be, more often than not, an integral part of their own community structure rather than the foreign body it had been in earlier years. It was run by their own school trustees and manned by their own teachers, mainly males of the Russländer group, many, if not most, of whom had received at least a part of their education in the Mennonite Collegiate Institute at Gretna or had come under its indirect influence.

High school and even university attendance by Mennonites was on the increase. Between 1932 and 1947, Mennonite enrollment in the University of Manitoba alone had jumped from 19 to 88, while others were studying outside the province, mainly in the United States. To this figure must be added many young Mennonites preparing for the teaching and nursing profession, one metropolitan hospital alone counting no less than 16 Mennonites among its nursing staff and student nurses in 1947.[12] Although the number of Mennonite graduates outside the field of teaching and nursing was as yet not great, it included missionaries, agriculturists, professors, community organizers, lawyers and physicians.

While public schools in the Mennonite colonies absorbed most of the Mennonite high school students, three private secondary schools were maintained in Manitoba under the auspices of the Mennonite church. The Mennonite Brethren Collegiate Institute in Winnipeg opened its doors in 1945 as an adjunct of the Mennonite Brethren Bible College. By 1946-47 it had an enrollment of 84, mostly children of Mennonite Brethren of Russländer extraction. Some years later a similar school was founded in Winnipeg under the auspices of the General Conference. The earlier story of the Mennonite Collegiate

---

[12] Cf. *Mennonitische Rundschau* 70 (April 16, 1947): 1.

Institute at Gretna has already been told.[13] Since the death of Heinrich Ewert in 1934, it had more and more been taken over by Russländer people affiliated with General Conference churches. After its function of preparing immigrant teachers for Canadian school certificates had terminated, enrolment had sunk from a high of 70 in the 1920's to a mere 22 in 1932; for Kanädier Mennonites, even those living in Gretna, preferred to send their children to public schools. But when the children of the Russländer immigrants had grown to high school age, the Gretna Institute experienced a triumphant comeback. From 50 in 1938-39, the number of students increased to as many as 154 in 1945-46; 60 per cent of these were girls, and 90 per cent belonged to the Russländer group coming from all parts of Canada between Ontario and the West Coast, mostly however from the smaller outlying settlements in Manitoba. Tuition and board amounted to $230-$270 a year, while the participating churches contributed 30 cents per church member, and the parents of the students $2 each a year. The Institute was among the "toughest" schools in the Province with a rigid, almost "Prussian," discipline. It required study programs in religion, church history, choir singing and German, in addition to the customary high school subjects, and permitted a failure rate of only 10 per cent as against the provincial average of 25 per cent. A thorough preparation for entry into the provincial Normal School at Winnipeg was still a major purpose of this institution, although its influence upon the religious life, culture and tastes of the Mennonite population in Manitoba was perhaps even more important than its academic achievements. The church historian Paul Schäfer has been its principal since 1947.

Impressive as the progress in general education had been, it did not solve the particular educational problems of a church which not only needs facilities for the religious instruction of the young like all churches but, in addition, requires the knowledge of a separate ritual language from its faithful, and some advanced training at least from those among whose ranks its lay ministers and preachers, deacons, Sunday school teachers and choir leaders are to be recruited. Although the law permits that one-half hour daily may be set aside for religious instruction in the public school, many school boards and teachers in Mennonite school districts did not avail themselves of this opportunity

---

[13] G. H. Peters, "Der Werdegang der Mennonitischen Lehranstalt zu Gretna," *Warte-Jahrbuch* 1 (1943): 20-26; and Paul J. Schäfer, "Der Neubau der Gretna Gemeindeschule," *Warte-Jahrbuch* 2 (1944): 15-17.

for various reasons. The private high schools, on the other hand, reached only a small fraction of future church members. This situation had been foreseen as early as 1925 by a group of former Bible school teachers in Russia, all of whom belonged to the Mennonite Brethren.[14] Under the able leadership of Professor A. H. Unruh, who had been principal of a junior college in the Crimea, a Bible school was founded in Winkler which, by the end of the war, had 3 full-time teachers and a student body of about 100, most of them between the ages of 20 and 30 years, who attended its four, two or one-year courses during the winter months, returning to their regular occupations during the fair season. Smaller Bible schools, more or less on an interdenominational basis, existed also in Altona and Steinbach.

The more advanced Mennonite Brethren College at Winnipeg was opened in 1944; its purpose was stated in the following words:

Advanced theological training and broad secular education must be required of our Bible school teachers if the schools are to survive and progress. The young men of our churches who are called to the teaching ministry should be offered an opportunity to attend an advanced Bible college or seminary. From those out of our midst, who have gone to schools of other denominations to receive this type of preparation, some have returned to us with ideals and interpretations foreign to our Mennonite Brethren principles of Spirit and Doctrine.[15]

The institution offered courses leading to the bachelor of divinity and various diplomas in religious education and sacred music, as well as a curriculum for missionaries. A few years later a similar school, the Mennonite Bible College in Winnipeg, was inaugurated by the General Conference, with Elder I. I. Friesen as president.

Charities

The break-down of the old solidaristic peasant community, new ideas taken over from the Canadian society at large, and the influence of the progressive Russländer immigrants had also brought about great changes in the field of charity. At the time of the Revolution, the Mennonites in Russia had fully adopted the modern principle of public welfare as the obligation of secular society wherever works of charity under church auspices failed to answer the need. They were far

---

[14] Clarence Fretz, "A History of Winter Bible Schools in the Mennonite Church," *Mennonite Quarterly Review* 16 (1942): 51-81; and J. H. Enns, "Mennonitische Bibelschulen in Kanada," *Warte-Jahrbuch* 1 (1943): 32-36.

[15] *Mennonite Brethren Bible College, Third Annual Catalogue*, 1946-1947.

advanced in the organization and maintenance of hospitals, asylums and homes of all kinds in their colonies. In contrast to them, the Manitoba Mennonites continued to rely on traditional methods of mutual aid, and where these proved insufficient, particularly in the field of medical and hospital care, they simply took advantage of the public institutions provided by the large society.

The Russländer immigrants found that whatever Mennonite charitable organizations there were in Manitoba, they proved unable to cope with the urgent needs created by the influx of indigent refugees who were scattered over the whole province, torn from their families and exposed to the moral dangers of city life. At the same time, they had a strong sense of national and group solidarity, and thus were hesitant to make use of non-Mennonite and non-German benevolences. They wished to keep their people, divided as they were among the many branches of the church, together at least as an ethnic unit, and feared loss through assimilation if they leaned too much on outside help. Unlike the Kanädier group, they had had experience in the administration of welfare agencies and had at their disposal trained personnel anxious to work again in their old occupations. As soon as economic conditions permitted, they set about to organize their own charitable institutions, some of which served strictly local needs, while others were conceived as centralized agencies for the whole Russländer community in the province. Among these should be mentioned several old folks and nursing homes in the towns of the Mennonite Reserves.[16] The large Bethania Home for the Aged and Infirm, on a beautiful estate outside of Winnipeg, was inaugurated in 1945, by the Mennonite Benevolent Association which, though inter-denominational, functioned under the leadership of a very active group of Russländer Mennonite Brethren. In 1946, 10 nurses under the supervision of Dr. Nicholas Neufeld, a Mennonite surgeon practicing at Winnipeg, cared for 62 inmates. Two homes for Mennonite girls, working or studying in the city, were maintained by different churches in Winnipeg.[17] These served not only as well-supervised boarding houses but as religious and recreational centers also, and as employment agencies, paralleling, as it were, the many activities of a YWCA.

---

[16] Cf. Abram Vogt, "Das Invalidenheim in Steinbach, Manitoba," *Warte-Jahrbuch* 1 (1943): 56-59.
[17] Cf. I. E. Enns, "Unser Mädchenheim 'Eben-Ezer' in Winnipeg," *Warte-Jahrbuch* 2 (1944): 32-34.

Within the Mennonite Reserves, public hospitals served as Mennonite community institutions in the same way as did the schools.[18] In addition, however, the Russländer group had provided for a central health organization to take care of the needs peculiar to its own members, particularly those living in outlying settlements and in Winnipeg. As early as 1928, they established a nursing home which four years later began to operate as a small nine-bed hospital with a Nebraska Mennonite matron in charge.[19] In 1933 the first non-profit hospitalization insurance in the province, operating very much along the lines of the Blue Cross system, was organized by the same Russländer group.[20] It remained the least expensive form of health insurance which could be obtained anywhere in Manitoba, although it was later expanded to include not only hospitalization but also medical care and periodic check-ups in a doctor's private office. In 1946 about 13 contract groups of 10 or more members each, covering 779 families and 57 unattached individuals, were in existence in various Russländer settlements. At the time, each family, regardless of the number of unmarried children still at home, paid $33 a year. Losses were at a minimum because membership was restricted to Mennonites, and each local group was held responsible collectively for the payment of contributions. The organization had succeeded in improving the general health among its members mainly by providing an incentive to clear up old cases whose cure is frequently neglected.

After several of the immigrant nurses and physicians who had been trained in Russia or Germany had finally obtained their Manitoba licenses, the Concordia Hospital moved to a larger 50-bed building in 1934. It has been able to offer its services at a lower cost than other city hospitals (about 70 per cent of the charge asked per bed in Winnipeg's General Hospital); for its staff, under the the direction of Dr. Nicholas Neufeld, was satisfied with small salaries, considering their work not only as a source of income but as an expression of

---

[18] Cf. A. D. Friesen, "Bethania Hospital." *Warte-Jahrbuch* 2 (1944): 30-31.

[19] *Die Entstehung und Entwicklung des Mennonitischen Krankenhauses Concordia zu Winnipeg* (Winnipeg, 1931); and H. J. Willems, "Concordia Hospital," *Warte-Jahrbuch* 1 (1943): 45-48.

[20] Also in their South American colonies have the Russian Mennonites developed a similar solidaristic system of medical care. In a recent report, for instance, we read that in all of their Paraguayan colonies prepayment plans are in operation. "It is assumed that income from patients will provide from 60 to 65 per cent of the total operating cost of the hospitals, and that the remainder will be borne by the colony." Doctors are paid a fixed fee or salary just as school teachers and other colony employees, but about from three to five times more than any other public servants. They "seem not to lose any incentive nor do they fail to perform service of the highest order." (J. W. Fretz, *Pilgrims in Paraguay*, p. 131f.).

Christian charity. In 1945 the hospital had 1,433 patients, 748 of whom were Mennonites, the balance Lutherans and Catholics, mostly of German origin. Over 5,010 days of hospitalization were provided under contract, and 7,832 under some other payment plan. The following reason was given for the maintenance of a separate Mennonite hospital by its administrators:

We are, and shall be, probably for many years to come, considered as foreigners in this country which we have chosen as our home. We are being treated as such, even if we have fulfilled all that is required from us just as well as any other citizen. Even if we have no more language difficulties we shall always prefer our own institutions which offer us a better treatment.

Like the French-Canadians, the Mennonites in times of distress turn to the Christian charity offered to them by their own kin rather than to public health services provided as a matter of contractual obligation.

The Press

Like other ethnic groups, the Mennonites maintained their own press partly in order to supplement religious instruction, partly to preserve language and culture, and also to strengthen social ties between scattered settlements. One of the first papers read among Manitoba Mennonites was the *Herold der Wahrheit,* published under the auspices of the Mennonites in the Eastern United States in Elkhart, Indiana, and edited by J. F. Funk, a prominent promoter of the first immigration of Russian Mennonites to America. In 1877 Funk founded the *Mennonitische Rundschau* which became very popular among the Russian Mennonites in America as well as in Russia itself. In 1923 the paper was sold to a publishing company in Winnipeg. In 1947 its circulation was 5,485 copies, with subscribers, mostly Russian Mennonites, in Canada, the United States, Mexico and Paraguay. In its make-up and content it followed the conventional pattern of parish and church papers, with religious articles and church news prominent but including also items about Mennonite activities throughout the world. Besides the widely read *Rundschau,* every branch of the Mennonite church tended to maintain its own little bulletin, particularly for the young. Sometimes these contained English sections, or were, though rarely, completely printed in the English language. By 1947 nine such church and youth magazines, in addition to an almanac, were published in Manitoba with a total circulation of almost 10,000 copies.

Apart from the religious press, several secular newspapers served Manitoba's Mennonite population. The oldest Mennonite weekly was the *Steinbach Post*, founded in 1913, which thirty years later had a circulation of 4,111, with 928 subscribers in the East Reserve, 1,511 in the West Reserve, 301 in outlying Manitoba settlements, 750 in Saskatchewan, 37 in Alberta, 71 in British Columbia, 15 in the United States, 59 in Paraguay, and 449 in Mexico. While the *Post* was a favorite with the older Kanädier generation, the Russländer people preferred *Der Bote,* a weekly published in Rosthern, Saskatchewan. Since 1941 D. W. Friesen and Sons Ltd. published the *Altona Echo* in English which gained a wide circulation in the West Reserve.

Several cultural magazines have been published by Russländer Mennonites in Manitoba, stressing the ethnic unity of the group and German national values. The *Mennonitische Warte* of the 1930's was later continued by its editor, Arnold Dyck, of Steinbach, under the form of the *Warte-Jahrbuch für die Mennonitische Gemeinschaft in Kanada.* After World War II, the *Mennonitische Welt* began publication under Victor Peters, superseding the *Mennonitische Lehrerzeitung,* while the Echo Verlag, headed by Dyck, was publishing scholarly studies on Mennonite History in Russia, in addition to some fiction. Besides publishing houses, there also were several Mennonite book stores in Manitoba. The leading firm was D. W. Friesen and Sons Ltd., in Altona, which specialized in German literature, both religious and secular, and in Mennonitica.

The Manitoba Mennonites, as a whole, were avid readers although the older folks confined their reading mostly to some German weekly, a church paper, the Bible and a few volumes of sixteenth and seventeenth-century Anabaptist religious literature. Among the middle-aged generation, those of the Kanädier group read many English books which they found easier to understand, while those of the Russländer group were often well acquainted with German classical and modern literature. Mennonite history probably had the widest appeal to Mennonite readers. Next in importance were travel books and non-fiction of various kinds, while fiction and poetry were more rarely represented in a typical Mennonite library. Several fine book collections were found in Mennonite homes; the libraries included many rare items dealing with Mennonitism. Music was another favorite Mennonite pastime. Although singing in parts had at one time been forbidden by the churches, Mennonites liked to sing not only religious tunes, but many German folk songs and had a good ear for harmonizing once it was awakened by some school teacher.[21] Jazz and other modern music was generally rejected, either as "worldly" or as contrary to good taste, or both. Mennonite musical festivals had become an annual event for school children and adolescents. Long restricted by a Puritanical tradition, the Mennonites have not developed any style of their own, either in literature[22] or the fine arts, but have as a rule followed the example of the larger society with which they were in cultural contact. They are rationally inclined rather than artistically creative, while sentiment finds its outlet mostly in religious emotionalism.

The Family

Amidst all this change in economic and community life, in education and even in the expression of religious convictions, the family remained the foundation and nucleus of the Mennonite group. Not that it had been untouched by the vicissitudes of time and external conditions, but in 1947 it occupied precisely the same pivotal place in the whole social structure as it had occupied in 1877. In the minds of the Mennonites themselves the whole ethnic community was still felt as being composed of so and so many families, more or less closely related by countless blood ties and intermarriages. This impression was supported by the fact that the vast majority of Russian Mennonites answer to no more than approximately 300 family names. The discussion of family trees was still one of the favorite pastimes at social gatherings within or without one's family circle. The position of any member of the group in the web of kinship ties could quickly be spotted by his family name, his middle name taken from the maternal family name, and, if this did not suffice, by ascertaining his ancestral background in one of the Russian colonies. A man without an identifiable genealogy was barely considered a true Mennonite.

While other social activities in the Mennonite communities had suffered a marked decline in recent years, visiting relationships with family members were still maintained as of old. The afternoons of high feast days, especially, were set aside for family groups to call on the parents of both, father and mother. These gatherings often included

---

[21] Cf. Victor and Elizabeth Peters, "Our Heritage of Music in Manitoba, *Mennonite Life* 3 (1948): 23-26.

[22] J. H. Janzen, "Die Belletristik der Kanadischen Russlanddeutschen Mennoniten, I" *Warte-Jahrbuch* 1 (1943): 83-89.

twenty or more relatives, some of whom might have travelled hundreds
of miles to be present. Weddings and funerals were other occasions of
family reunions, again with many coming from distant places. During
the summer months there were few Mennonite homes in Manitoba
which did not welcome relatives from other parts of Canada or the
United States, occasionally even from overseas and Latin America.
These family affairs were the favorite social functions, in fact, they
were the only ones besides church meetings, school picnics and festivals,
agricultural fairs and conventions, which were tolerated by the Mennonite churches. For, with the exception of the town cafe (in a few
instances also the beer parlor), radio, car rides, and by the more sophisticated an occasional concert in the city, most modern amusements
such as spectator sports, dances, or even movies still remained taboo
for the majority of Manitoba Mennonites.

Because of the traditional form of dividing estates in equal shares
among the surviving male and female heirs, the typical Mennonite
household rarely comprised more than two generations. A high respect
for the human personality and a democratic organization had been
preserved in Mennonite families. Their women had a very modest
and gentle way of leaving to the men what is considered their part of
life, although the responsibility for the education of the children was a
responsibility shared by both spouses. The children themselves appeared docile and well-behaved, yet without servility or shyness. They
respected their parents without question as superiors and benefactors.
Even among the returned war veterans, no signs of a young generation
in revolt could be discovered. It may be true, however, that their
elders themselves had grown more indulgent with regard to attitudes
and behaviour learned from the large society which, even if contrary
to strict traditions, did not directly endanger group coherence. The
children, although enjoying greater freedom than before, remained
closely integrated in the kinship group, also after leaving their parental
home. Child bearing, child rearing and home making were still considered the main objective of a woman's life although unmarried women
were gainfully employed in about the same degree as among other
Canadians. Household duties were treated neither as a pastime nor
as a drudgery, and these were not as a rule shared with the husbands,
mainly because the women themselves achieved a deep sense of satisfaction from their awareness of how crucial their work was for the
family economy and welfare.

CHART X—AGE-SEX DISTRIBUTION OF SELECTED POPULATIONS*

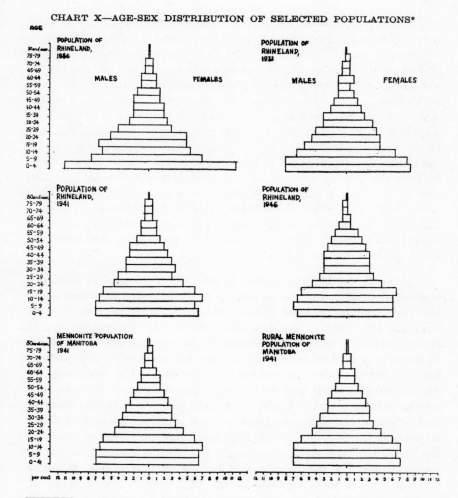

* Based on published and unpublished data of the Canadian Bureau of Statistics.

The family among the Manitoba Mennonites had remained intact except in one vital point: birth control. Decreasing birth rates are bound to have a far-reaching effect upon the maintenance and structure of an ethnic minority whose coherence is so dependent on strong family ties and social interaction between kinship members as the Mennonite group. The trend itself is by no means unusual, for other culture groups in America with a higher than average birth rate, too, have shown a tendency toward a more rapid decrease in birth rates than in the large society, until the general level has been reached. According to an estimate based on recent census figures, the crude birth rate among Mennonites was still greater by 2.64 than that of the total population of Manitoba, while the death rate was less by .23, so that the rate of natural increase among the Mennonites exceeded that of the total population by 1.87. Nevertheless, the Mennonite population pyramid, which was perfectly regular in 1931, ten years later showed a significant shrinkage in the relative size of the age groups under ten years, although infant mortality and mortality in general had decreased rather than increased. A comparison of fertility ratios told a similar story. While in 1886 the fertility ratios in the Mennonite population of Manitoba and in the total population of Manitoba were almost identical and rather high, since 1931 the fertility ratio of the Mennonites, though still unusually high for modern conditions, had decreased much more rapidly than among the total population, paralleling somewhat the trend in the Province of Quebec.

There is hardly any doubt in the minds of experts that this downward trend was primarily a result of birth control measures which had been adopted by some Mennonites, particularly the younger ones since the Depression. This was also indicated by the smaller size of young families in recent years despite lower marriage ages, and by the higher ages of mothers at the birth of their first child, while the intervals between births showed a tendency to increase. The knowledge of contraceptive methods had deliberately been introduced by some outsiders, such as a public health nurse and physicians in the Reserves and in Winnipeg. What the practice might do to the group as a whole is not difficult to infer, if one considers that the inner strength of the Mennonite farm economy is largely the result of an adequate labour supply within the family, and that lack of interest in the biological survival and in the continuity of the individual family is likely to weaken attachment to an ethnic group which is conceived primarily as an historical continuum of succeeding generations. On the other hand, of course, the extrapolation of population trends is always a precarious matter, and does not permit any definite prognosis in as far as unexpected factors may at any time alter existing conditions.

A much more favorable situation prevailed with regard to losses as a result of out-marriage. Apart from war brides brought back by returning Mennonite veterans, as late as 1946 intermarriages were confined very largely to those between Mennonites and German Lutherans. In Winkler, between 1935 and 1942, for instance, out of 187 couples having at least one Mennonite partner, we found only 16 where one partner was a German Lutheran, 2 where the wives were of Anglo-Saxon descent, and 1 where the wife was a Ukrainian. For the Municipality of Stanley as a whole, only 11 marriages between Mennonites and German Lutherans were recorded, in addition to 2 between Mennonites and Anglo-Saxons, and 2 between Mennonites and Ukrainians. Moreover, a number of half-Mennonites with Mennonite mothers had contracted marriages with non-Mennonites. A check of birth certificates brought substantially identical results.

Acculturation and Assimilation

Thus we come to the conclusion that, at least until shortly after the end of the second World War, acculturation among the Manitoba Mennonites (that is, the acceptance of culture traits from the large society) had by no means led to any significant degree of assimilation (whereby individual members of a minority are transferred into the host society with permanent loss to the ethnic group). We found hardly any rejection of non-Mennonites on religious grounds but there was a greater awareness of ethnic distinctions. Although most Kanädier Mennonites were now more familiar with English than German as the literary language, the Low German vernacular was not only understood by all members of the group but for most of them it had remained the language of family intercourse, although some of the Russländer families preferred High German. A survey of 40 Mennonite students enrolled at the University of Manitoba in 1946-47, all but one belonging to the Russländer group, revealed that English alone was the language spoken in only three homes, although one would expect that the sample included some of the most assimilated individuals among the whole Mennonite group. Sixteen used High German exclusively, and only two used Low German alone in their families. All but five declared that they understood Low German without any difficulty. Both High German and English was used in six families, English and Low German in two, while all three languages were spoken in one home. The answers to the questionnaire indicated that, where English was used at all, it was spoken by the siblings among themselves, while the parents were addressed exclusively in German.

Mennonites living in compact settlements, and the majority of them continued to reside in predominantly Mennonite communities, or at least neighbourhoods, did not to any considerable extent mingle with Canadians of different backgrounds, mainly because their colonies and towns had, if anything, become more homogeneous ethnically than they had been twenty years earlier. Proselytizing among the Mennonites had not led to any appreciable loss in total church membership, but some shifts between different branches of the Mennonite church had occurred, and revivalistic practices had been taken over from other Protestant denominations. When the one Mennonite member of the Provincial Legislature retired to his medical practice, he did not find any successor among his own people. Mennonite participation in politics expressed itself indirectly in the use of the weight and influence of such non-political organizations as the Manitoba Federation of Agriculture or the coöperatives, in which Mennonites had acquired considerable influence. By and large, it seemed as if the process of wholesale acculturation had been arrested for the time being, and group coherence and solidarity had been strengthened as a result of the events of the past decade.

When we look for the factors responsible for the striking revival and continuance of Mennonite group solidarity in Manitoba we are thinking first of the three basic elements of their social fabric: the region, the church and the family. The Mennonite Reserves are sufficiently big to supply all basic needs if necessary, and thus enable the people to stand aloof from society at large. They also constitute focal points of social organization for the outlying settlements of the Russländer immigrants, and in a way for all Russian Mennonites scattered throughout the world. The local pattern is in part supported by the concentration of certain branches of the Mennonite church in definite sections of the Reserves. Ecclesiastical divisions do foster particularistic tendencies to the extent that knowledge of what is going on "across the river" is often surprisingly sketchy. Yet, such particularism is difficult to keep up when few local communities have remained homogeneous with regard to church affiliation. Mennonites belonging to different branches of the church go to the same public school, do business with each other, meet at social affairs and intermarry. Frequently, the prevalence of non-religious interests and the development of a distinct ethnic we-feeling have further weakened attachment to any one particular branch of the church. Private schools, charities and the press are often inter-denominational Mennonite, and such common emergencies as the defence of conscientious objectors or the arrival of refugees have led to closer coöperation. Moreover, there is a core of religious principles and practices which differentiates all branches of the Mennonite church from non-Mennonite religious bodies and thus necessarily draws them together, once the chips are down.

Even those Mennonites to whom religion has become but a thin veneer have retained value orientations which are in the Mennonite religious tradition, and which are felt to be intimately related to its institutional expression in the various branches of the Mennonite church. As long as a Mennonite remains part of a local community in which such values are still dominant, neither secularization nor even apostasy are able to destroy his religious heritage entirely, or to eliminate altogether the social controls exercised by the church. This connection is further strengthened by a keen and wide-spread sense of historical and biological continuity. History, more than anything else, provides the Mennonites with an intelligible explanation of the fact that they have remained distinct from their neighbours. It gives them a feeling of being something better than all the others. Mennonite church history emphasizes their common origin, the sufferings which befell all the various branches of their church, and the ideals common to them, though they may have sought their realization in many different ways. Their historical literature thus provides the Mennonites with an effective social myth that transcends all particularistic subdivisions and conceives the whole group as an indivisible unit.

The German vernacular is an added element of ethnic unification. Through it they are unquestionably differentiated from their Anglo-Saxon environment. A folk dialect which is not understood by others makes a minority a sort of secret order, while bilingualism in this situation conveys a sense of immunity from outside interference and of superiority over fellow citizens who know but one language. The tendency of some Russländer Mennonites to replace the folk dialect with High German perhaps indicates a wavering between loyalty to the Mennonite group and a rather recently acquired allegiance to the German nation. Otherwise, High German is valued as the traditional church language rather than as the vehicle of a national literature. Once the Kanädier Mennonites recognized that the adoption of English did not necessarily lead to a loss of group identity, they ceased to resist its use as a lingua franca and vehicle of cultural values, although they continued to cling to their West Prussian Platt as their true mother tongue and family language.

*

Some 400 years ago, the Mennonites set out to find Utopia. About 45,000 of their descendants are now living in Manitoba. Their religious faith has forged them into a solid community. They have changed, and still are changing, from a religious group to an ethnic group. But when culture change was forced upon them, they changed as a group thus sparing individual members the misery and mental agonies of the marginal man. Devices which had been invented in an attempt to reorganize rural life in Western society, such as coöperatives, appear in their system as young shoots springing forth from the green roots of an aged trunk whose top has been capped by the storms of time. Utopia is farther beyond the horizon than ever. But Manitoba's Mennonites have found social and psychological security in their well-organized communities, and sufficient wealth to give them a sense of satisfaction and contentedness.

Selected Readings

The following list contains only items which refer directly to the topic of this volume and which are accessible to the general reader. A more exhaustive bibliographical essay by the author was published in *Mennonite Quarterly Review* 27 (1953): 238-248. Rare Mennonitica will be found in the Historical Library at Goshen College, Goshen, Indiana, and in the Bethel College Library at North Newton, Kansas. Articles in the *Mennonite Quarterly Review* or *Mennonite Life* have not been listed here, and only a minimum of publications in the German language has been mentioned.

Das 60 jährige Jubiläum der mennonitischen Einwanderung in Manitoba, Canada, gefeiert am 1 August 1943 in Steinbach, Manitoba (Beiträge zur mennonitischen Geschichte, no. 1), Steinbach, 1935.

Dawson, C.A., *Group Settlement: Ethnic Communities in Western Canada*, Toronto, 1936.

England, Robert, *The Colonization of Western Canada*, Toronto, 1936.

Francis, E. K., "Mennonite Institutions in Early Manitoba: A Study on Their Origins," *Agricultural History* XXII (1948): 144-55.

Francis, E. K., "The Russian Mennonites: From Religious Group to Ethnic Group," American Journal of Sociology LIV (1950): 101-7.

Francis, E. K., "The Adjustment of a Peasant Group to a Capitalistic Economy," *Rural Sociology* XVII (1952): 218-28.

Fretz, J. Winfield, *Mennonite Colonization, Lessons from the Past for the Future*, Akron, Pa., 1944.

Friesen, I. I., The Mennonites of Western Canada with Special Reference to Education, unpublished Master's Thesis, University of Saskatchewan, 1934.

Gedenkfeier 1874-1949 (75) der Mennonitischen Einwanderung in Manitoba, Canada, North Kildonan, 1949.

Gingerich, Melvin, "Jacob Y. Shantz, The Mennonite Immigration to Manitoba," *From the Steppes to the Prairies*, Newton, 1949.

[Hamm, H. H.], *Sixty Years of Progress, 1884-1944: Diamond Jubilee [of] the Rural Municipality of Rhineland*, Altona, 1944.

Hildebrand, J. J., *Chronologische Zeittafel, 1500 Daten, historischer Ereignisse und Geschehnisse aus der Zeit der Geschichte der Mennoniten Westeuropas, Russlands und Amerikas . . .*, Winnipeg, 1945.

Krehbiel, H. P., *The History of the General Conference of Mennonites of North America*, 2 vols., St. Louis, Mo., 1898 and Hesston, Kans., 1938.

Lehmann, Heinz, *Das Deutschtum in Westkanada*, Berlin, 1939.

Lohrenz, John H., *The Mennonite Brethren Church*, Hillsbooro, Kans., 1950.

Schäfer, Paul J., *Woher? Wohin? Mennoniten! Lektionen für den Unterricht in der Mennonitengeschichte*, 3 vols., Altona, 1942-46.

Schäfer, Paul J., *Heinrich H. Ewert, Lehrer, Erzieher und Prediger der Mennoniten*, Altona, 1945.

Smith, C. Henry, *The Story of the Mennonites*, Berne, Ind., 1941.

Unruh, John D., *In the Name of Christ: A History of the Mennonite Central Committee and Its Service, 1920-1951*, Scottdale, Pa., 1952.

Willows, A., A History of the Mennonites, Particularly in Manitoba, unpublished Master's Thesis, University of Manitoba, 1924.

Index

The Index has been greatly simplified in order to reduce printing cost. Topics and phrases occurring throughout the book have been either omitted or marked "passim." Place names without any indication of country refer either to Manitoba or Europe. Please consult also tables of content.

Photos Courtesy of: John Driemen, Winnipeg, Bruno Derksen, Steinbach, George Sawatzky, Winkler, The Altona Echo.